CHAPTER 1

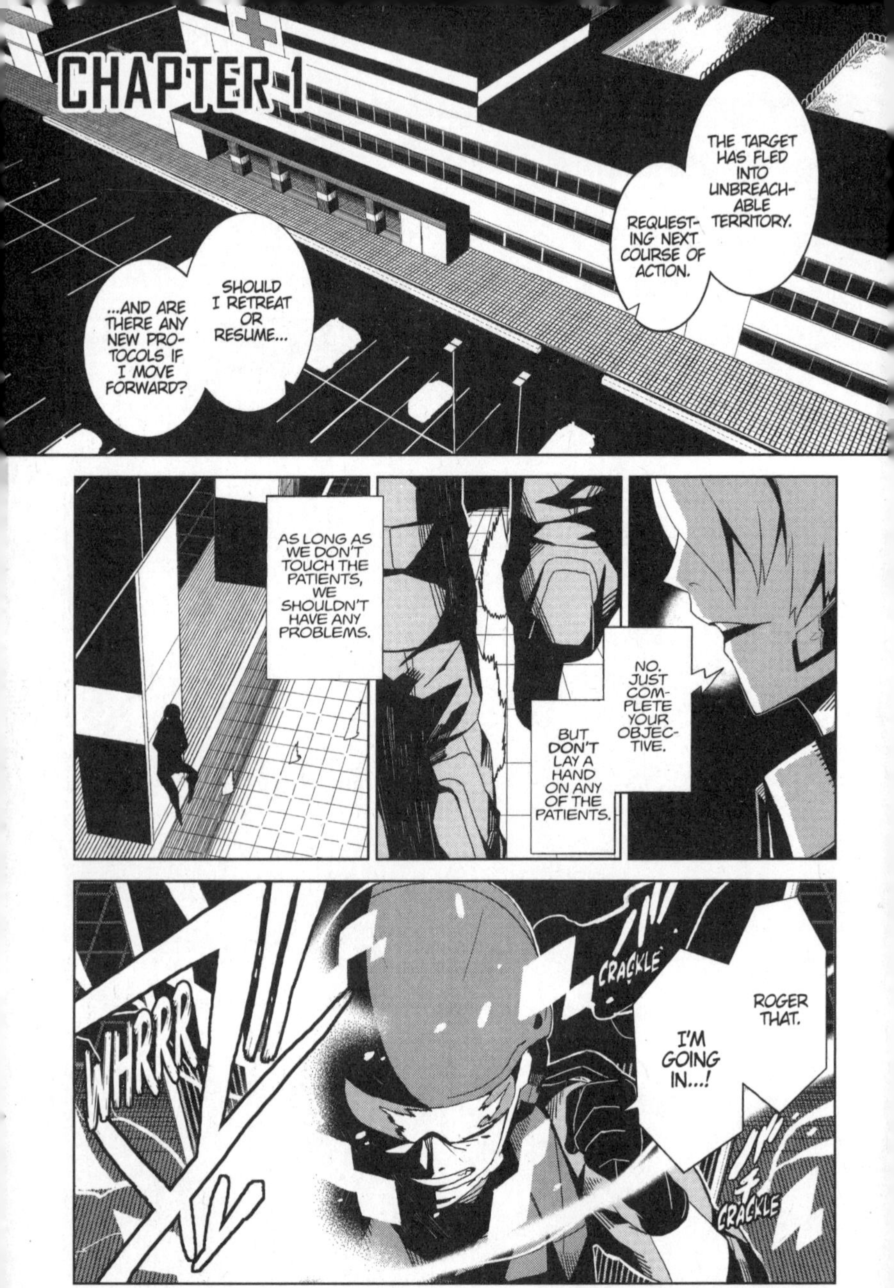

THE TARGET HAS FLED INTO UNBREACHABLE TERRITORY.
REQUESTING NEXT COURSE OF ACTION.
SHOULD I RETREAT OR RESUME...
...AND ARE THERE ANY NEW PROTOCOLS IF I MOVE FORWARD?
NO. JUST COMPLETE YOUR OBJECTIVE.
BUT DON'T LAY A HAND ON ANY OF THE PATIENTS.
AS LONG AS WE DON'T TOUCH THE PATIENTS, WE SHOULDN'T HAVE ANY PROBLEMS.
CRACKLE
ROGER THAT.
I'M GOING IN...!
CRACKLE
WHRRR

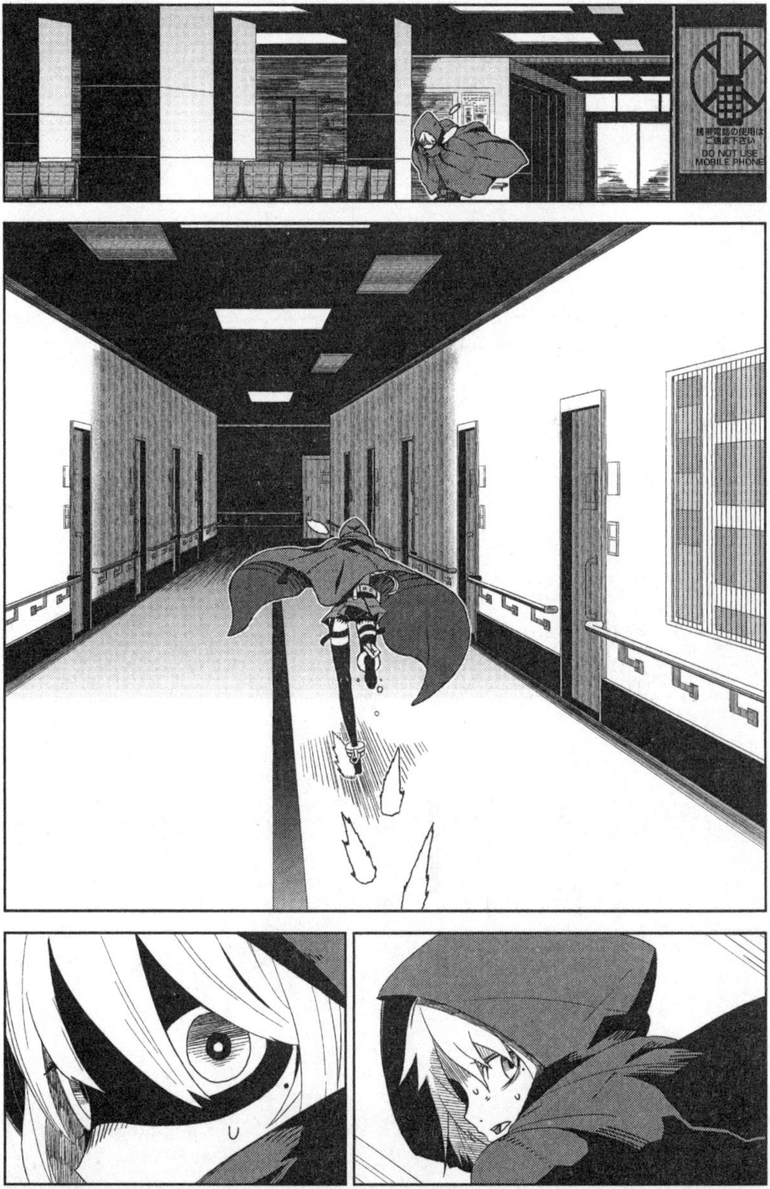
携帯電話の使用はご遠慮下さい
DO NOT USE MOBILE PHONE

CHAME-
LEON
CAMO-
FLAGE?!

CRACKLE

WHRRRR

CRACKLE

RRGH!
HE
DID
COME
FOR
ME!

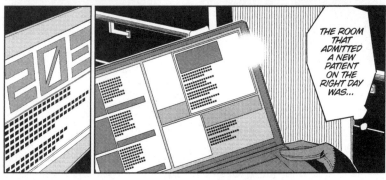

THE ROOM
THAT
ADMITTED
A NEW
PATIENT
ON THE
RIGHT DAY
WAS...

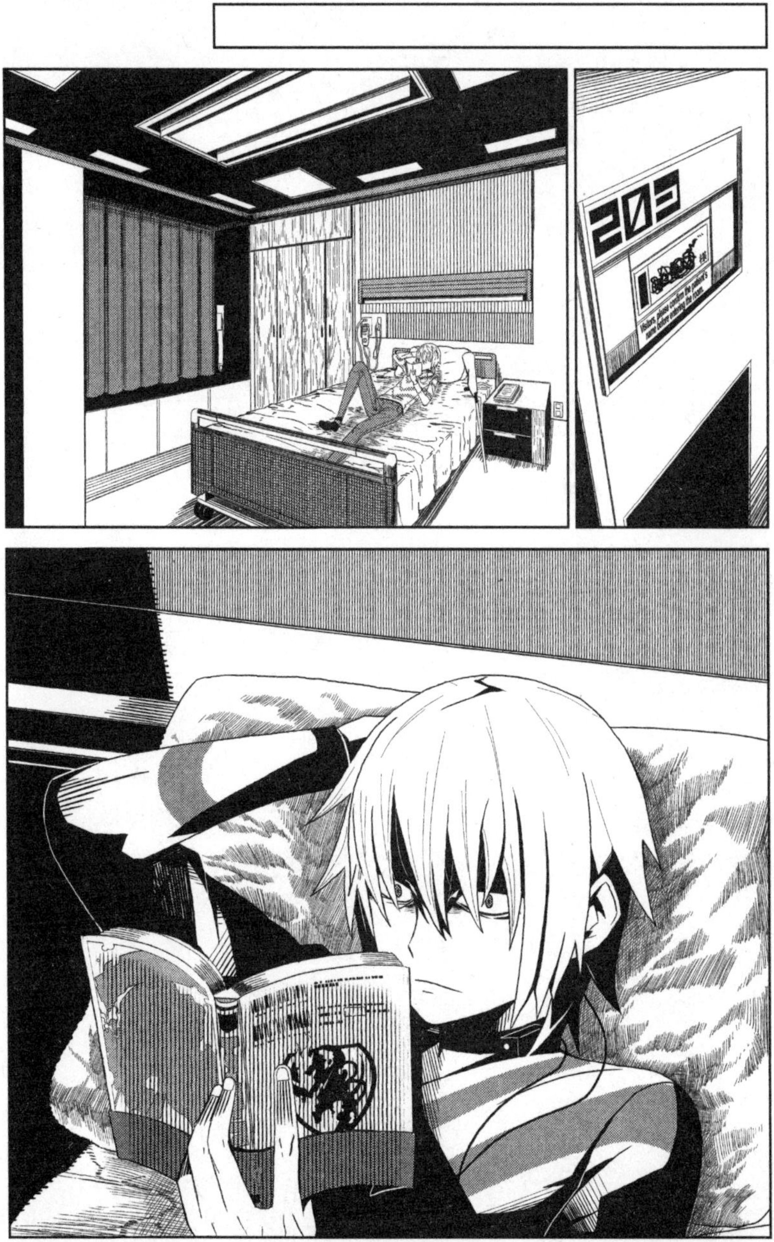
203
様
Visitors, please confirm the patient's name before entering the room.

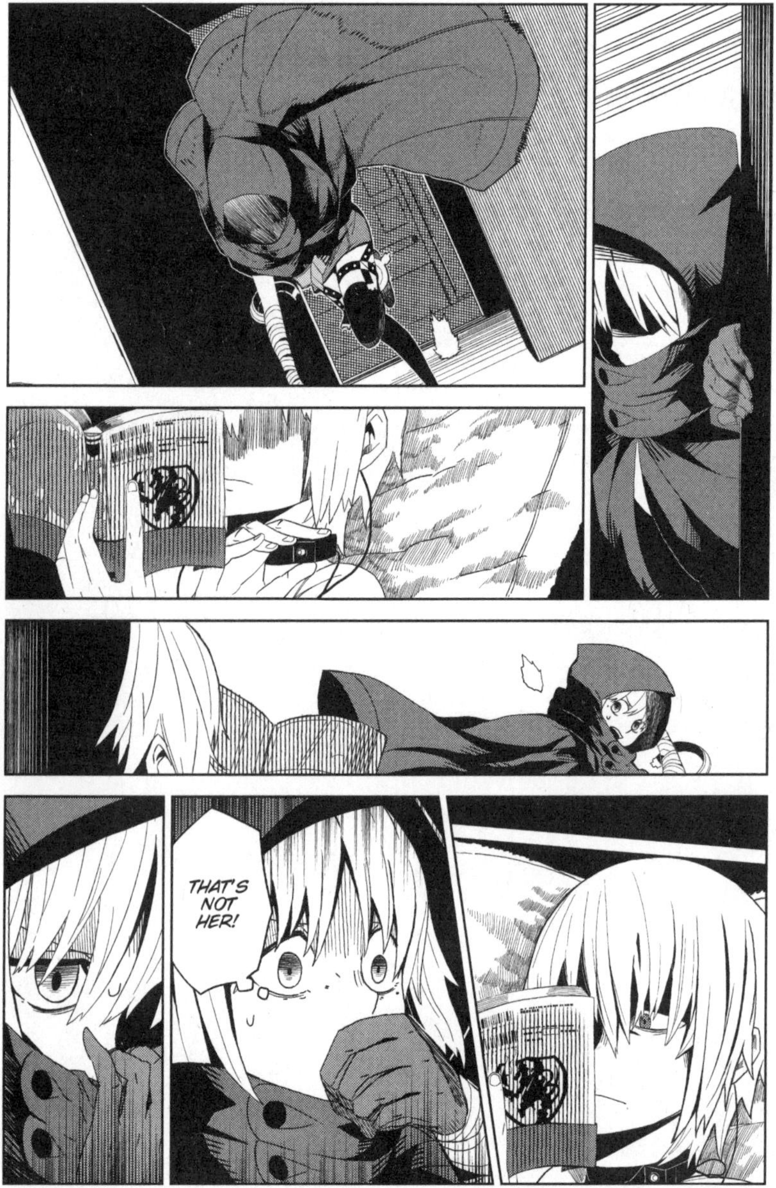
THAT'S NOT HER!

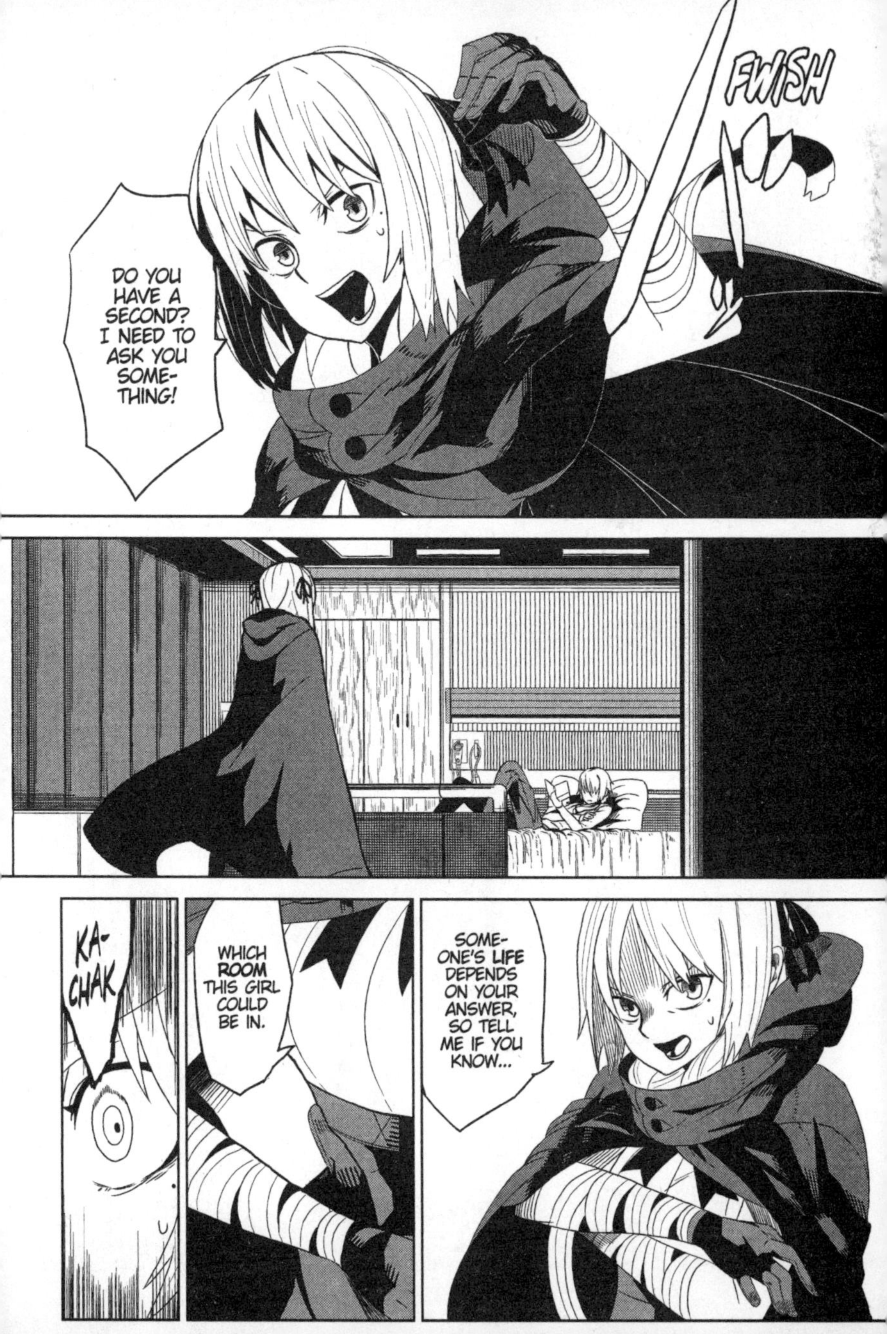
FWISH
DO YOU HAVE A SECOND? I NEED TO ASK YOU SOME-THING!
SOME-ONE'S LIFE DEPENDS ON YOUR ANSWER, SO TELL ME IF YOU KNOW...
WHICH ROOM THIS GIRL COULD BE IN.
KA-CHAK

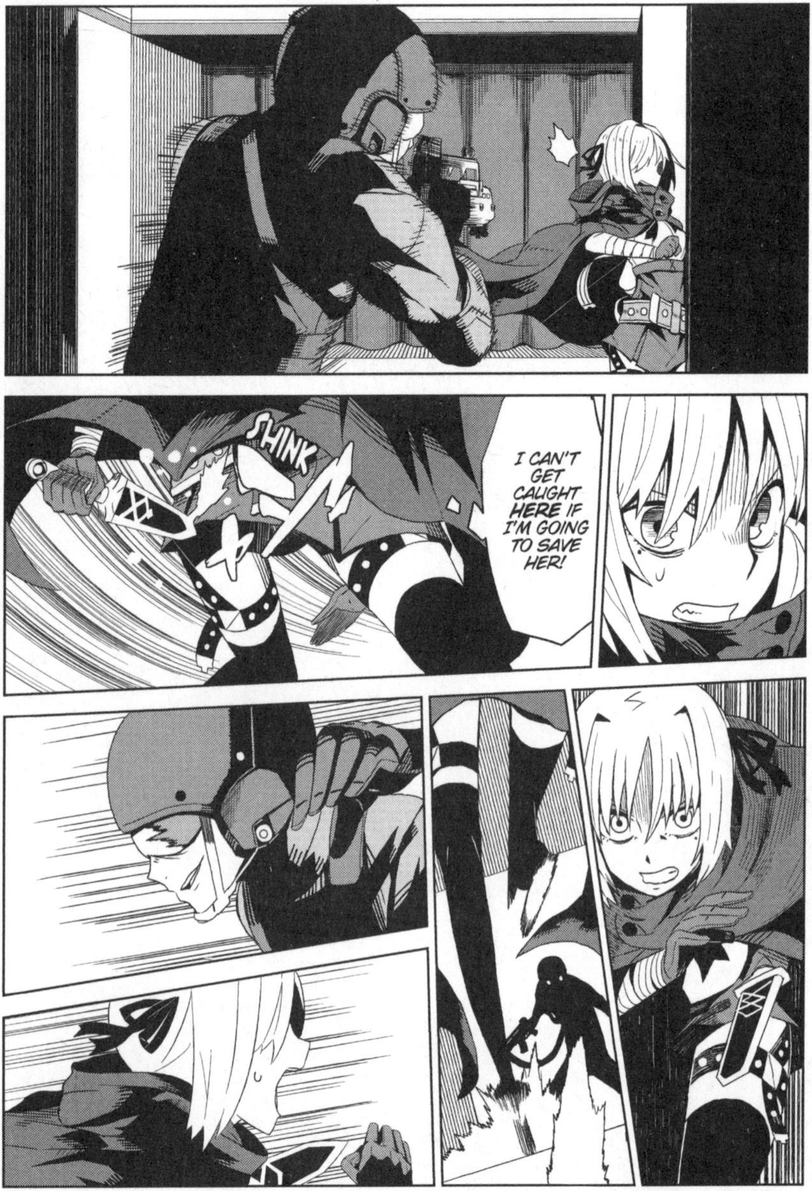
I CAN'T GET CAUGHT HERE IF I'M GOING TO SAVE HER!
SHINK

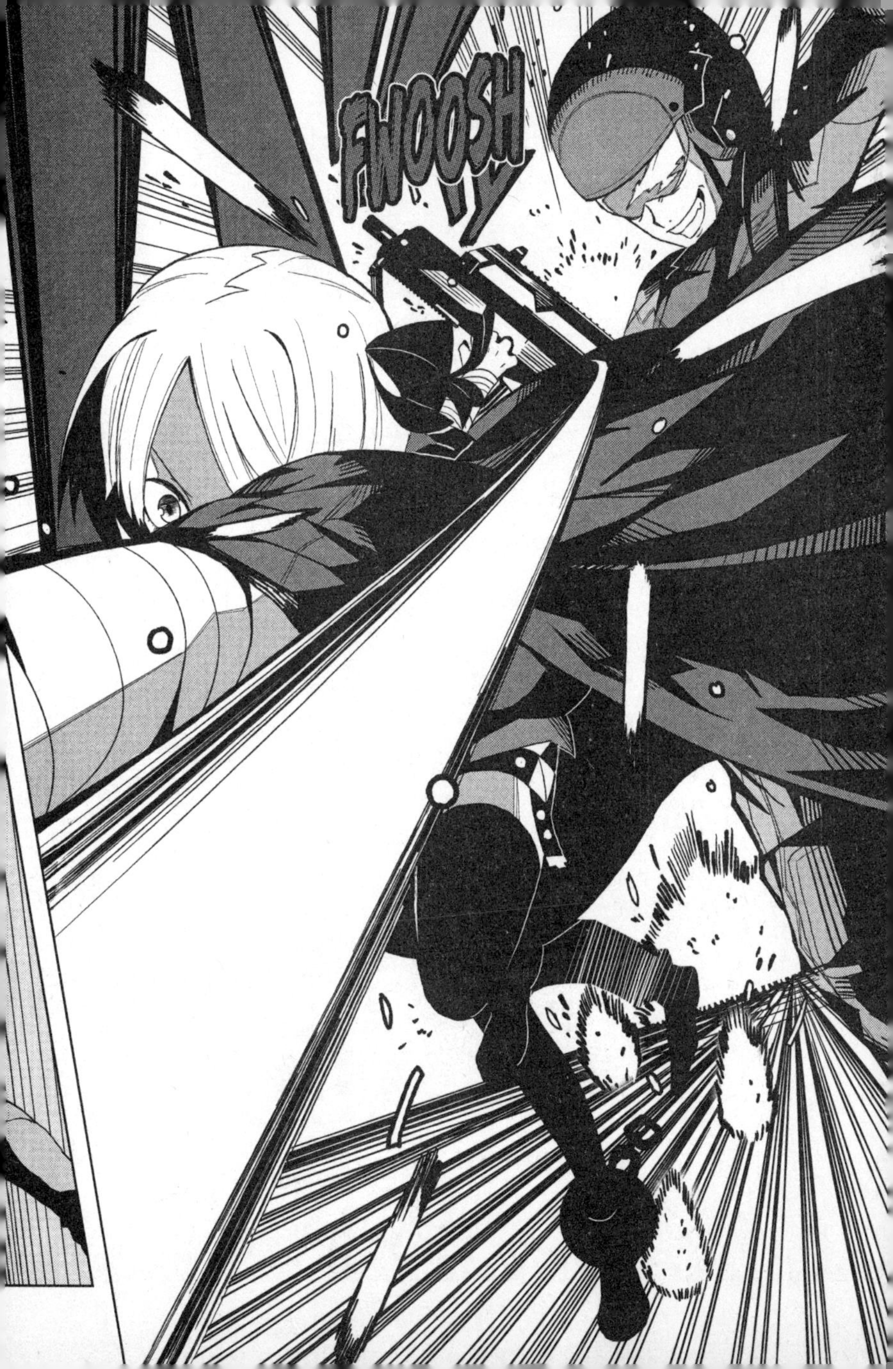
FWOOSH

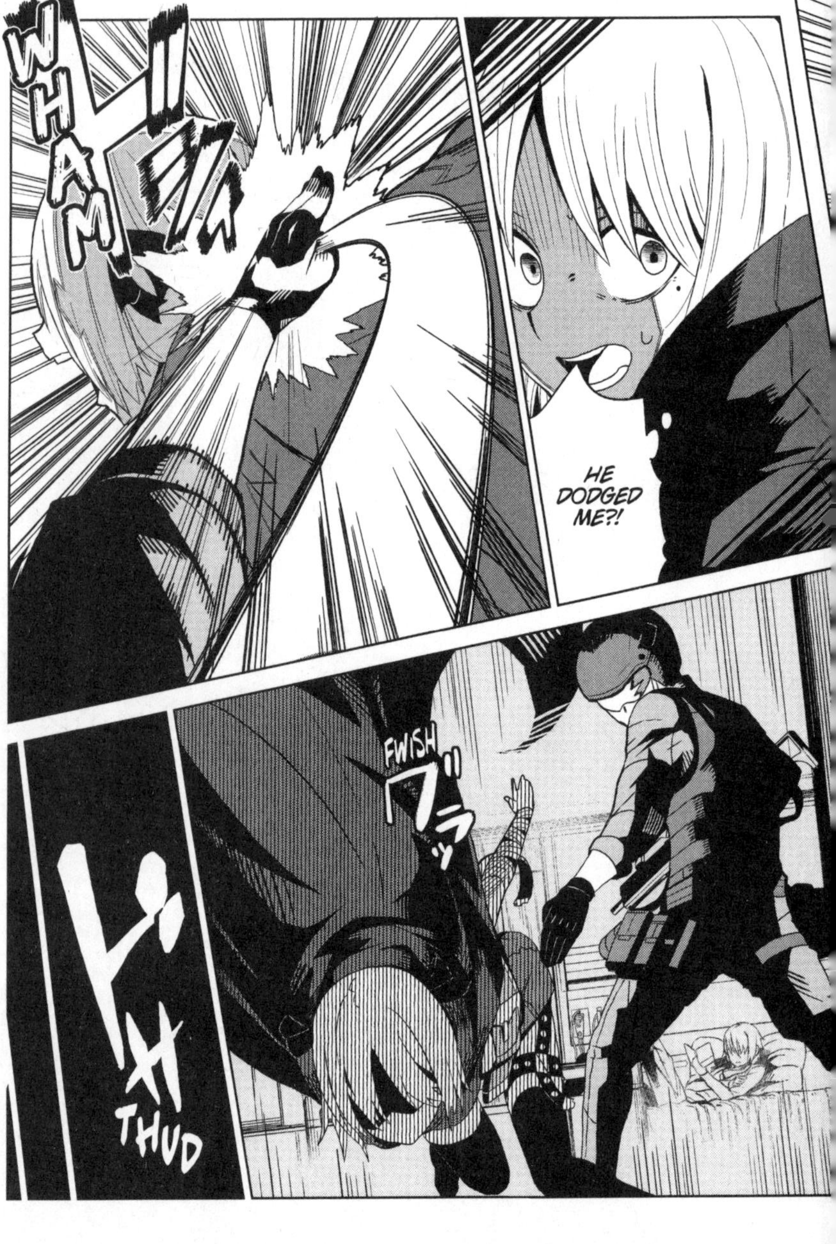
HE DODGED ME?!
WHAM
FWISH
THUD

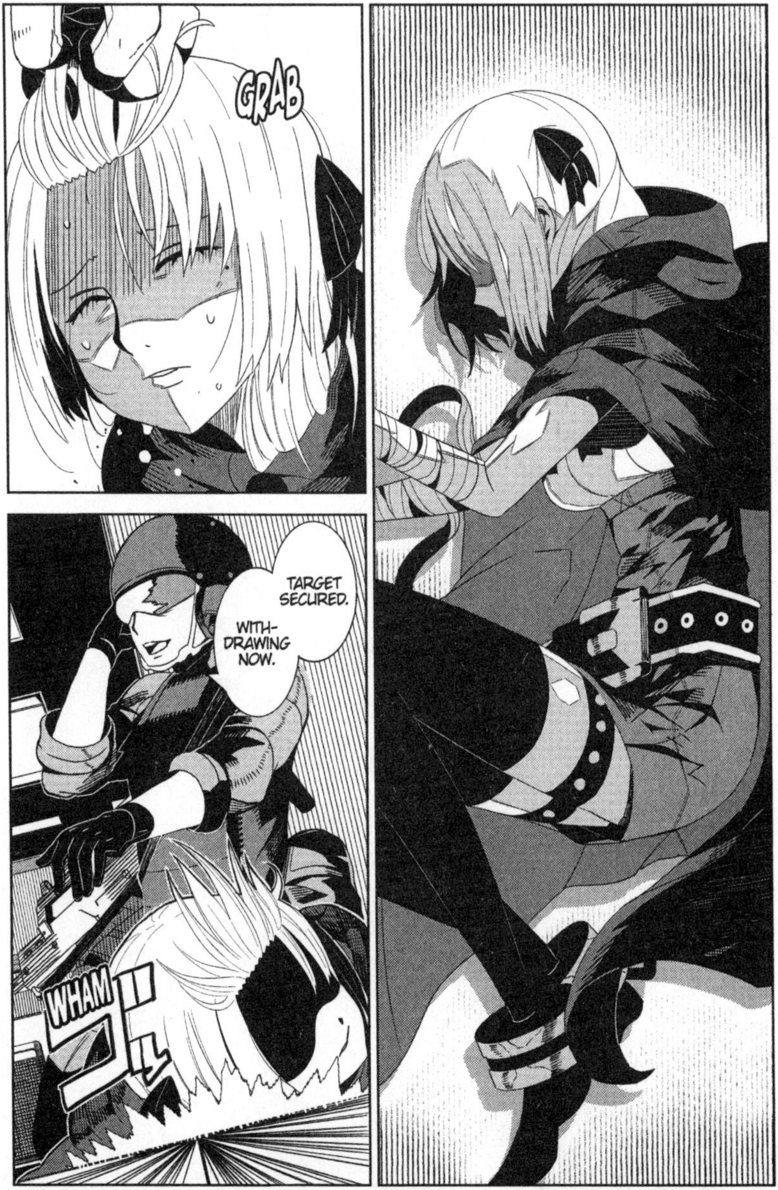
GRAB
TARGET SECURED.
WITH-DRAWING NOW.
WHAM

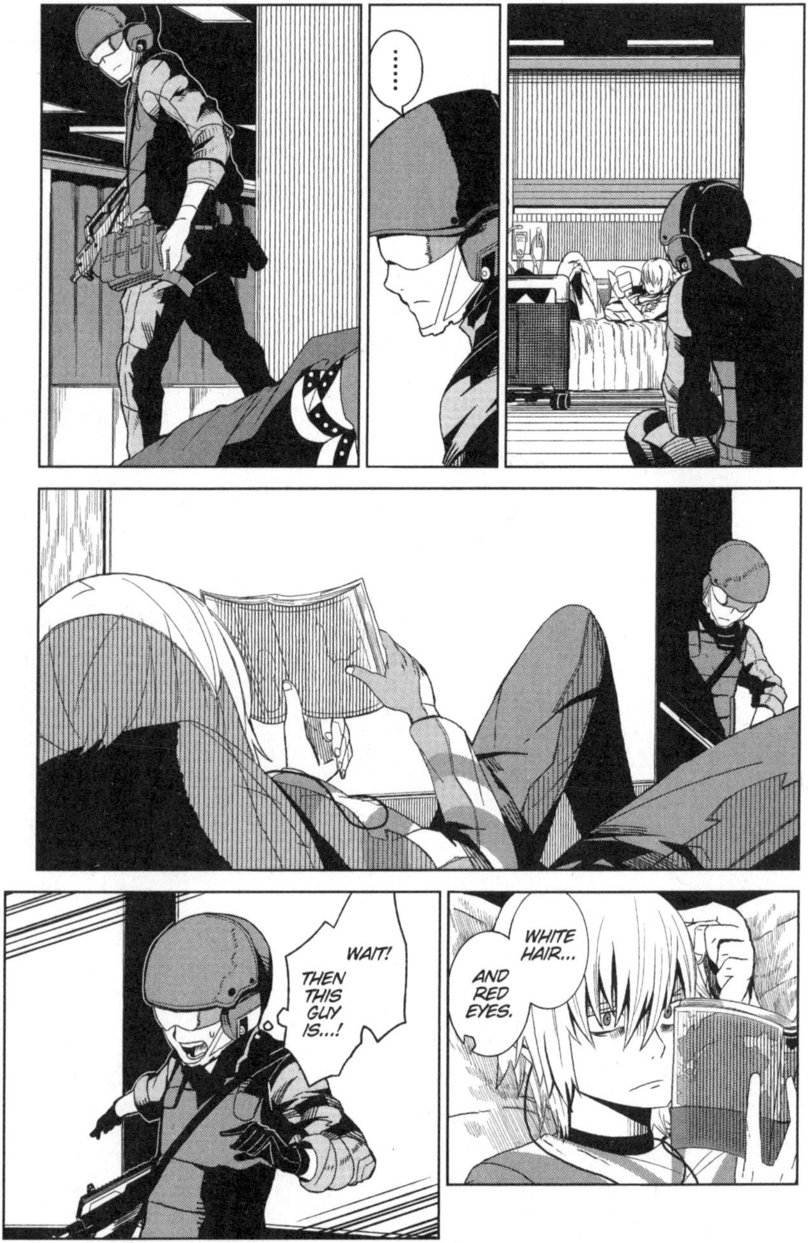
……
WHITE HAIR...
AND RED EYES.
WAIT!
THEN THIS GUY IS...!

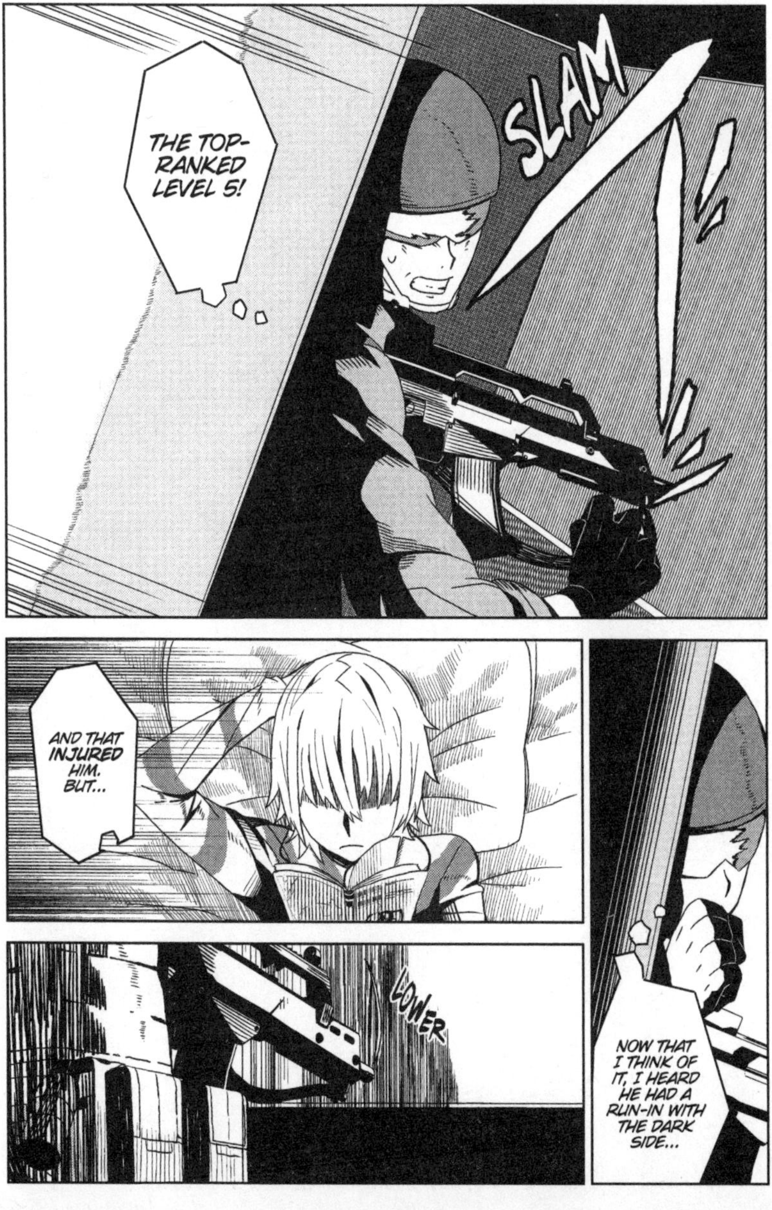
SLAM
THE TOP-RANKED LEVEL 5!
AND THAT INJURED HIM. BUT...
NOW THAT I THINK OF IT, I HEARD HE HAD A RUN-IN WITH THE DARK SIDE...
LOWER

IS HE FEIGNING TOTAL INDIFFERENCE SO HE CAN AVOID THE HASSLE IN FRONT OF HIM?

WHAT A PIECE OF *GARBAGE.* IT'S USUALLY MY JOB TO REFORM TRASH LIKE THAT.

HE'S LUCKY I'M ON ANOTHER MISSION RIGHT NOW.

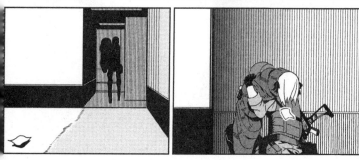

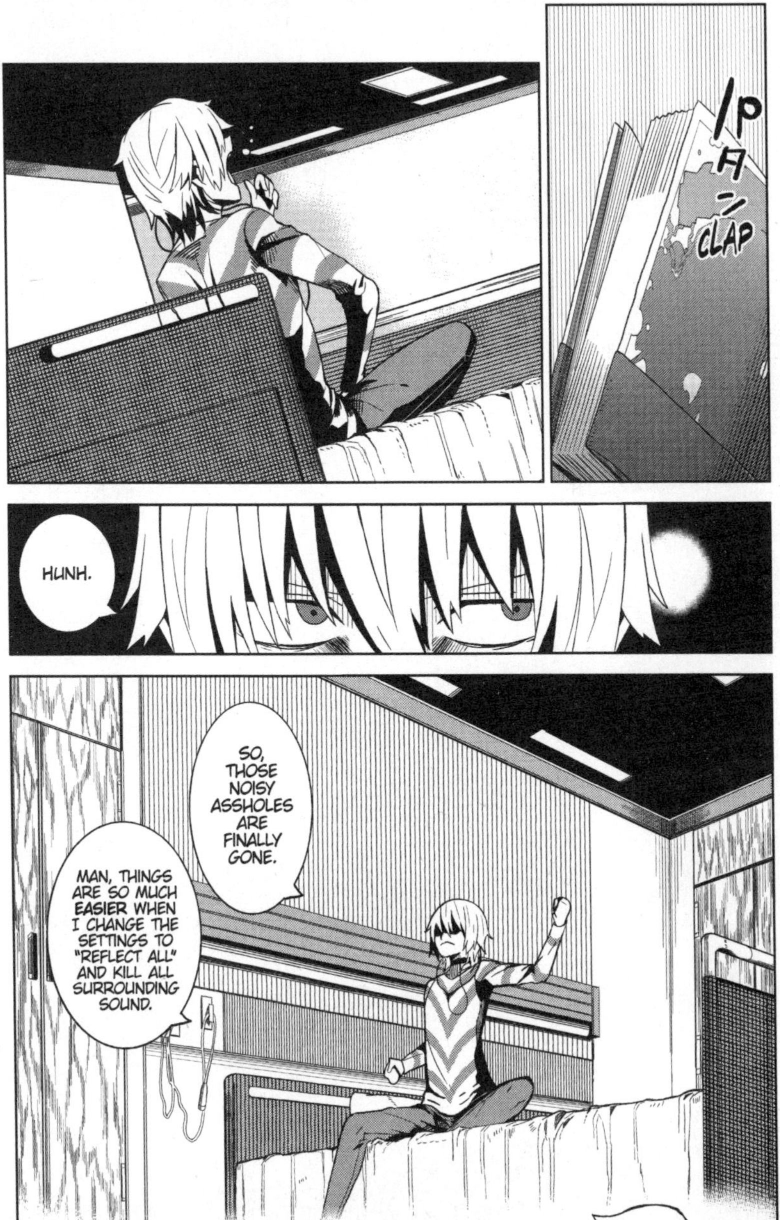
CLAP
HUNH.
SO, THOSE NOISY ASSHOLES ARE FINALLY GONE.
MAN, THINGS ARE SO MUCH EASIER WHEN I CHANGE THE SETTINGS TO "REFLECT ALL" AND KILL ALL SURROUNDING SOUND.

HM?

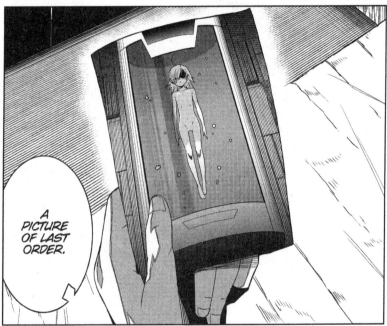

A PICTURE OF LAST ORDER.

DID THOSE GUYS LEAVE THIS?

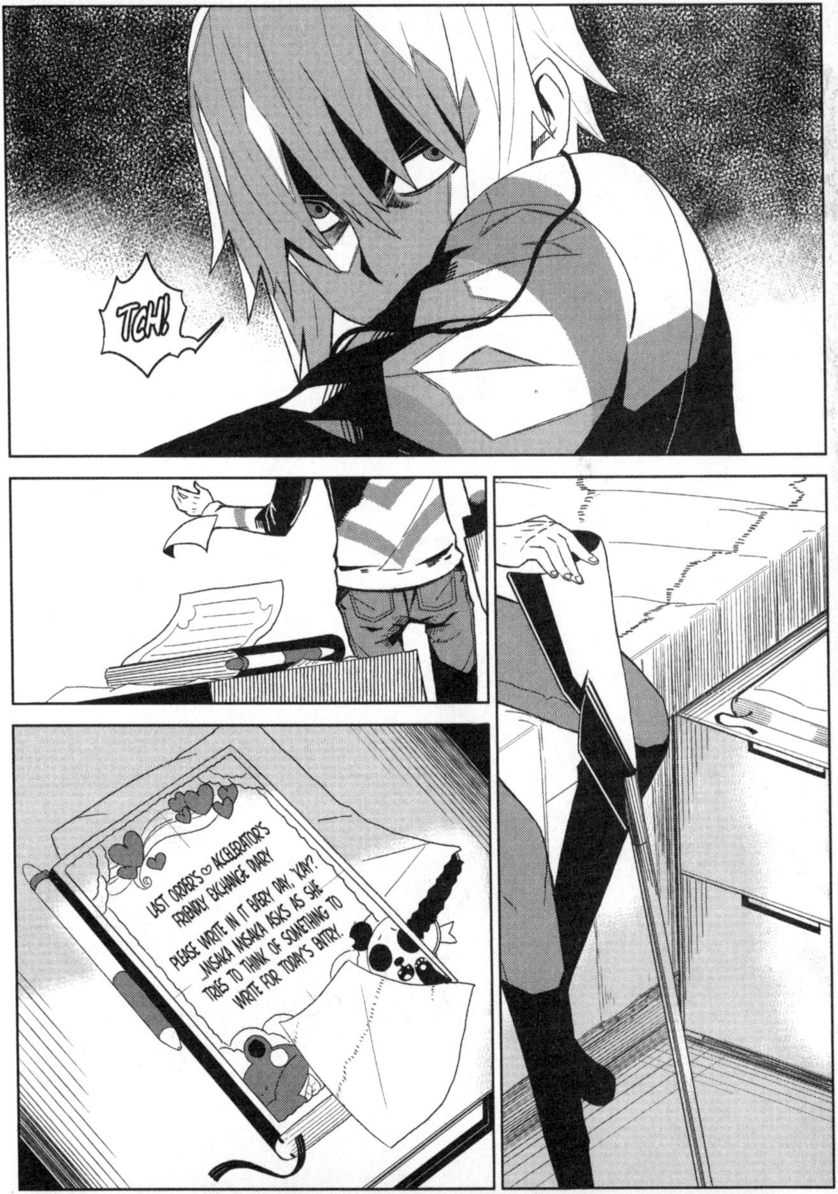
TCH!
LAST ORDER'S ♡ ACCELERATOR'S FRIENDLY EXCHANGE DIARY
PLEASE WRITE IN IT EVERY DAY, 'KAY? ...MISAKA MISAKA ASKS AS SHE TRIES TO THINK OF SOMETHING TO WRITE FOR TODAY'S ENTRY.

THE TARGET ATTEMPTED CONTACT WITH AN UNEXPECTED ENTITY...

BUT IT'S STILL UNCLEAR IF THAT WAS THE TARGET'S PLAN ALL ALONG.

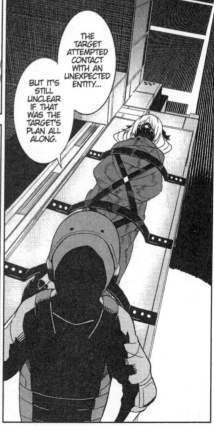

SAID ENTITY DIDN'T RESPOND, SO THERE WAS NO PROB--

HEY.

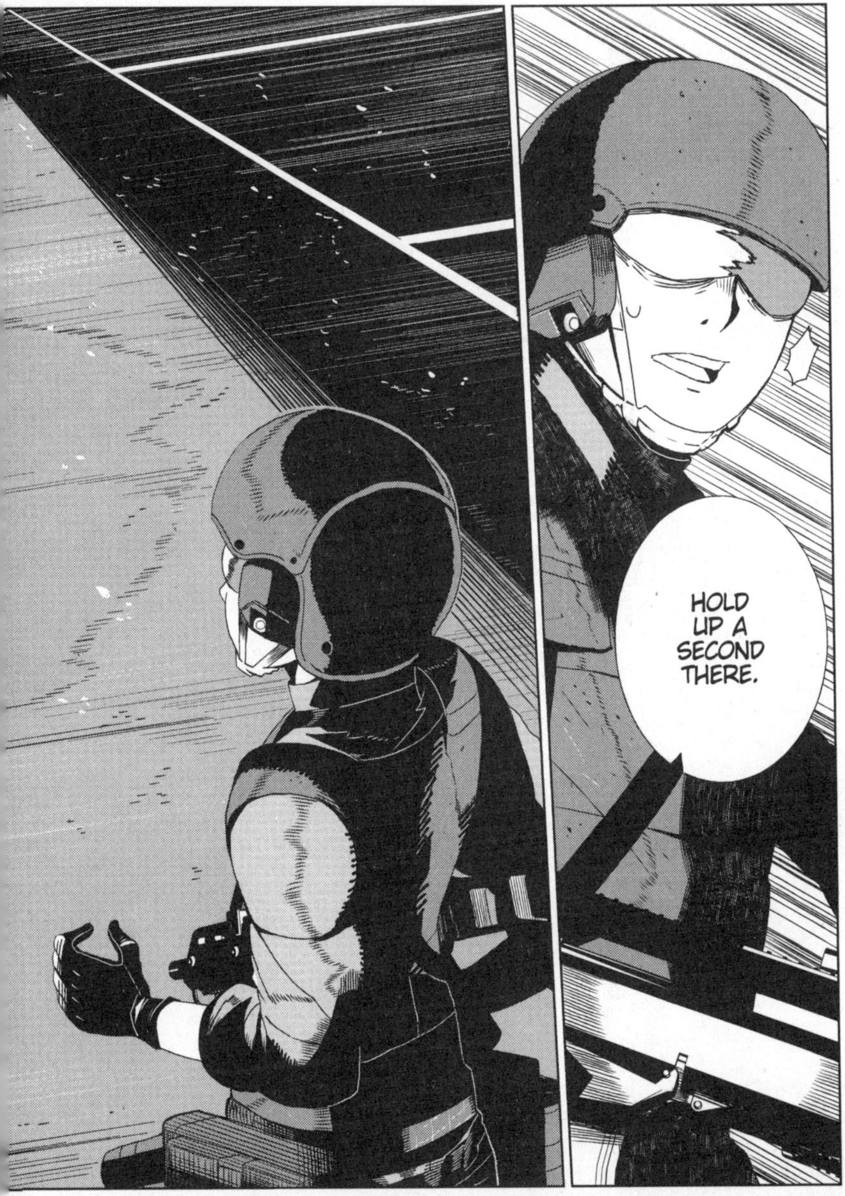
HOLD UP A SECOND THERE.

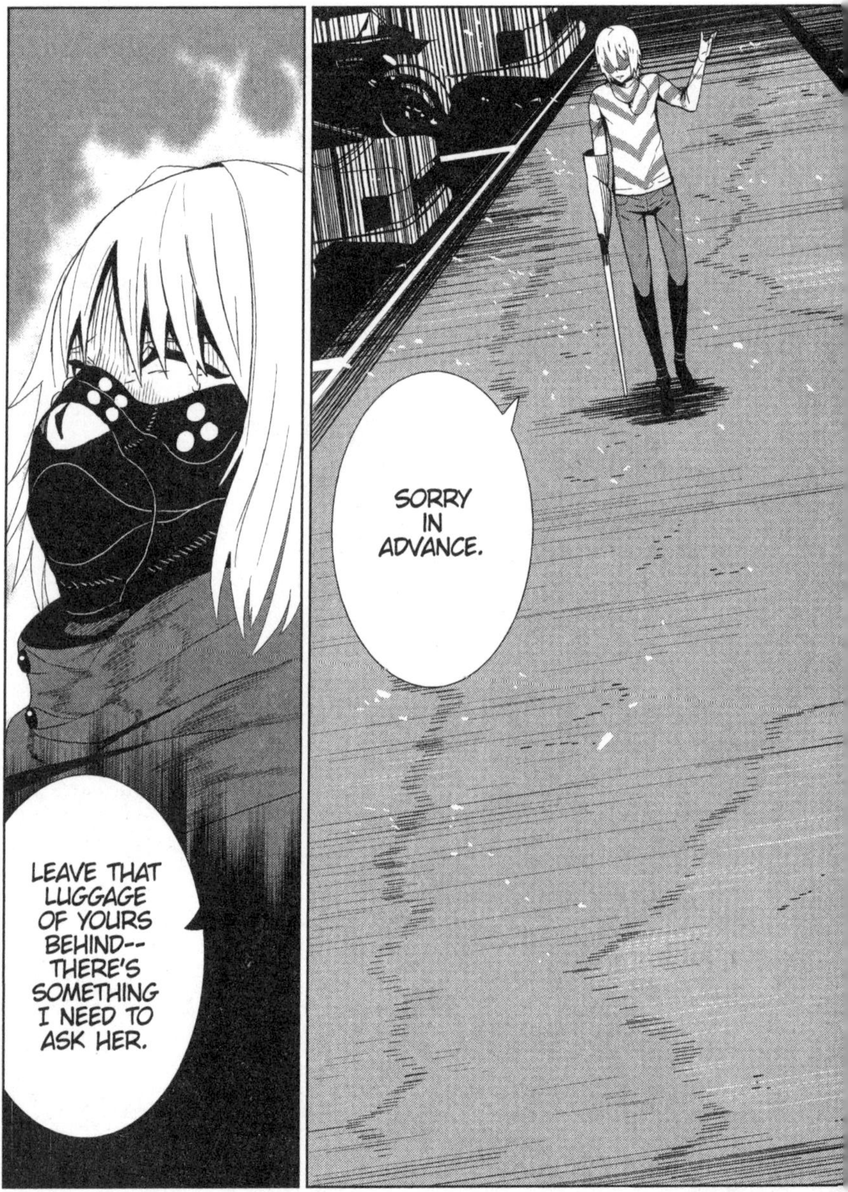
SORRY IN ADVANCE.
LEAVE THAT LUGGAGE OF YOURS BEHIND-- THERE'S SOMETHING I NEED TO ASK HER.

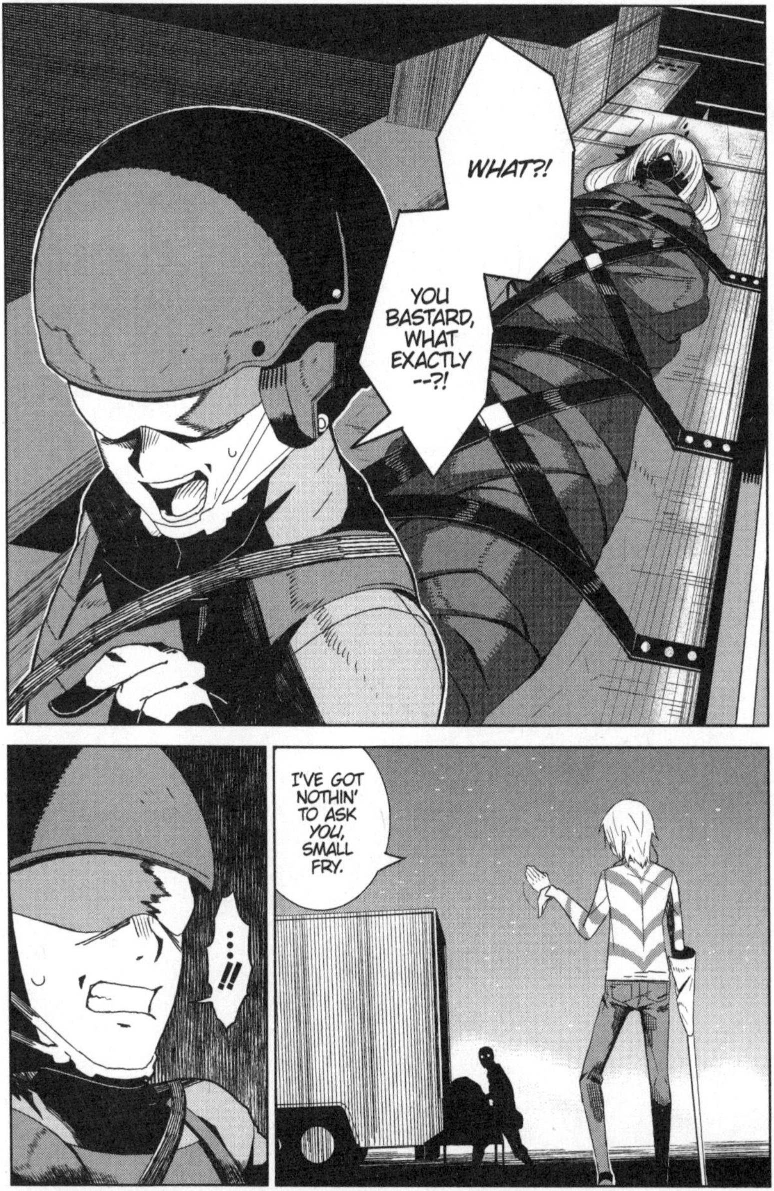
WHAT?!
YOU BASTARD, WHAT EXACTLY --?!
I'VE GOT NOTHIN' TO ASK YOU, SMALL FRY.
....!!

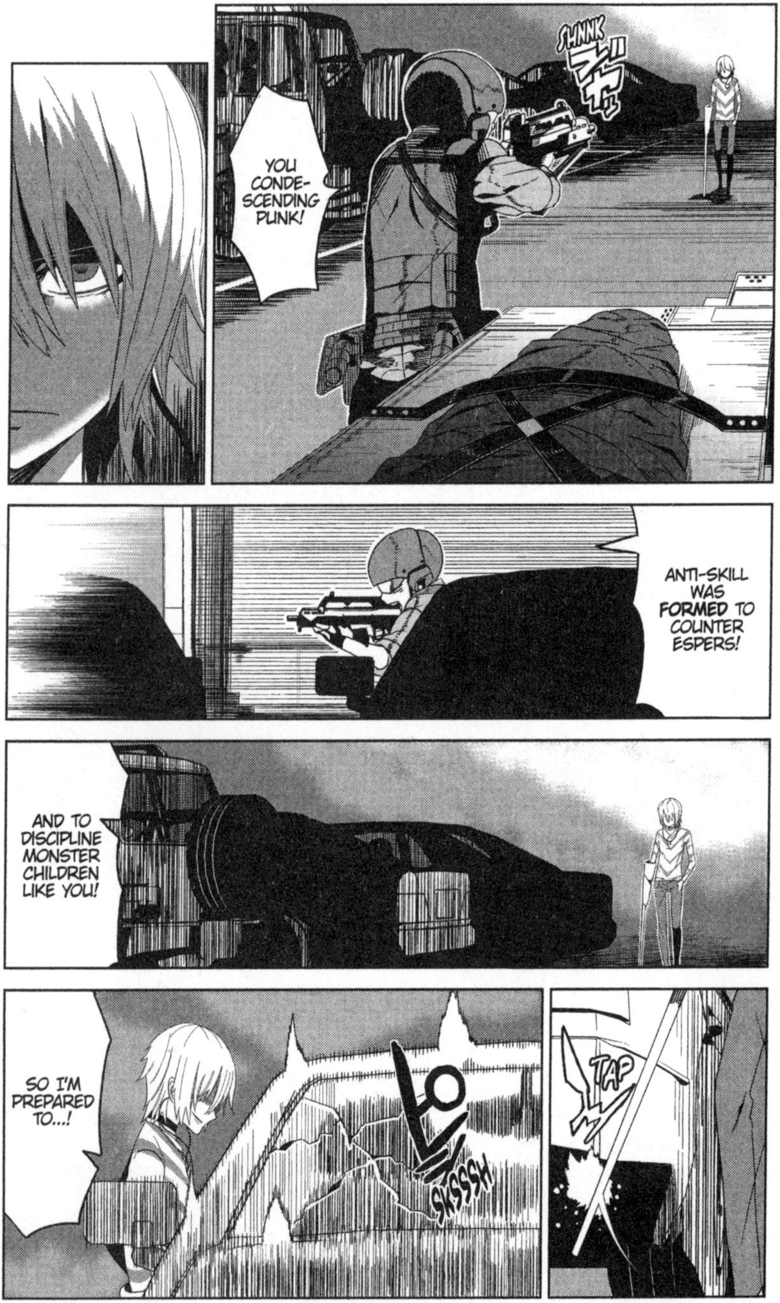
SHNNK
YOU CONDE-SCENDING PUNK!
ANTI-SKILL WAS **FORMED** TO COUNTER ESPERS!
AND TO DISCIPLINE MONSTER CHILDREN LIKE YOU!
TAP
SO I'M PREPARED TO...!
SKSSSH

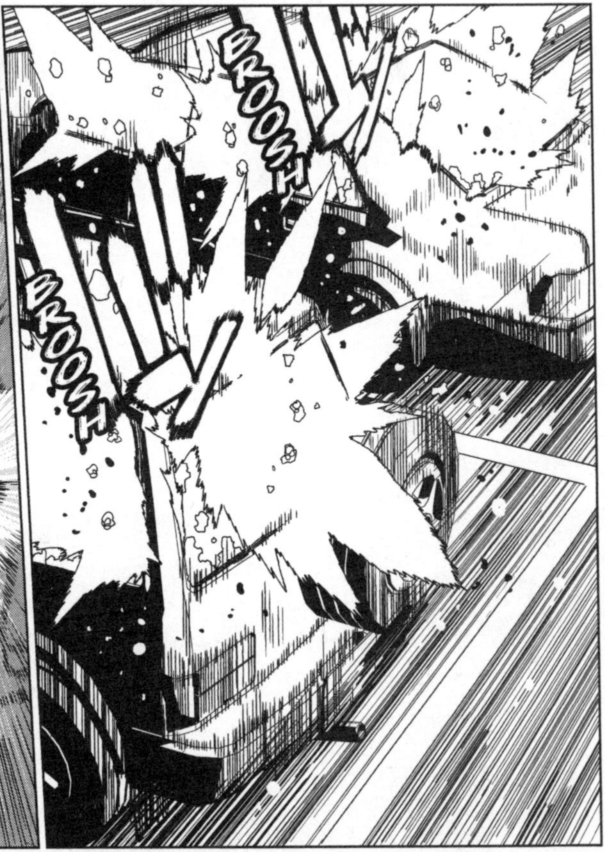
BROOSH
BROOSH

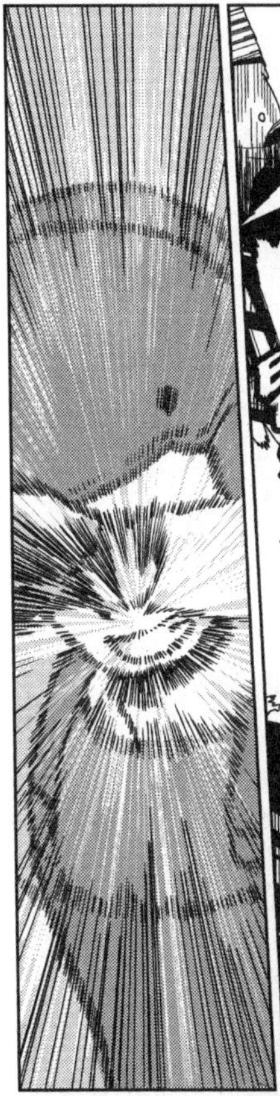

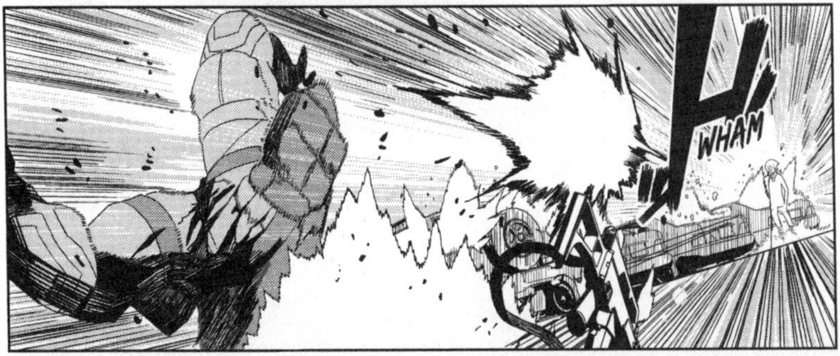
WHAM

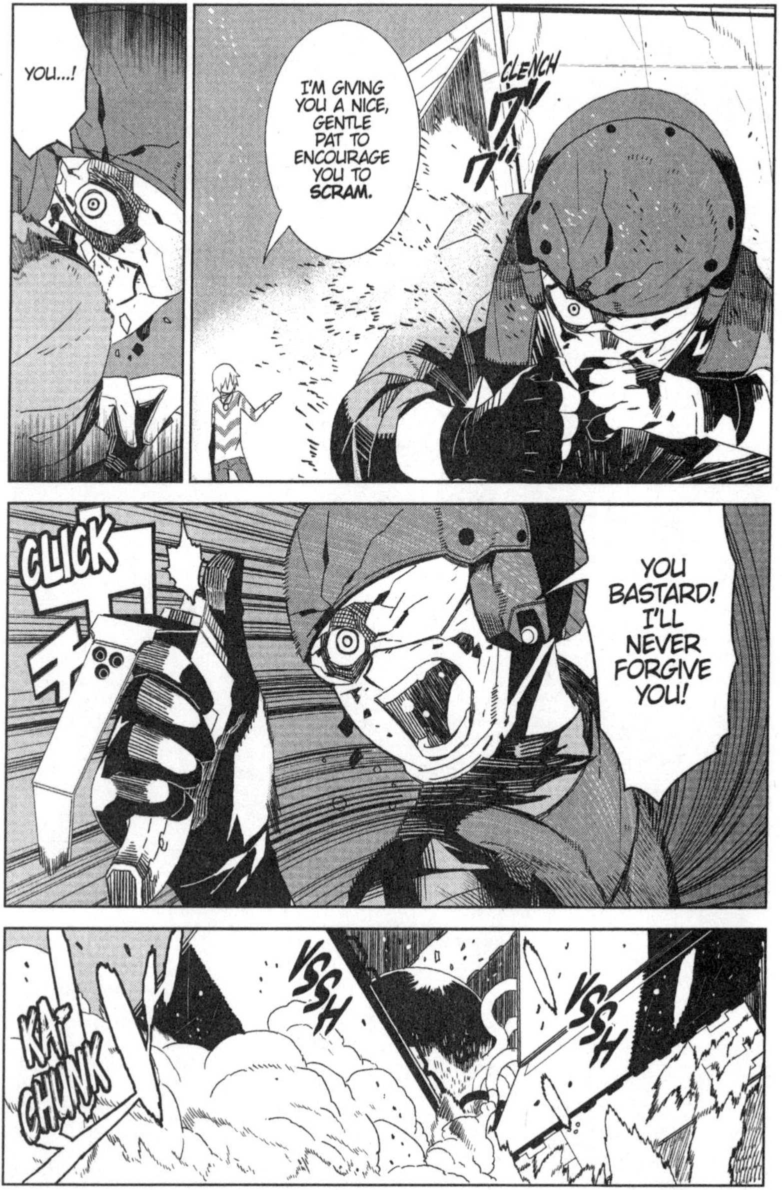
CLENCH
I'M GIVING YOU A NICE, GENTLE PAT TO ENCOURAGE YOU TO SCRAM.
YOU...!
YOU BASTARD! I'LL NEVER FORGIVE YOU!
CLICK
VSSH
VSSH
KA-CHUNK

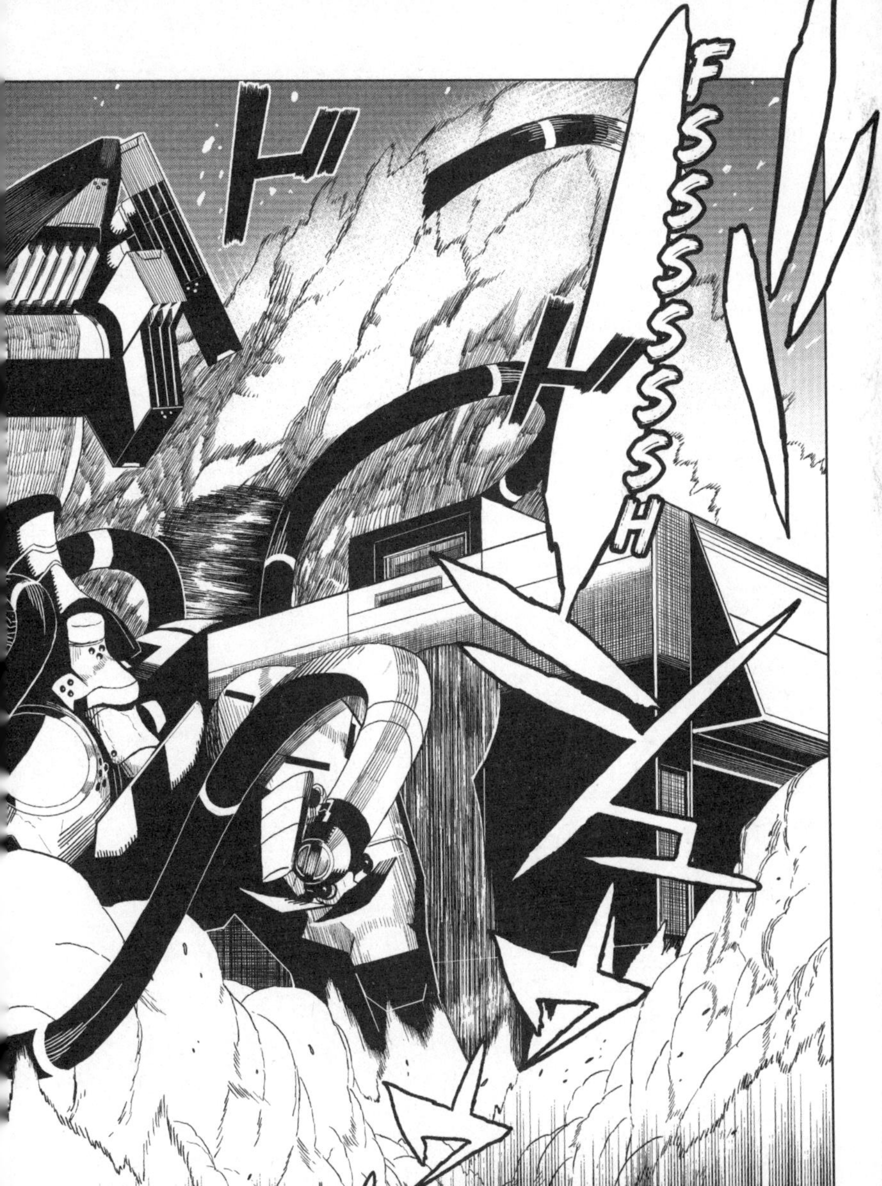
FSSSSSSSH

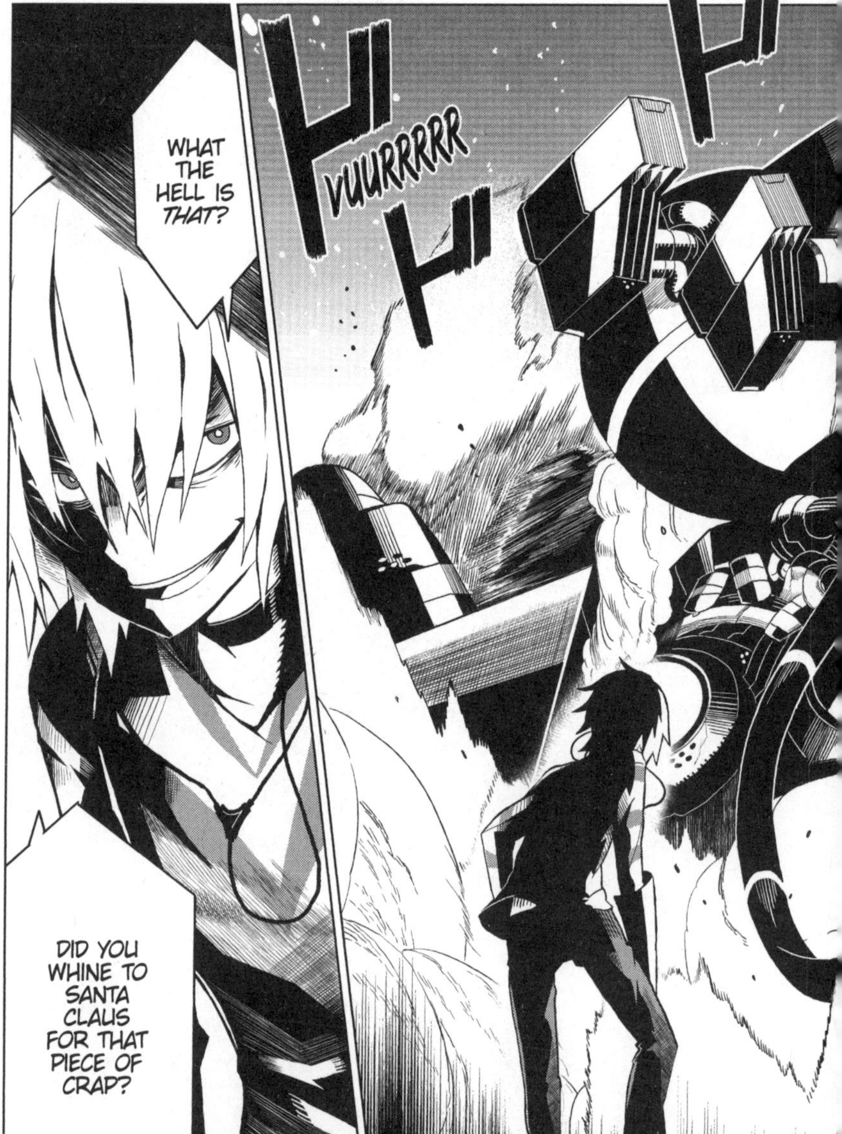
VUURRRRR
WHAT THE HELL IS *THAT?*
DID YOU WHINE TO SANTA CLAUS FOR THAT PIECE OF CRAP?

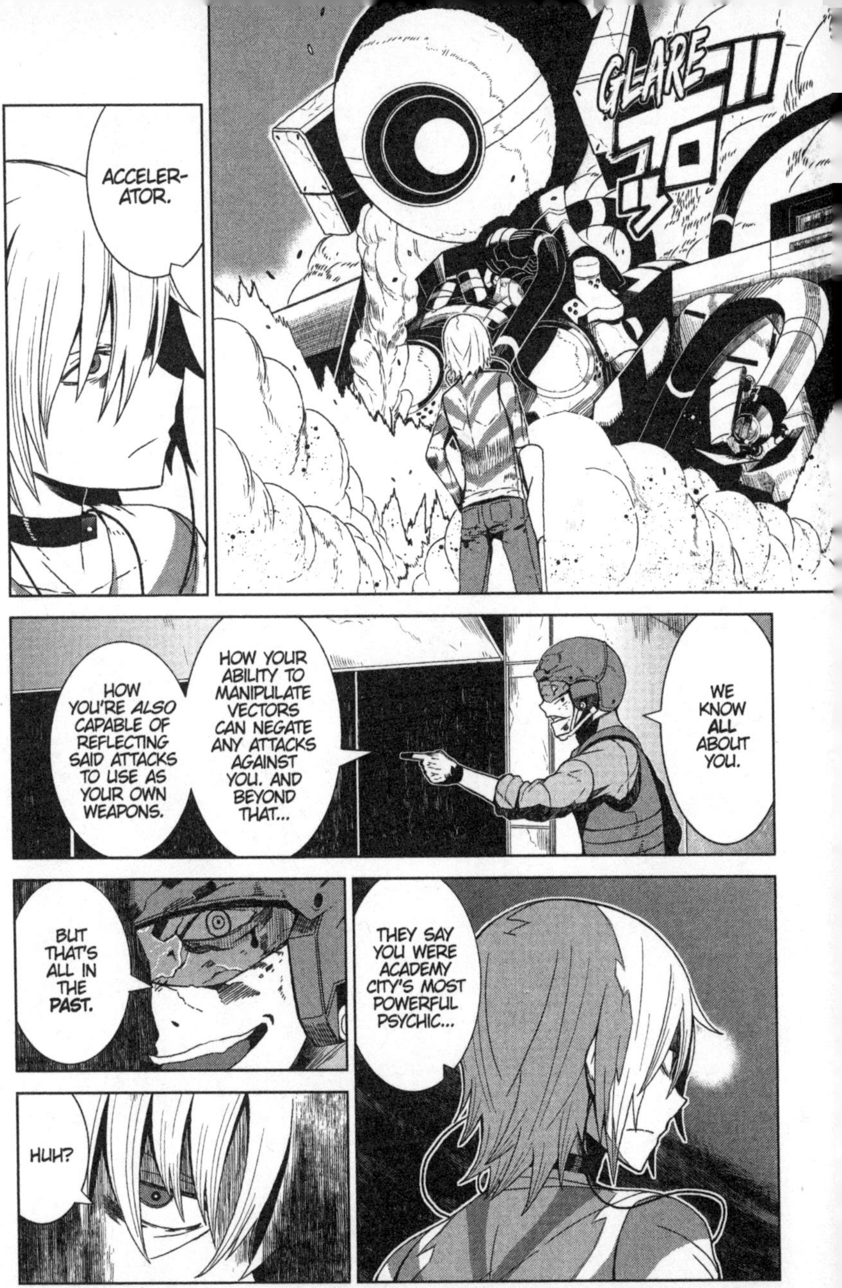
GLARE
ACCELER-ATOR.
WE KNOW ALL ABOUT YOU.
HOW YOUR ABILITY TO MANIPULATE VECTORS CAN NEGATE ANY ATTACKS AGAINST YOU. AND BEYOND THAT...
HOW YOU'RE *ALSO* CAPABLE OF REFLECTING SAID ATTACKS TO USE AS YOUR OWN WEAPONS.
THEY SAY YOU WERE ACADEMY CITY'S MOST POWERFUL PSYCHIC...
BUT THAT'S ALL IN THE **PAST.**
HUH?

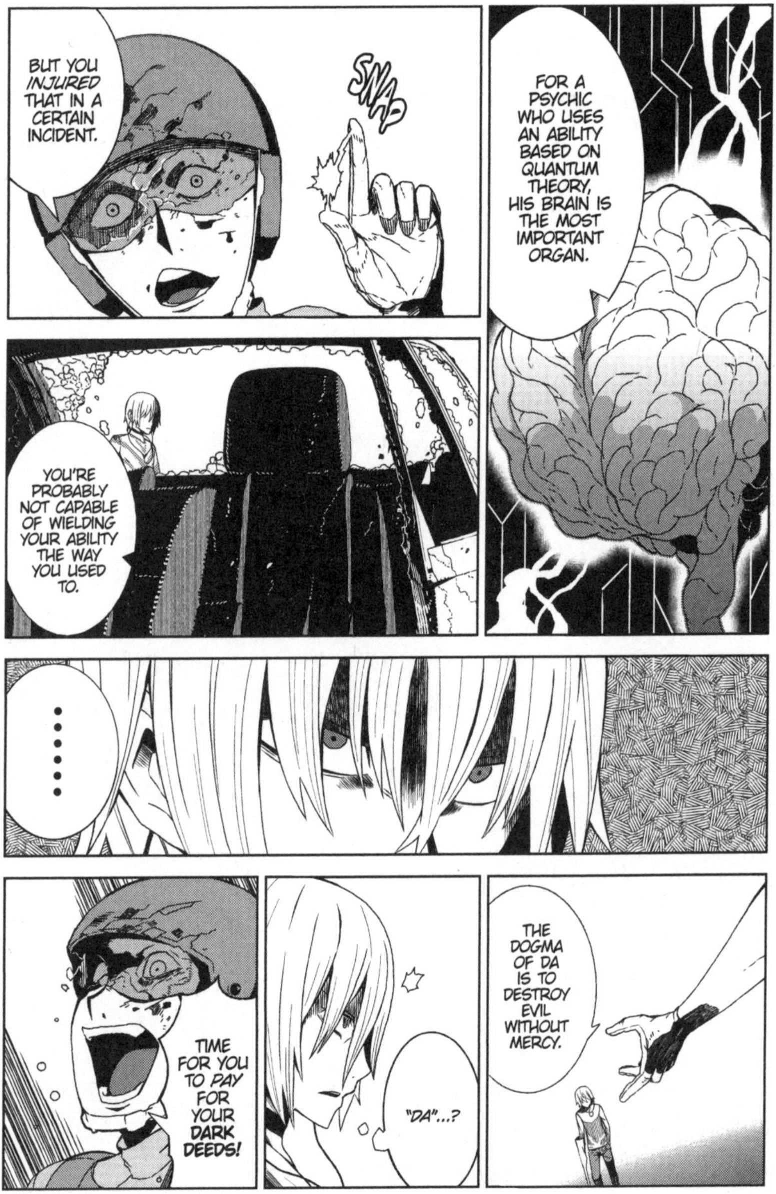
FOR A PSYCHIC WHO USES AN ABILITY BASED ON QUANTUM THEORY, HIS BRAIN IS THE MOST IMPORTANT ORGAN.
SNAP
BUT YOU *INJURED* THAT IN A CERTAIN INCIDENT.
YOU'RE PROBABLY NOT CAPABLE OF WIELDING YOUR ABILITY THE WAY YOU USED TO.
......
THE DOGMA OF DA IS TO DESTROY EVIL WITHOUT MERCY.
"DA"...?
TIME FOR YOU TO *PAY* FOR YOUR **DARK DEEDS!**

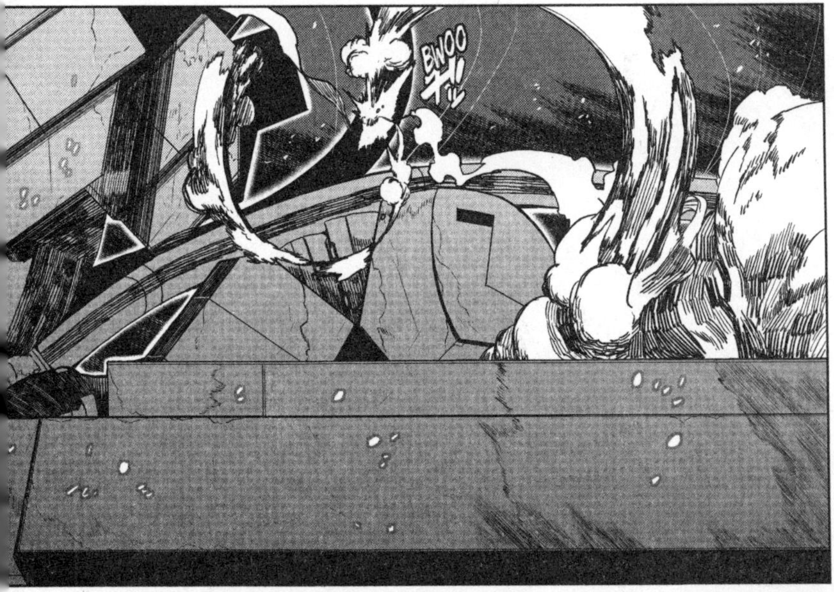
BWOO
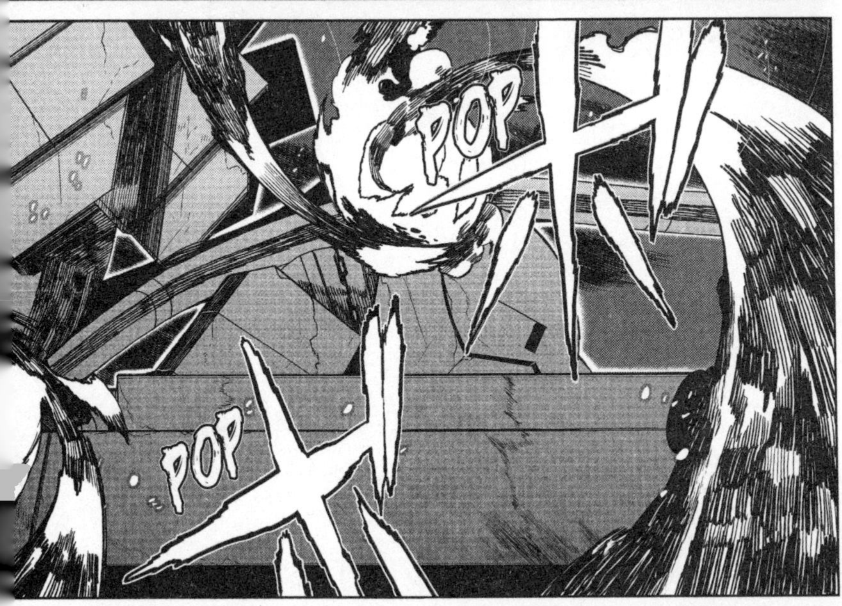
POP
POP

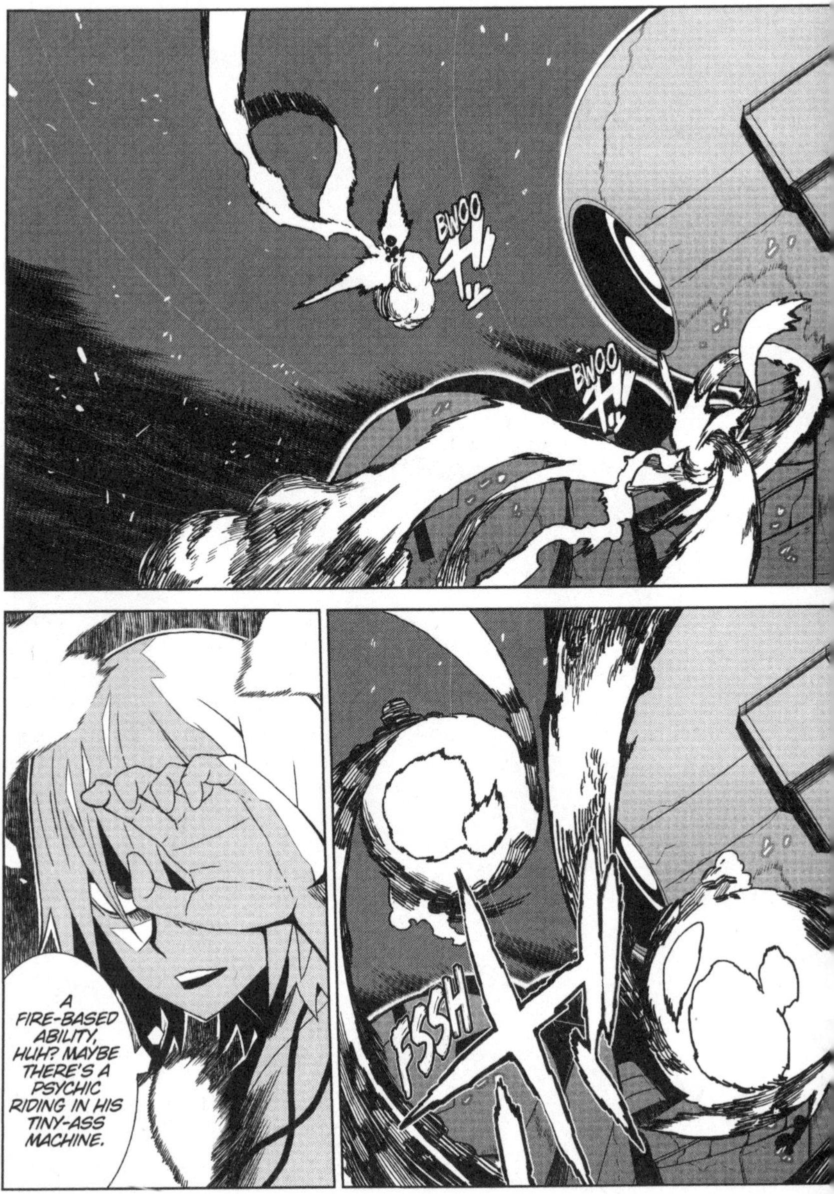
BWOO
BWOO
FSSH
A FIRE-BASED ABILITY, HUH? MAYBE THERE'S A PSYCHIC RIDING IN HIS TINY-ASS MACHINE.

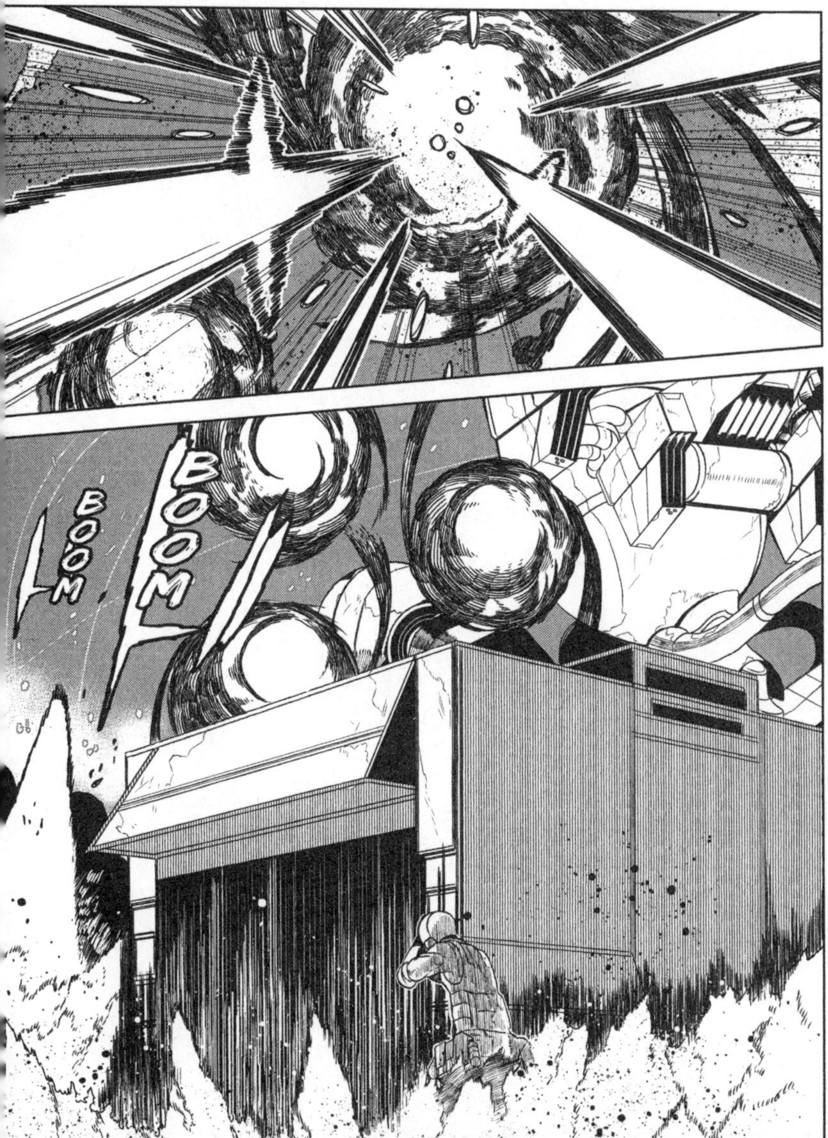
BOOM
BOOM

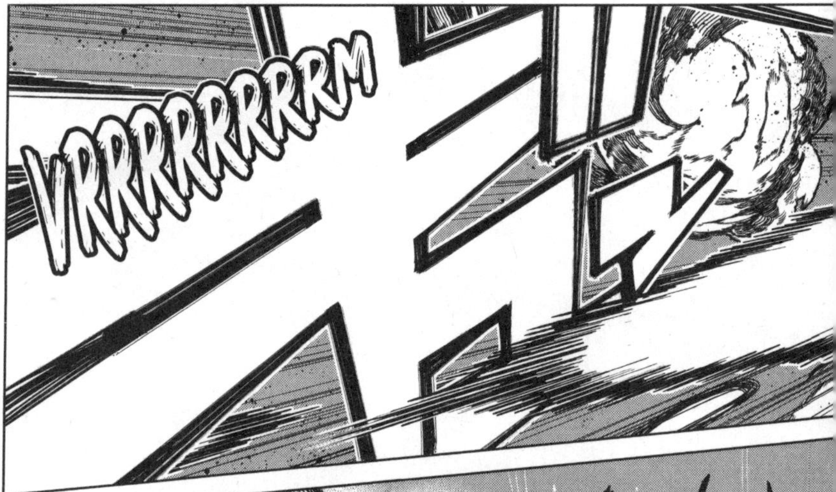
VRRRRRRRRM

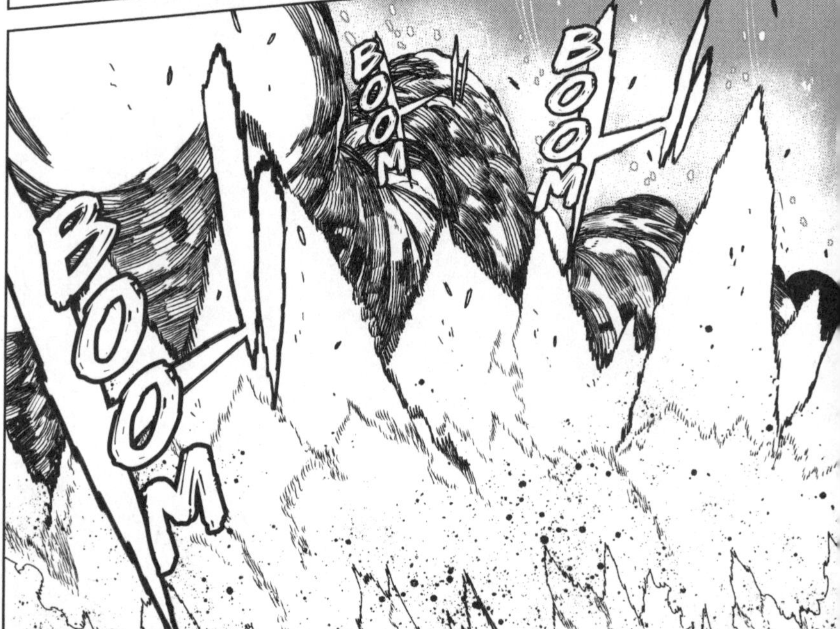
BOOOM
BOOOM
BOOOM

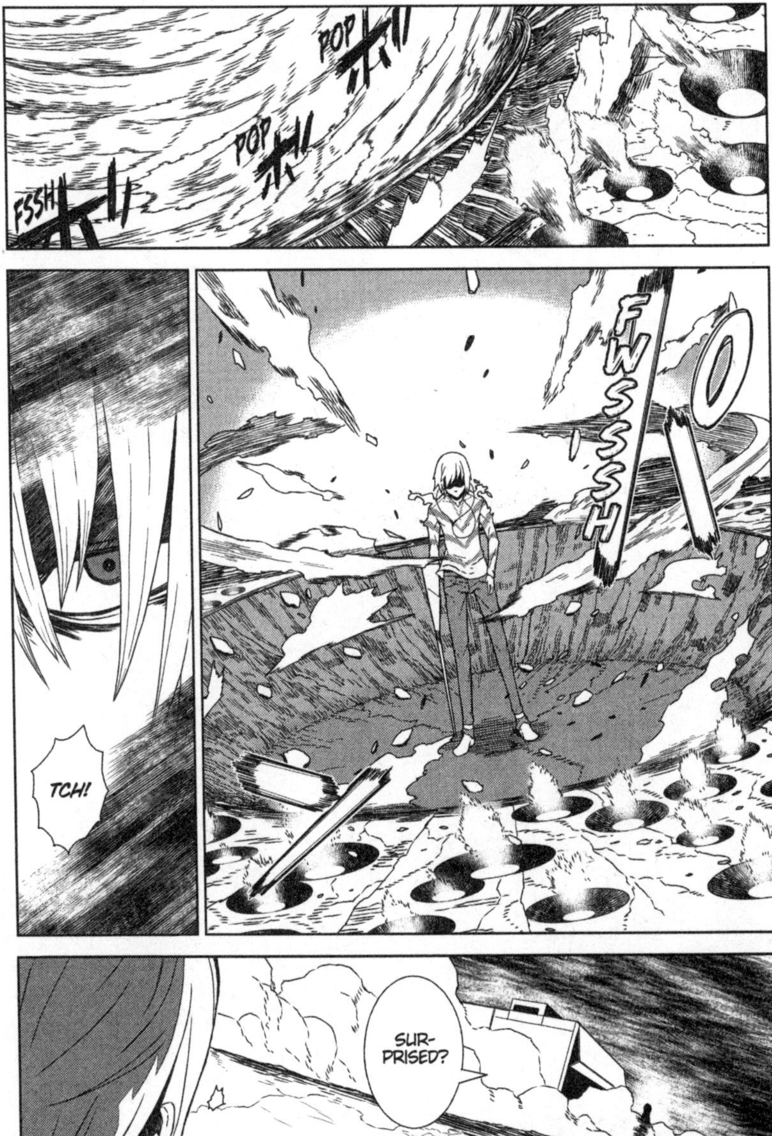
POP
POP
FSSH
FWSSSH
TCH!
SUR-PRISED?

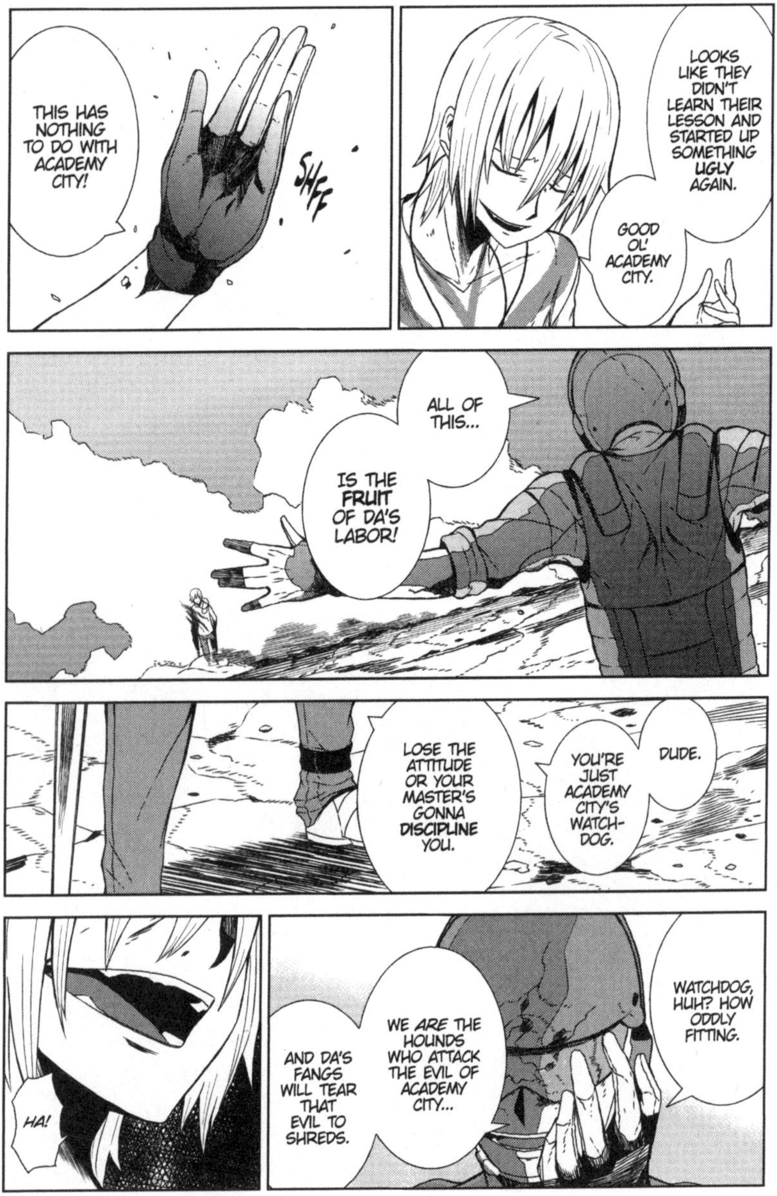
LOOKS LIKE THEY DIDN'T LEARN THEIR LESSON AND STARTED UP SOMETHING UGLY AGAIN.
GOOD OL' ACADEMY CITY.
THIS HAS NOTHING TO DO WITH ACADEMY CITY!
SHFF
ALL OF THIS...
IS THE FRUIT OF DA'S LABOR!
DUDE.
YOU'RE JUST ACADEMY CITY'S WATCH-DOG.
LOSE THE ATTITUDE OR YOUR MASTER'S GONNA DISCIPLINE YOU.
WATCHDOG, HUH? HOW ODDLY FITTING.
WE ARE THE HOUNDS WHO ATTACK THE EVIL OF ACADEMY CITY...
AND DA'S FANGS WILL TEAR THAT EVIL TO SHREDS.
HA!

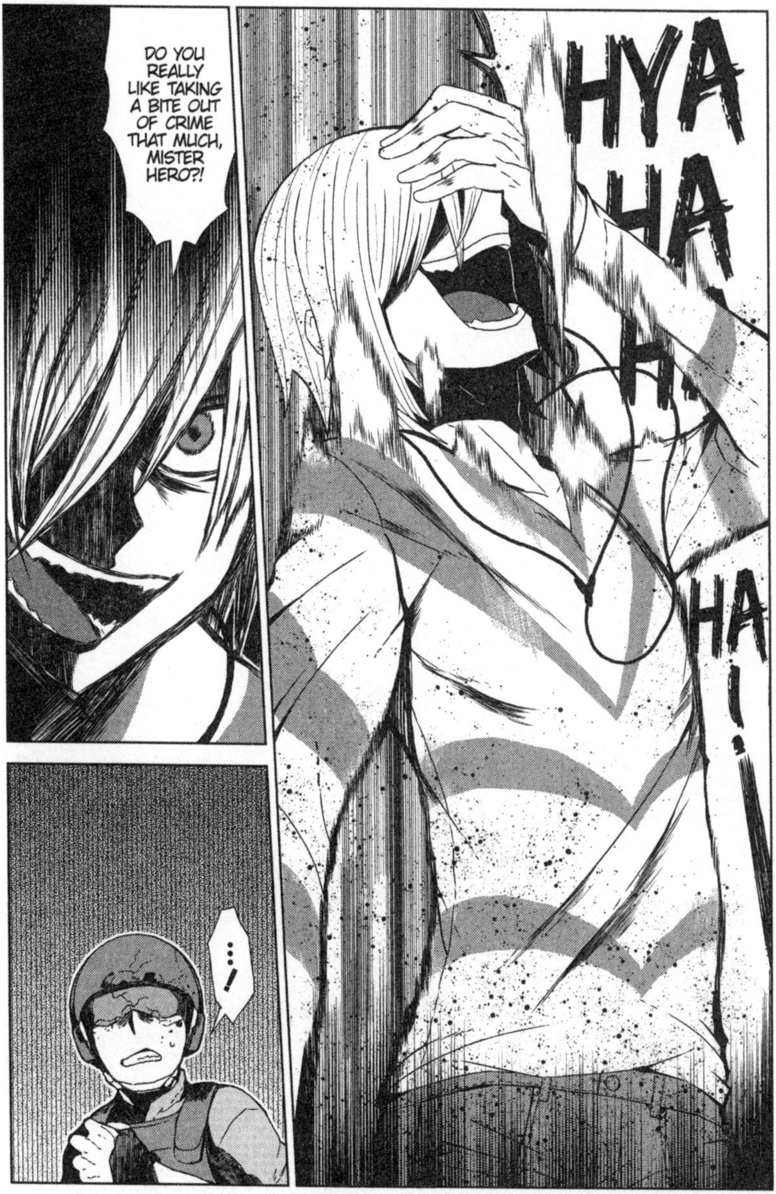
HYA HA HA HA!
DO YOU REALLY LIKE TAKING A BITE OUT OF CRIME THAT MUCH, MISTER HERO?!
...!

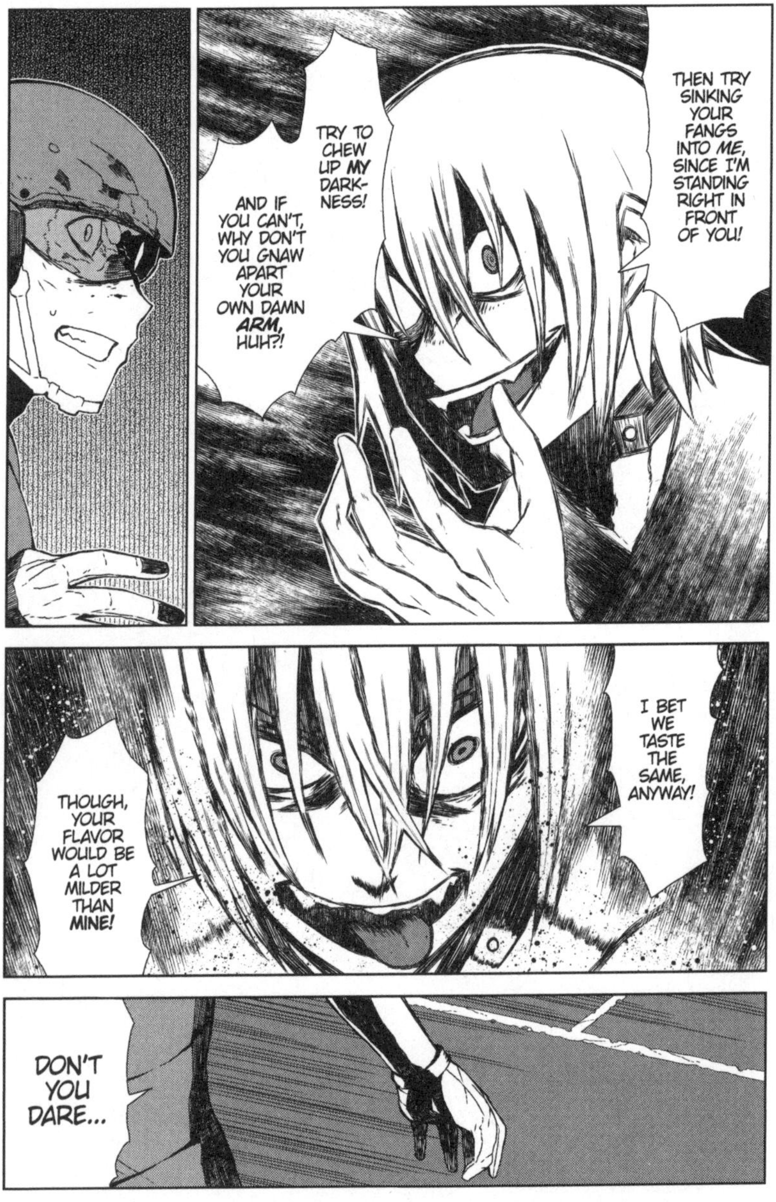
THEN TRY SINKING YOUR FANGS INTO *ME*, SINCE I'M STANDING RIGHT IN FRONT OF YOU!
TRY TO CHEW UP **MY** DARKNESS!
AND IF YOU CAN'T, WHY DON'T YOU GNAW APART YOUR OWN DAMN ***ARM***, HUH?!
I BET WE TASTE THE SAME, ANYWAY!
THOUGH, YOUR FLAVOR WOULD BE A LOT MILDER THAN **MINE**!
DON'T YOU DARE...

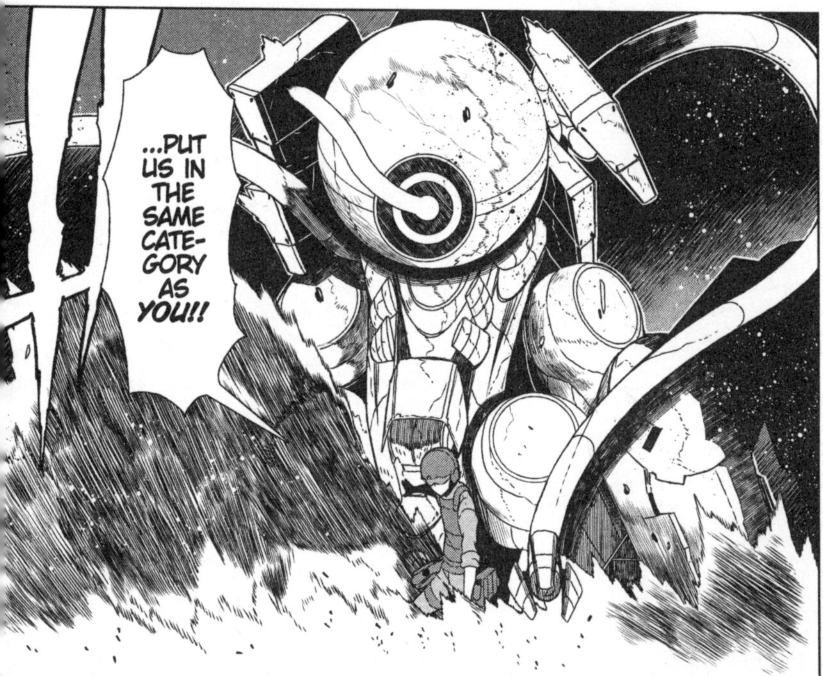
...PUT US IN THE SAME CATE-GORY AS YOU!!
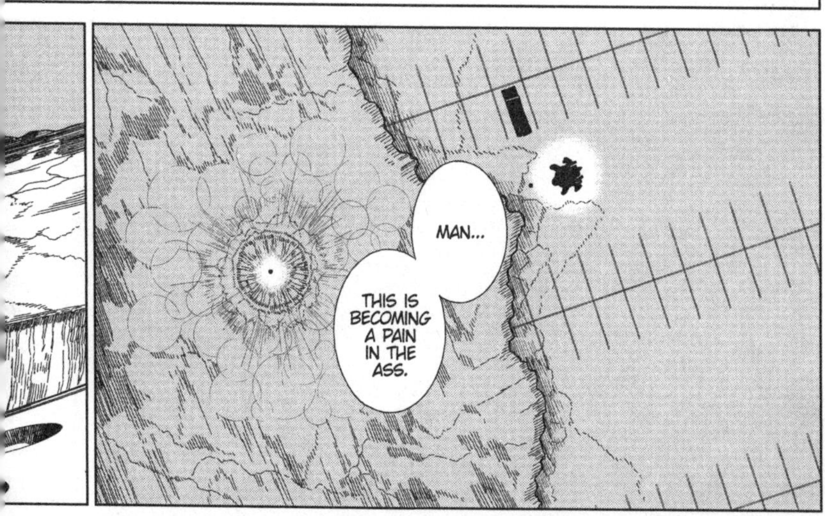
MAN...
THIS IS BECOMING A PAIN IN THE ASS.

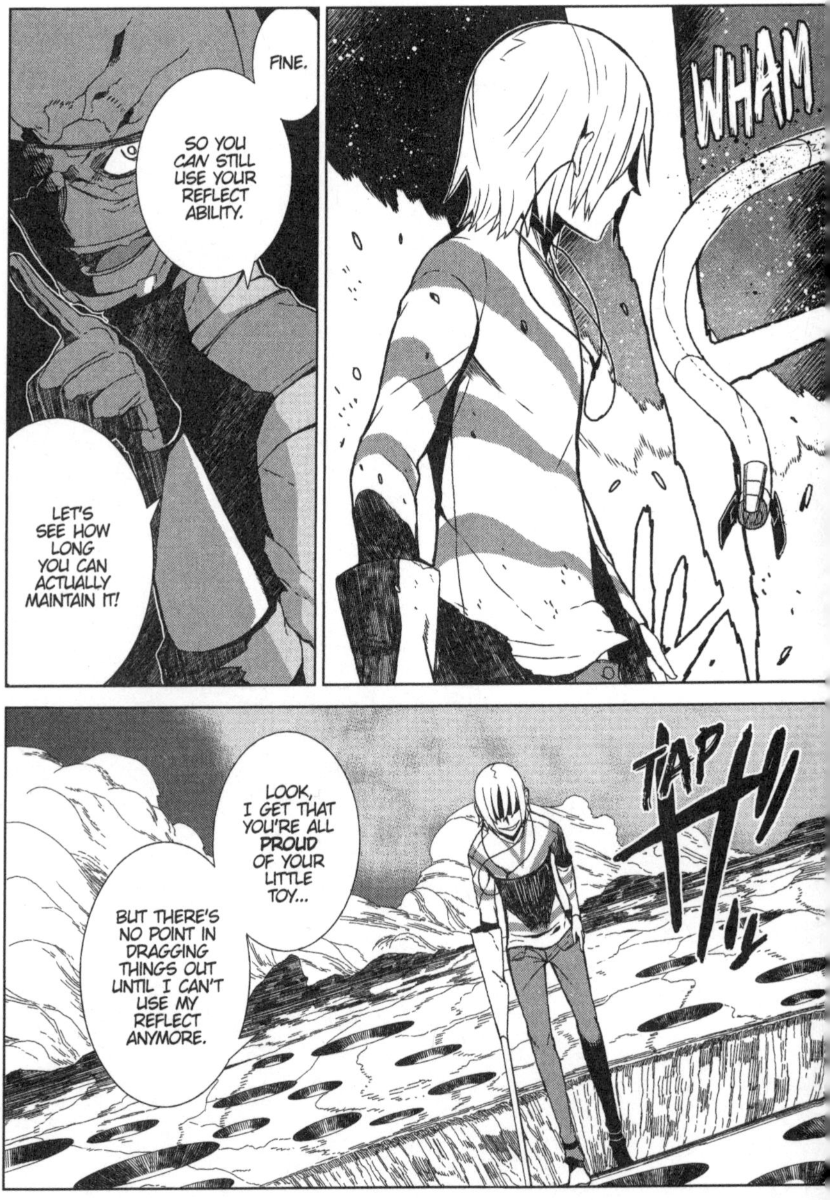
WHAM
FINE.
SO YOU CAN STILL USE YOUR REFLECT ABILITY.
LET'S SEE HOW LONG YOU CAN ACTUALLY MAINTAIN IT!
TAP
LOOK, I GET THAT YOU'RE ALL **PROUD** OF YOUR LITTLE TOY...
BUT THERE'S NO POINT IN DRAGGING THINGS OUT UNTIL I CAN'T USE MY REFLECT ANYMORE.

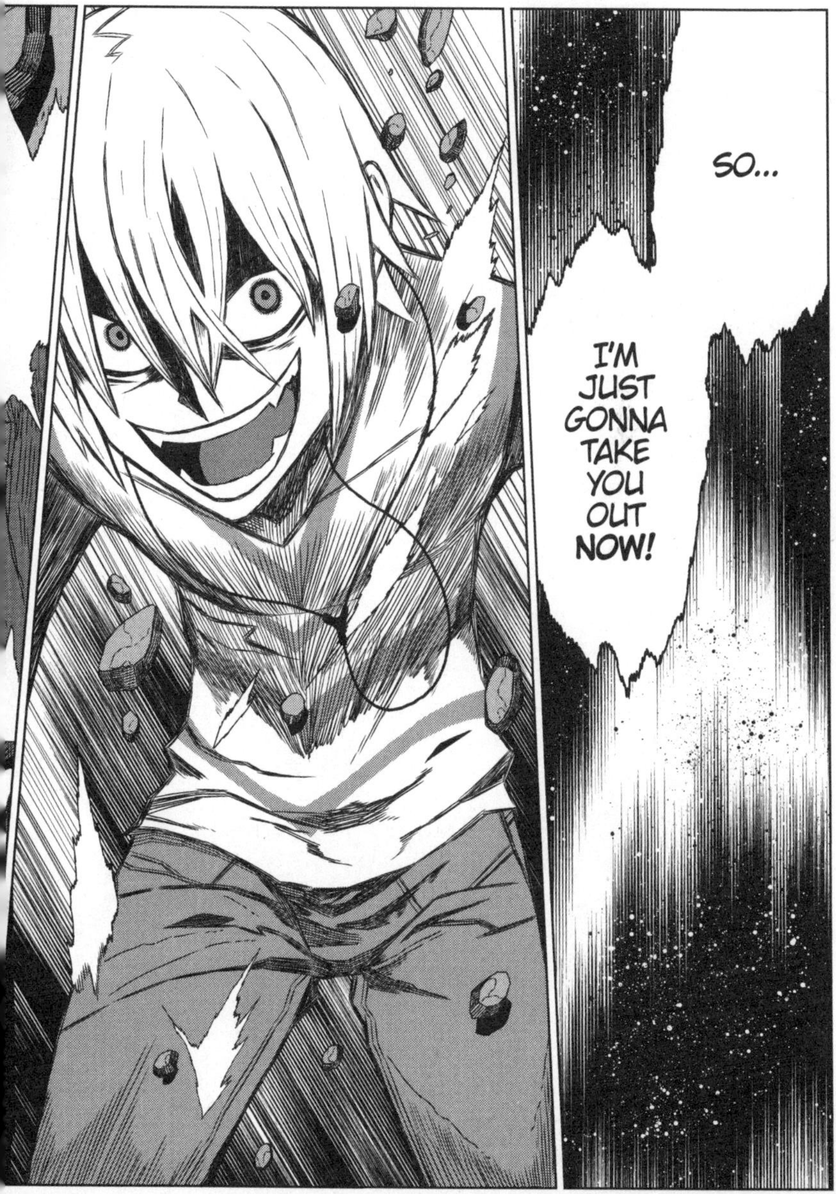
SO...
I'M JUST GONNA TAKE YOU OUT NOW!

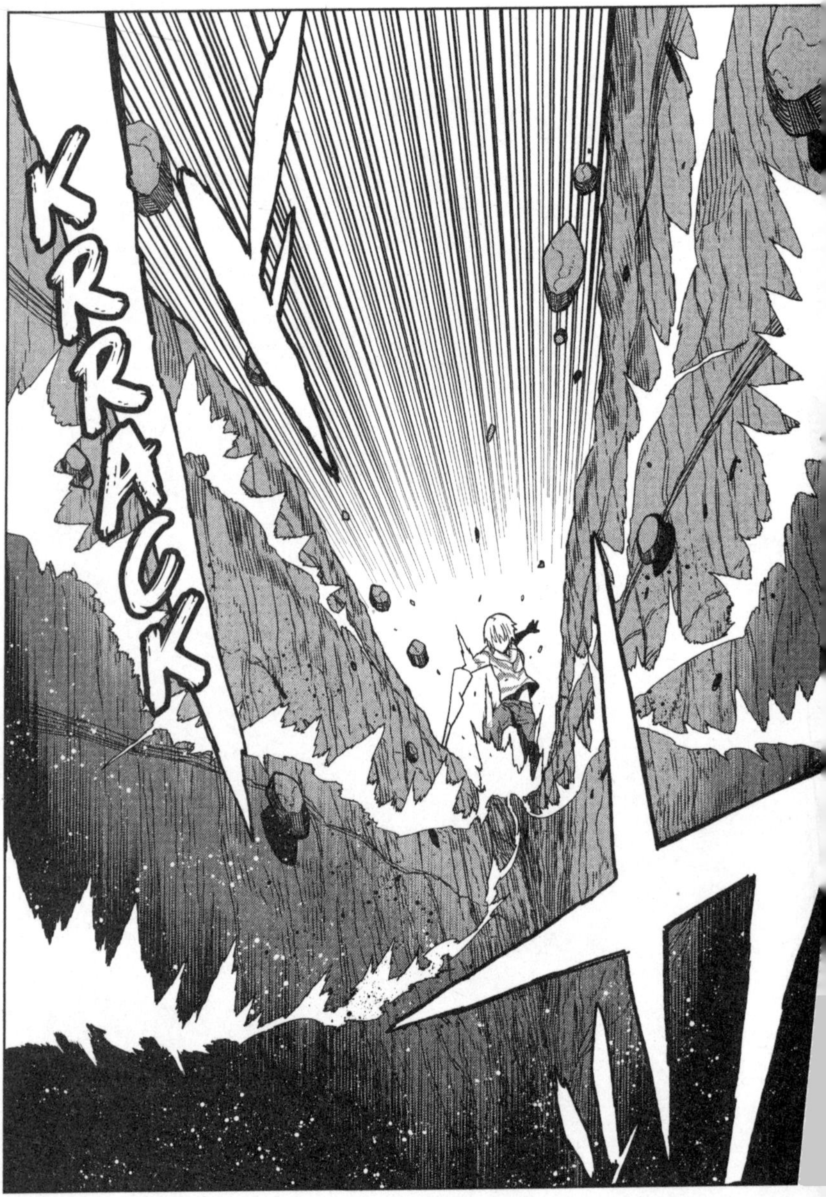
KRRACK

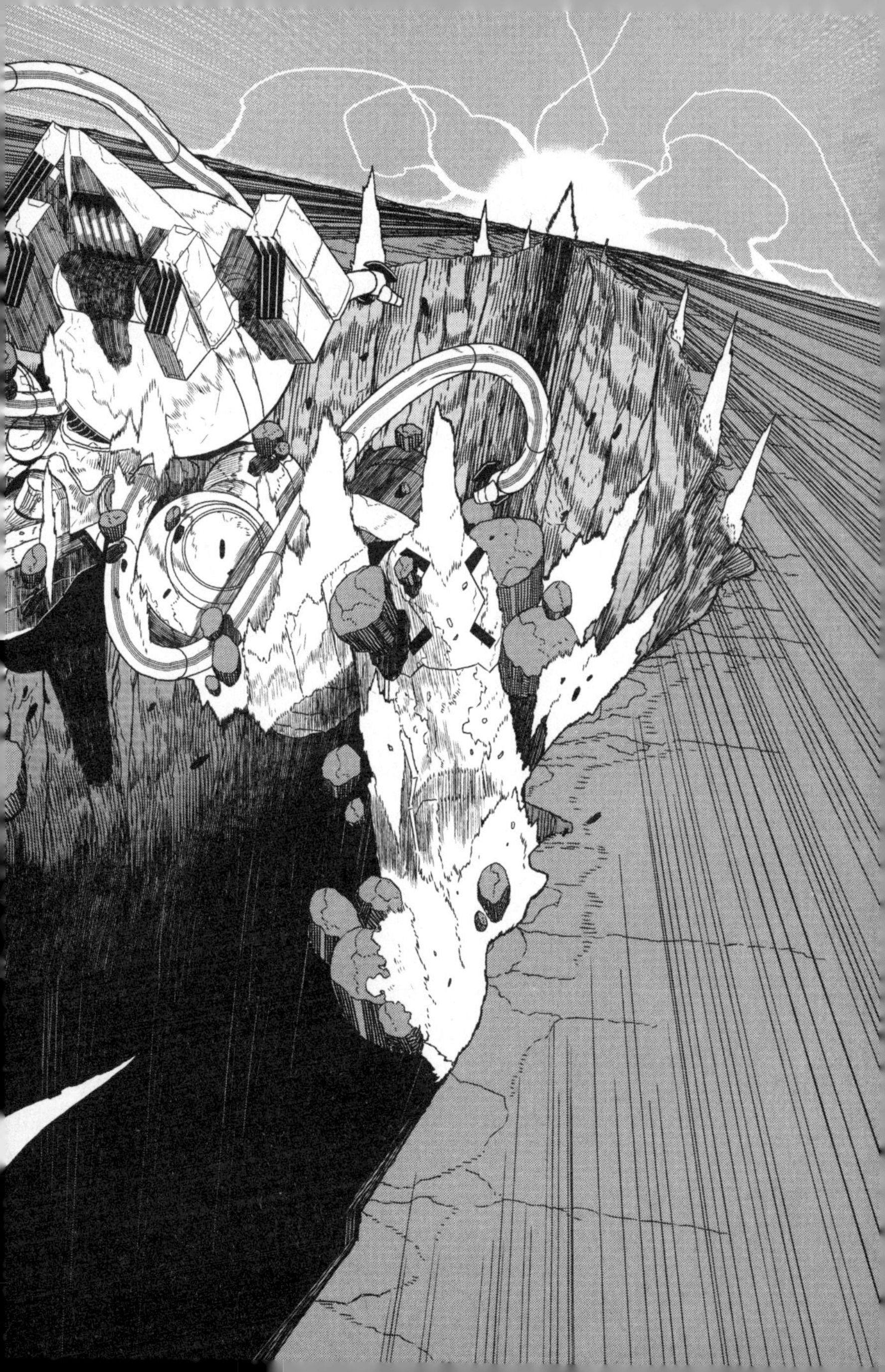

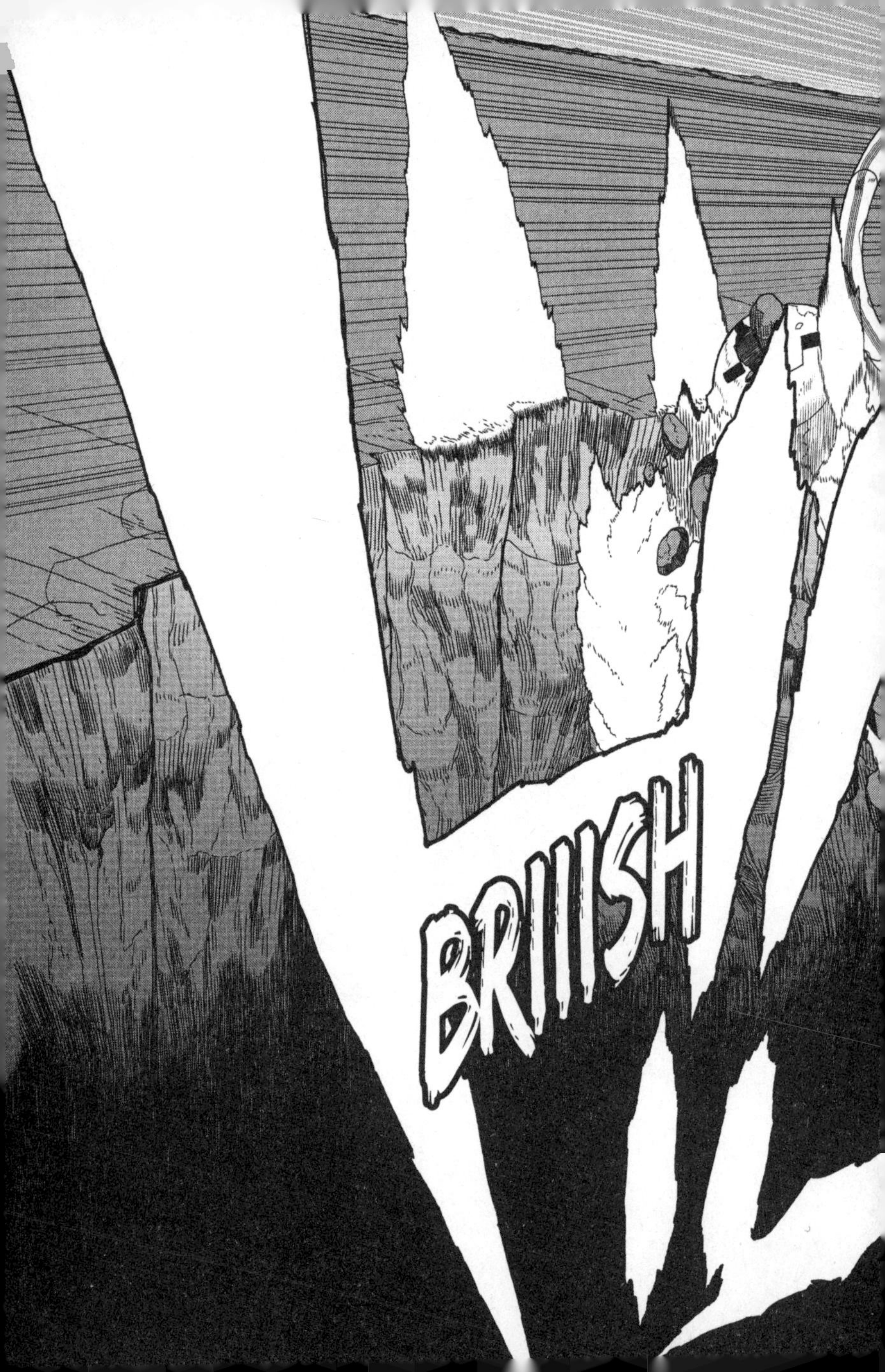
BRIIISH

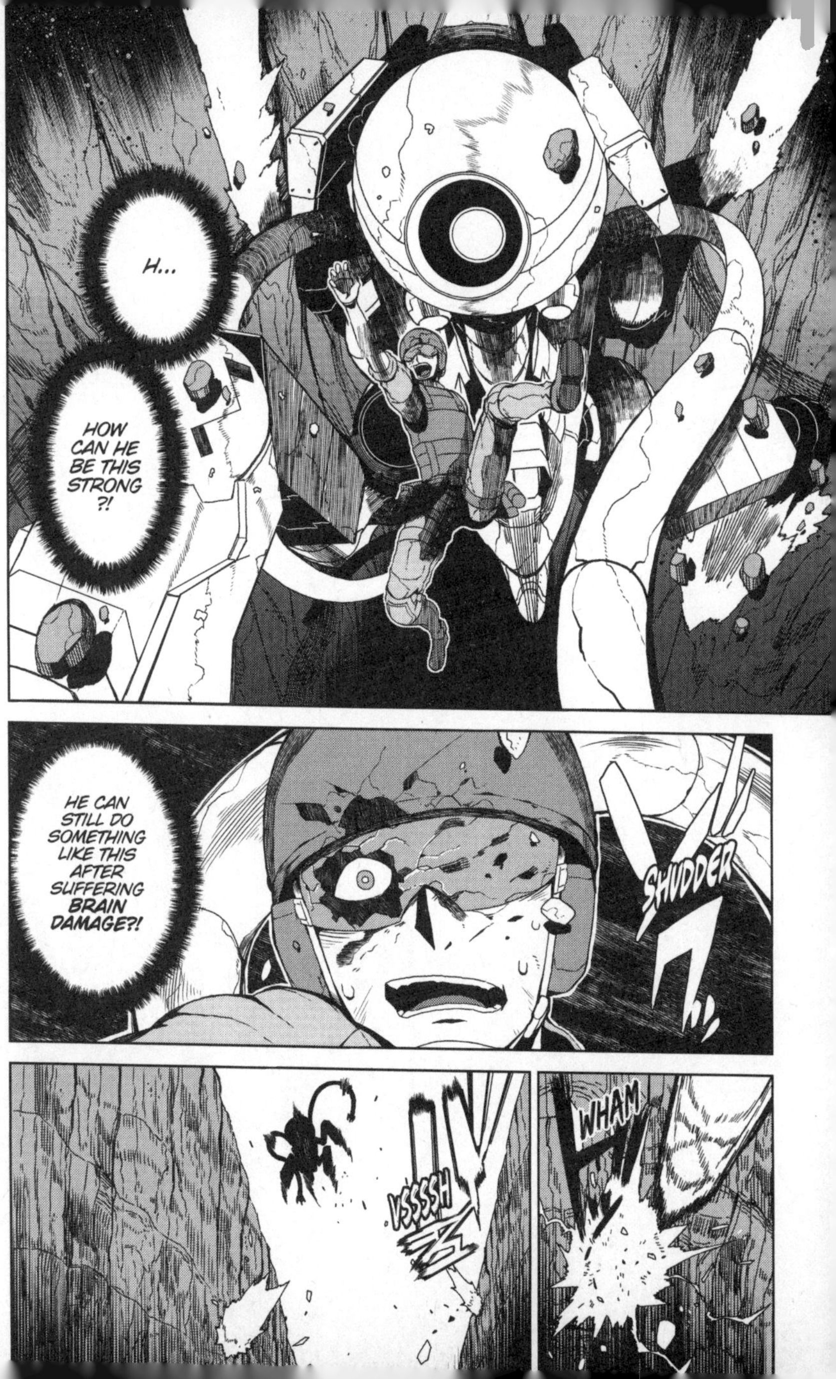
H...
HOW CAN HE BE THIS STRONG ?!
HE CAN STILL DO SOMETHING LIKE THIS AFTER SUFFERING BRAIN DAMAGE?!
SHUDDER
VSSSSH
WHAM

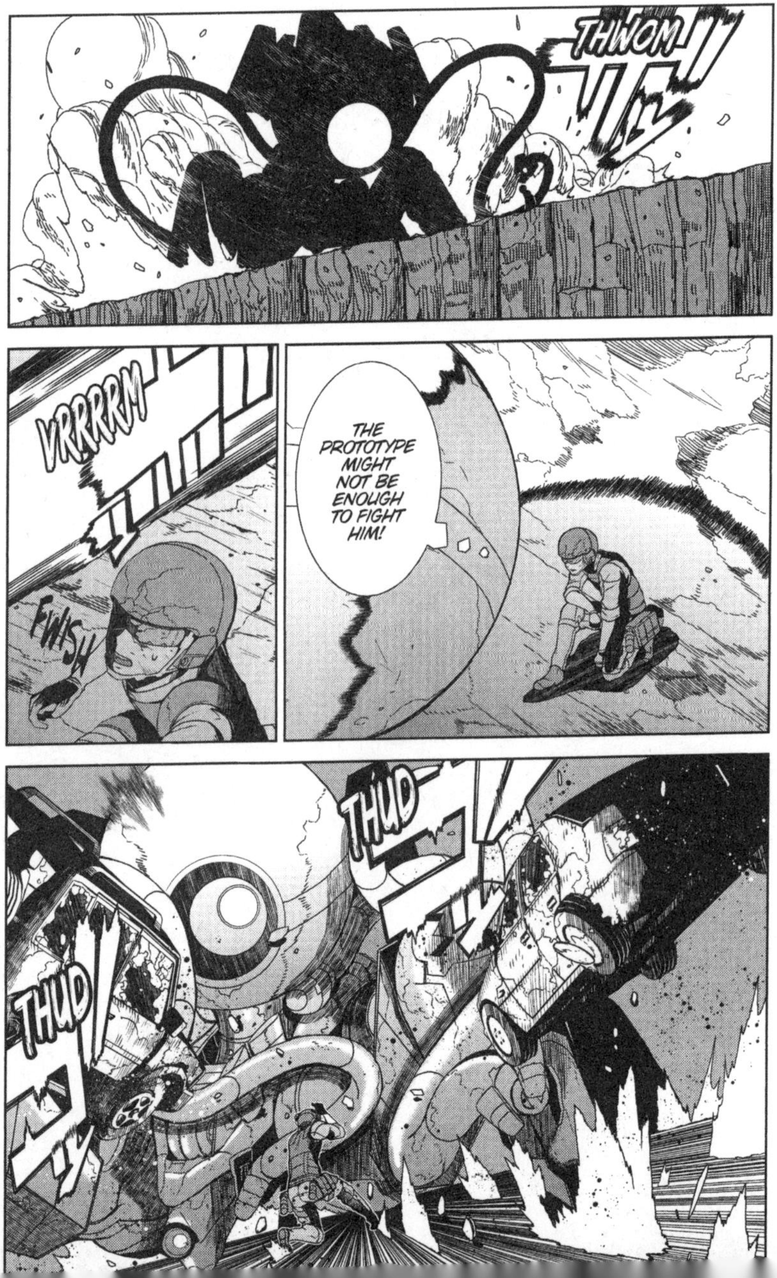
THWOM
THE PROTOTYPE MIGHT NOT BE ENOUGH TO FIGHT HIM!
VRRRRM
FWISH
THUD
THUD

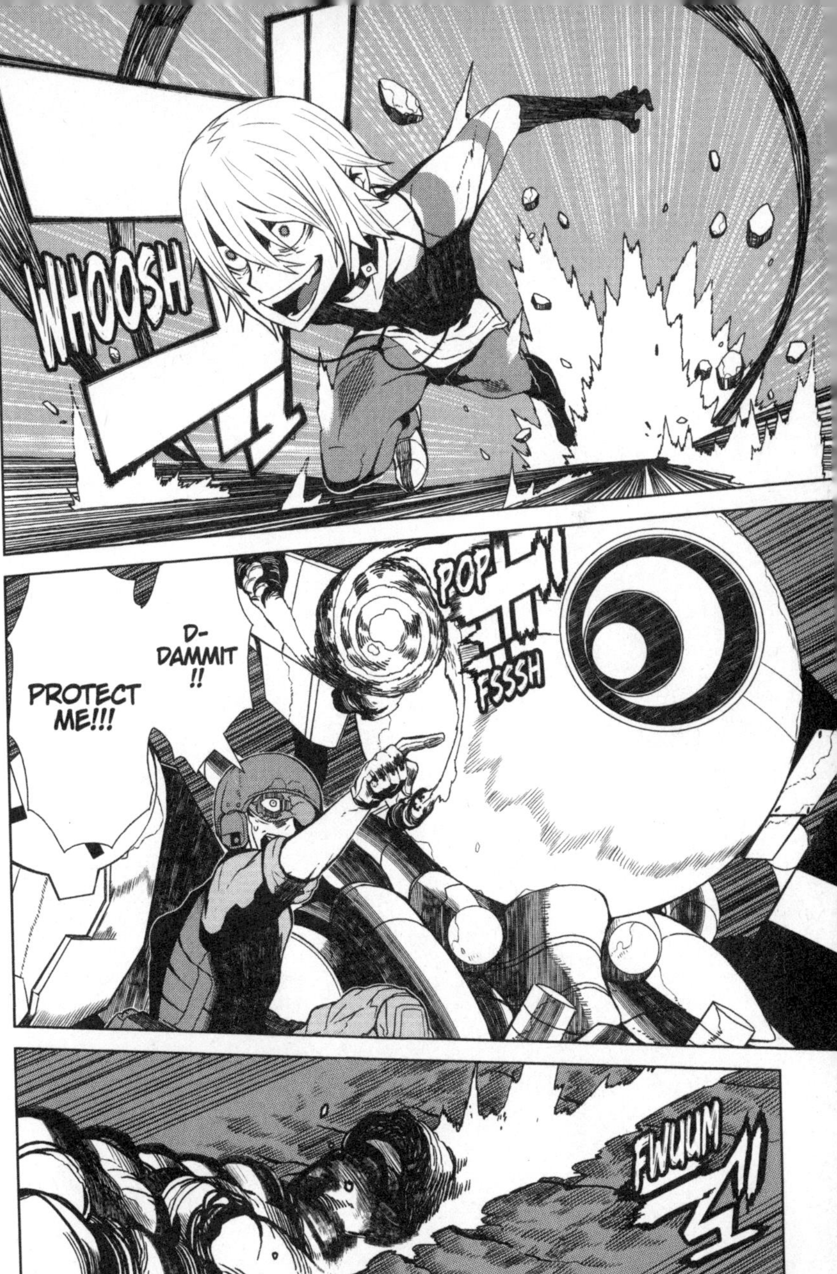
WHOOSH
POP
FSSSH
D-DAMMIT!!
PROTECT ME!!!
FWUUM

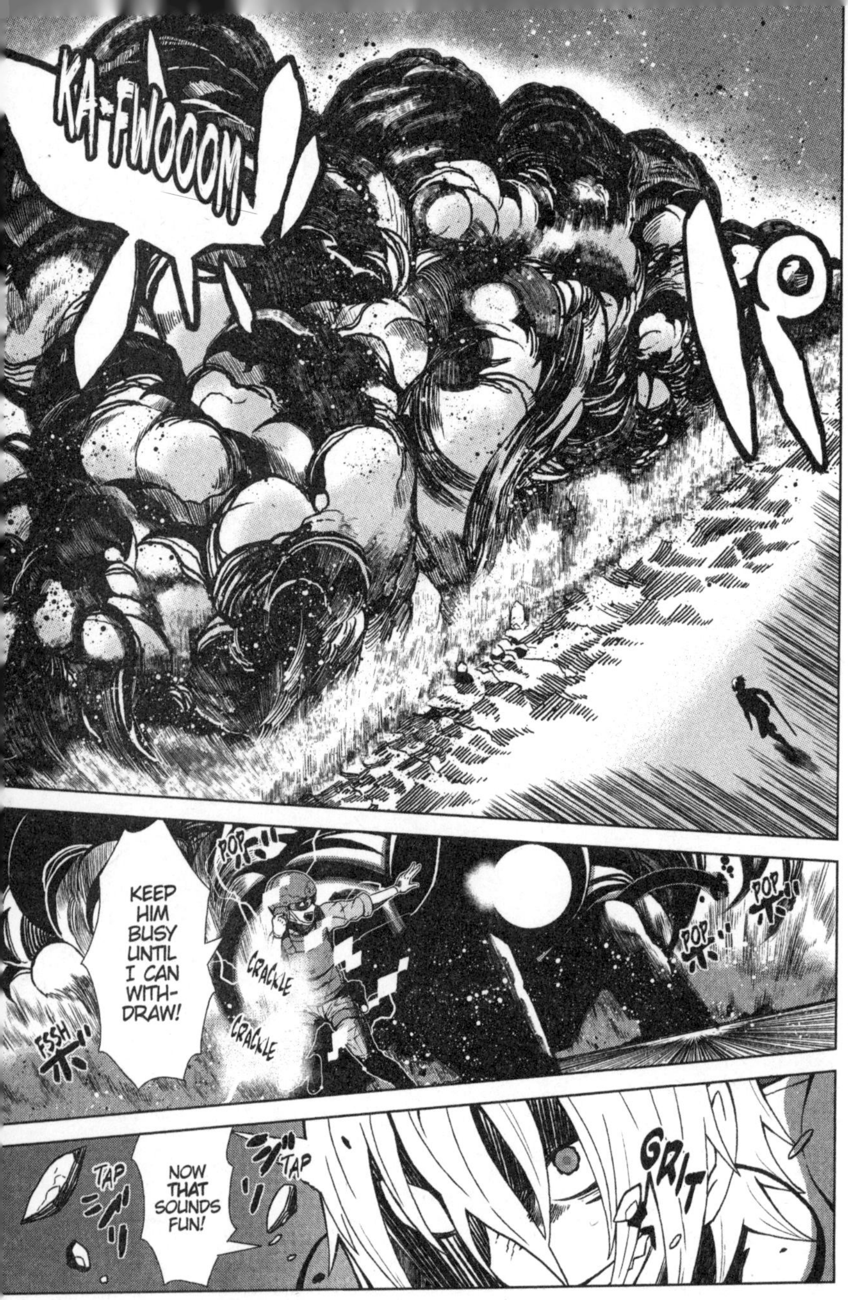
KA-FWOOOM
POP
POP
POP
POP
KEEP HIM BUSY UNTIL I CAN WITH-DRAW!
CRACKLE
CRACKLE
FSSH
GRIT
TAP
NOW THAT SOUNDS FUN!
TAP

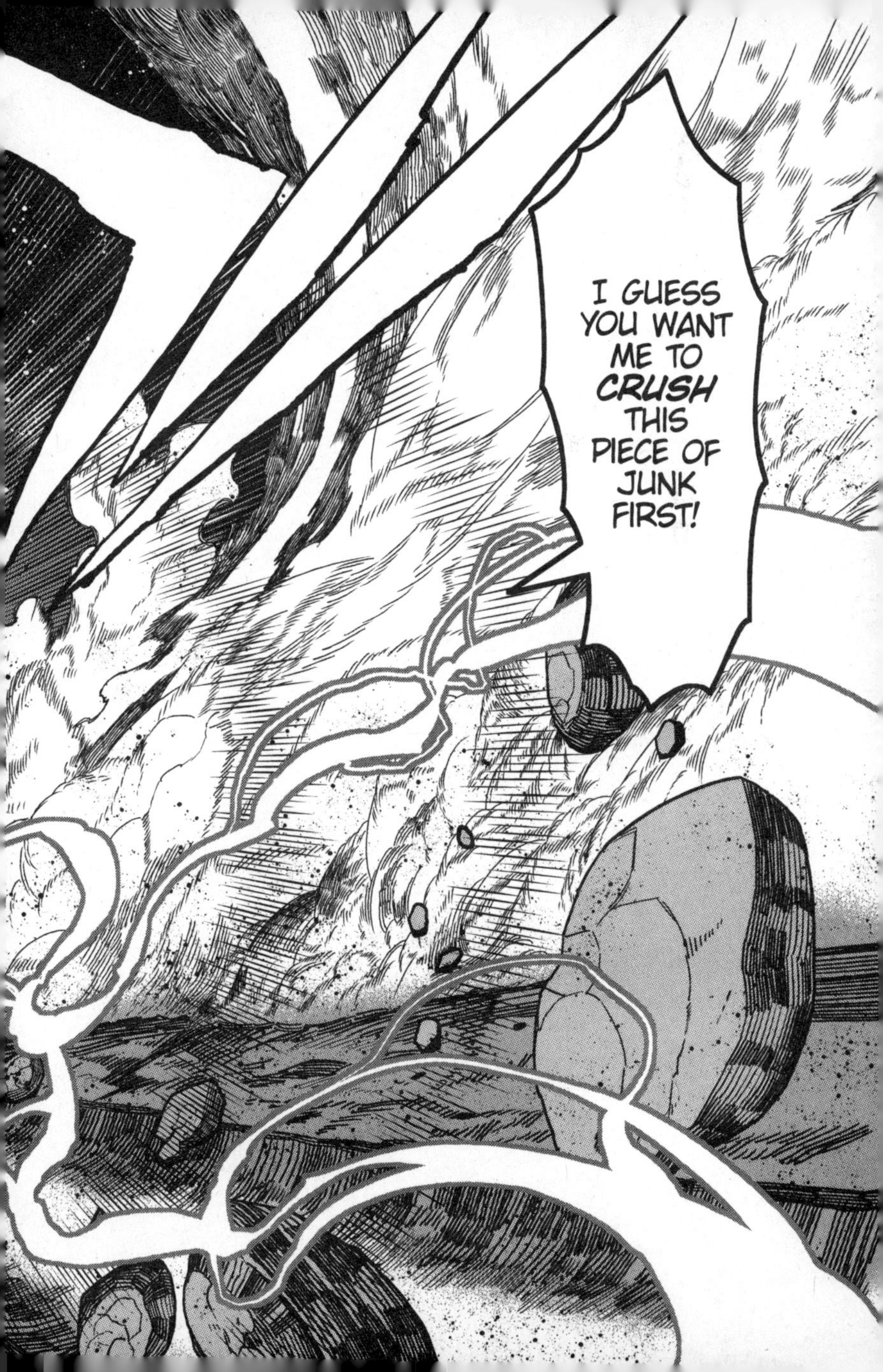
I GUESS YOU WANT ME TO CRUSH THIS PIECE OF JUNK FIRST!

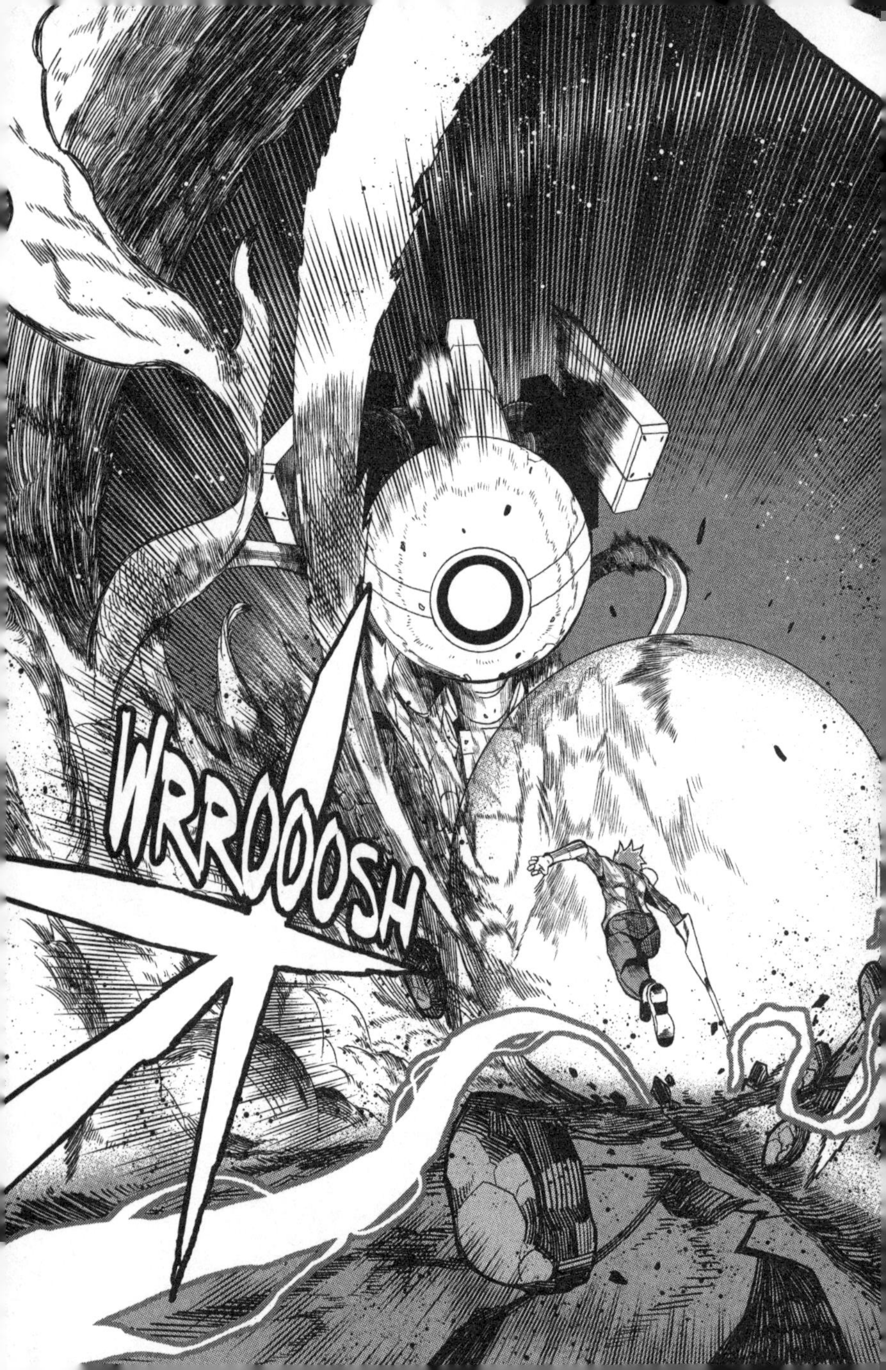
WRROOOSH

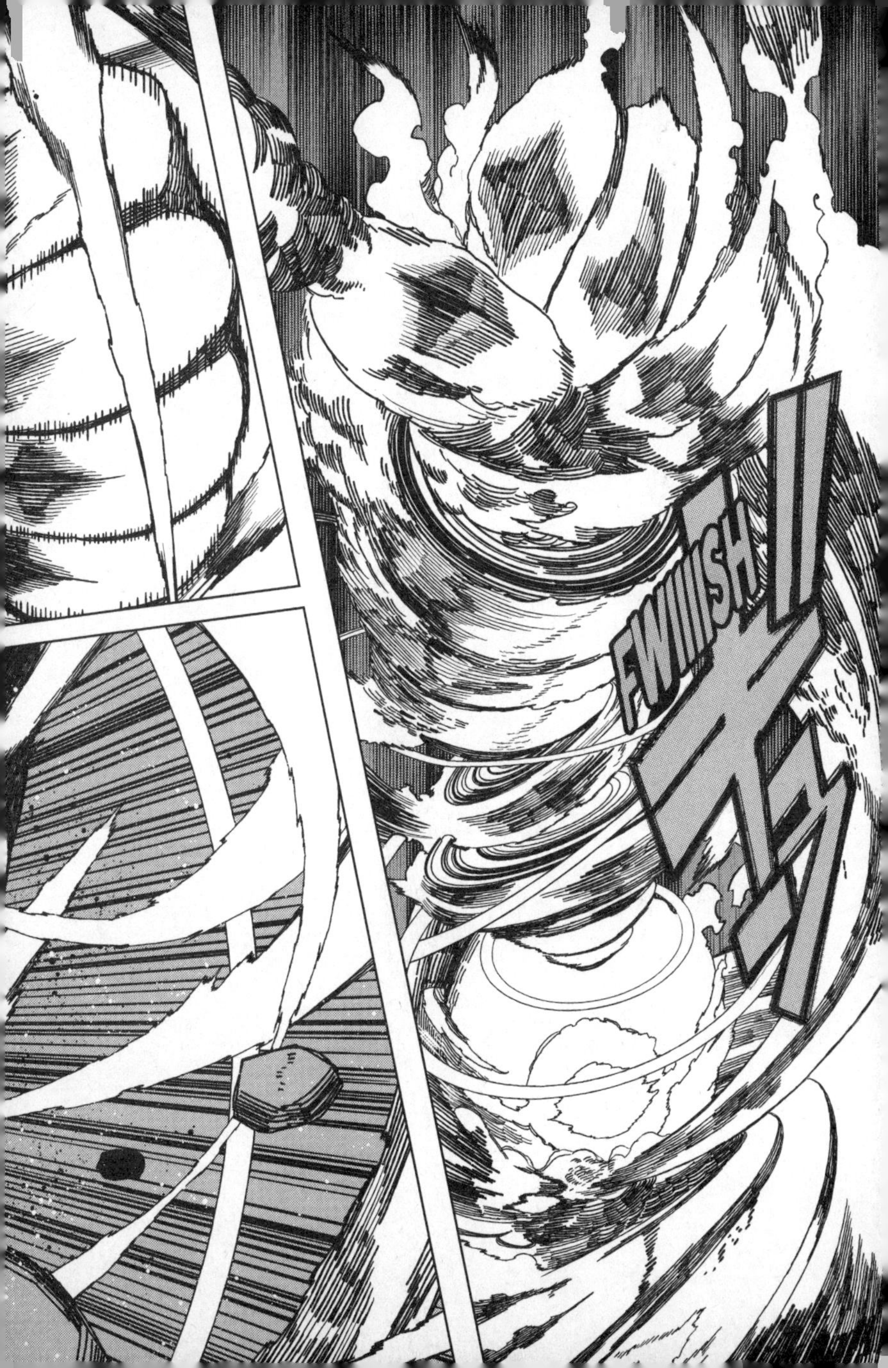
FWIIIISH!!

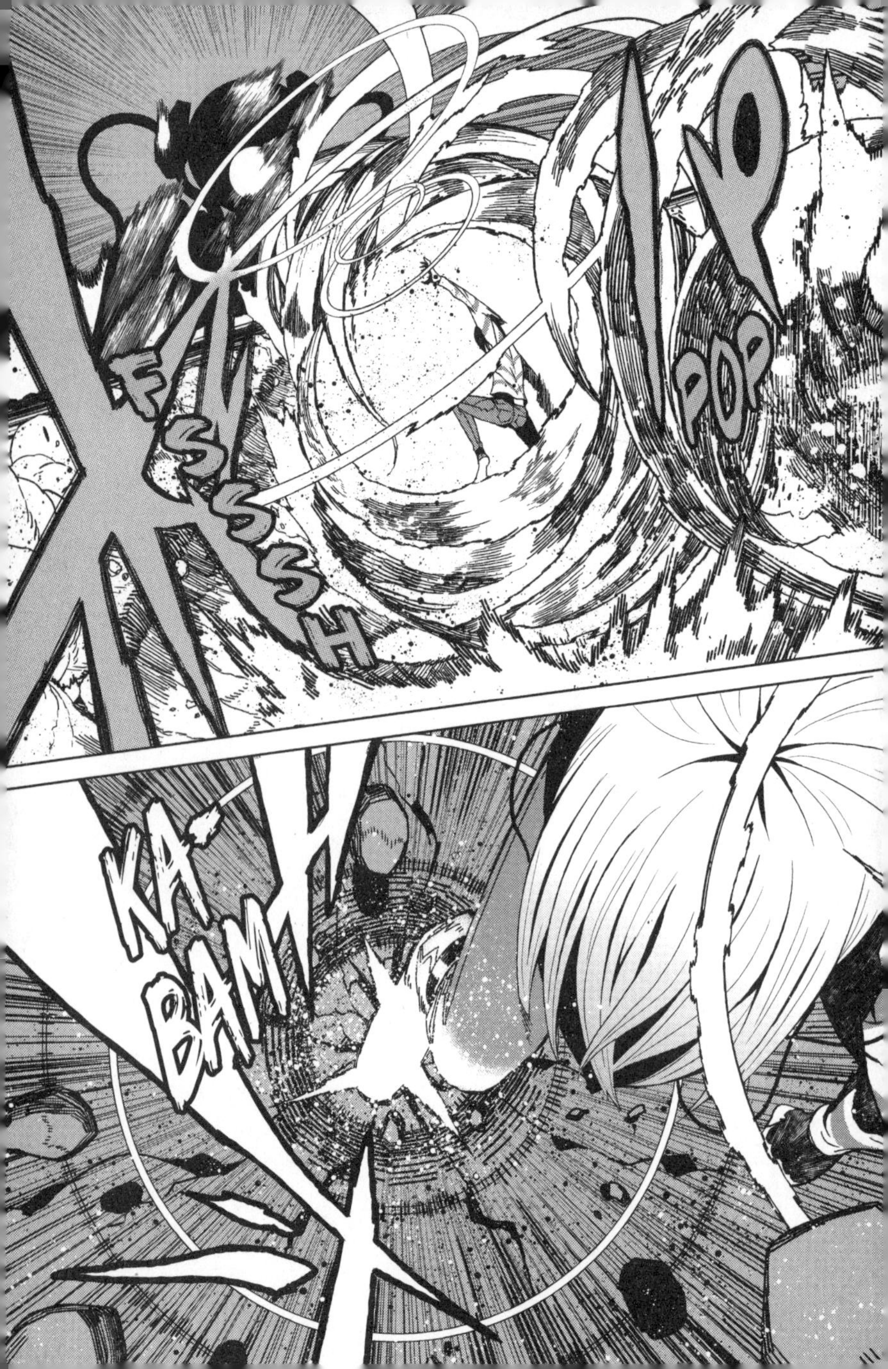
POP
POP
FSSSSH
KA
BAM

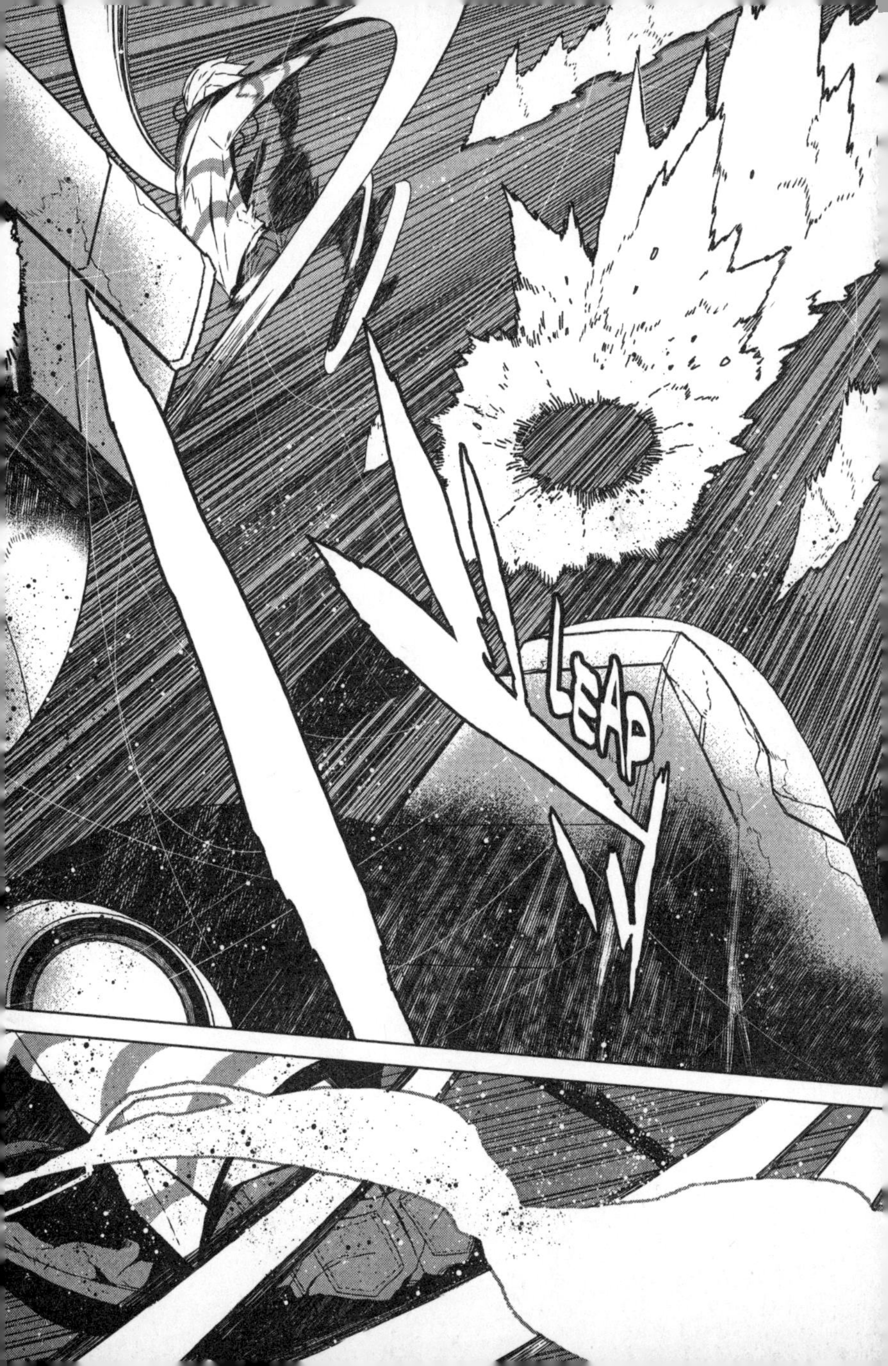
LEAP

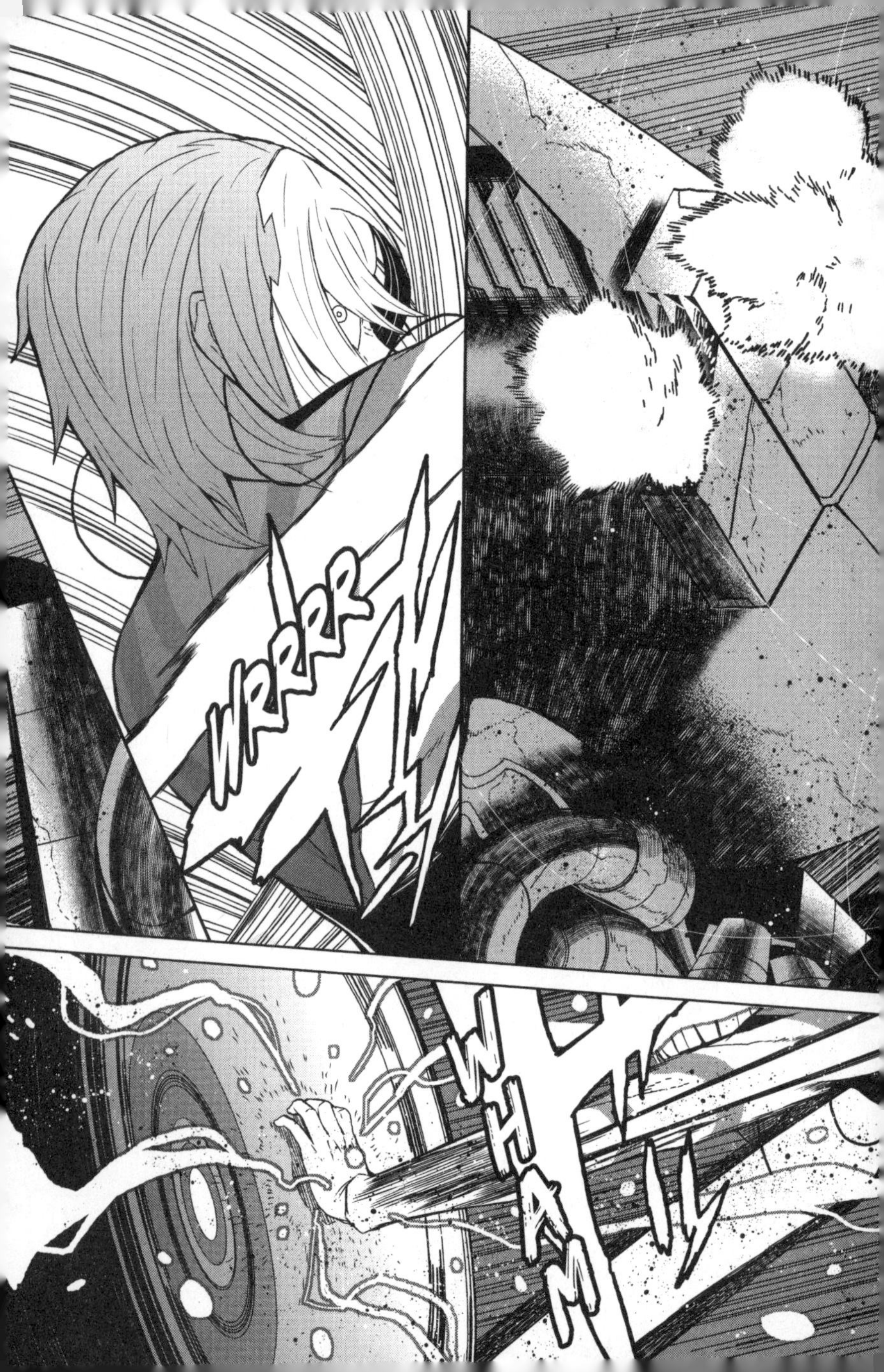
WRRRR
WHAM

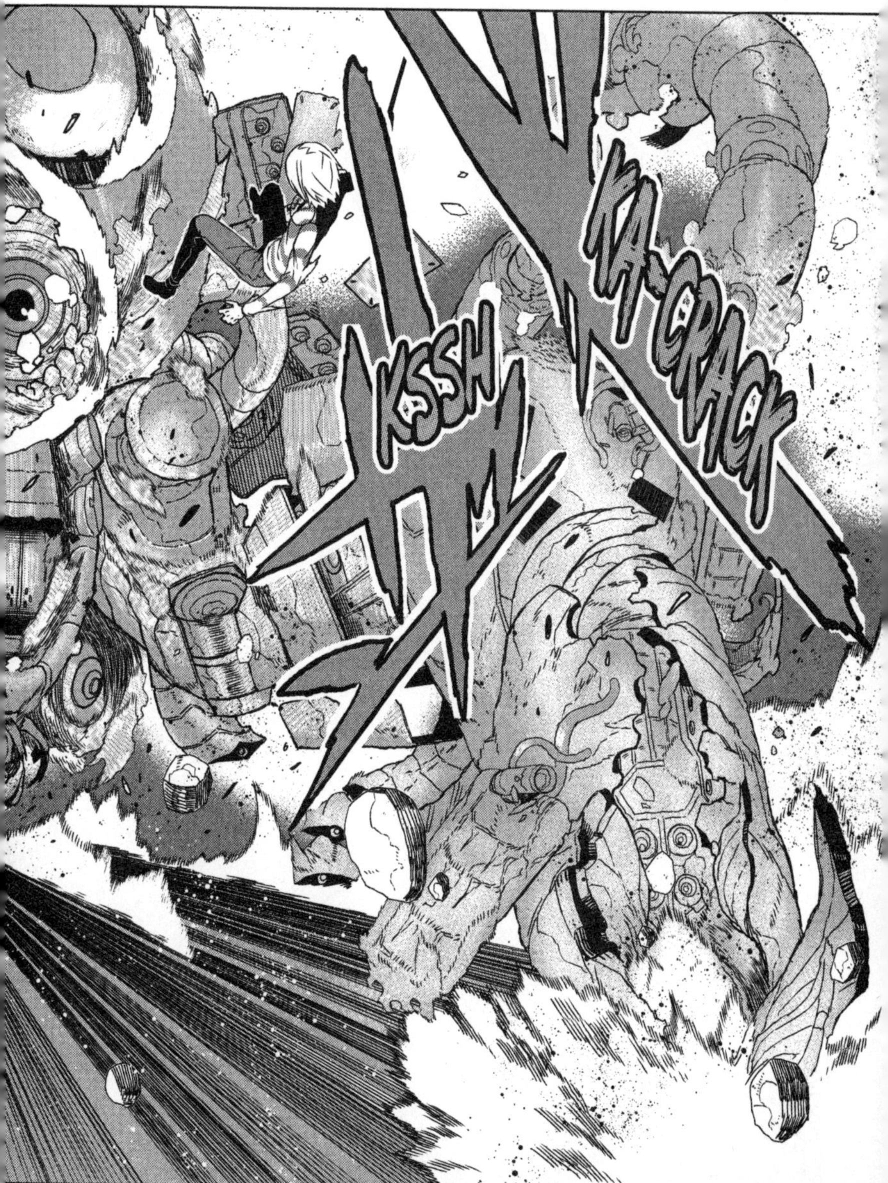
KA-CRACK
KSSH

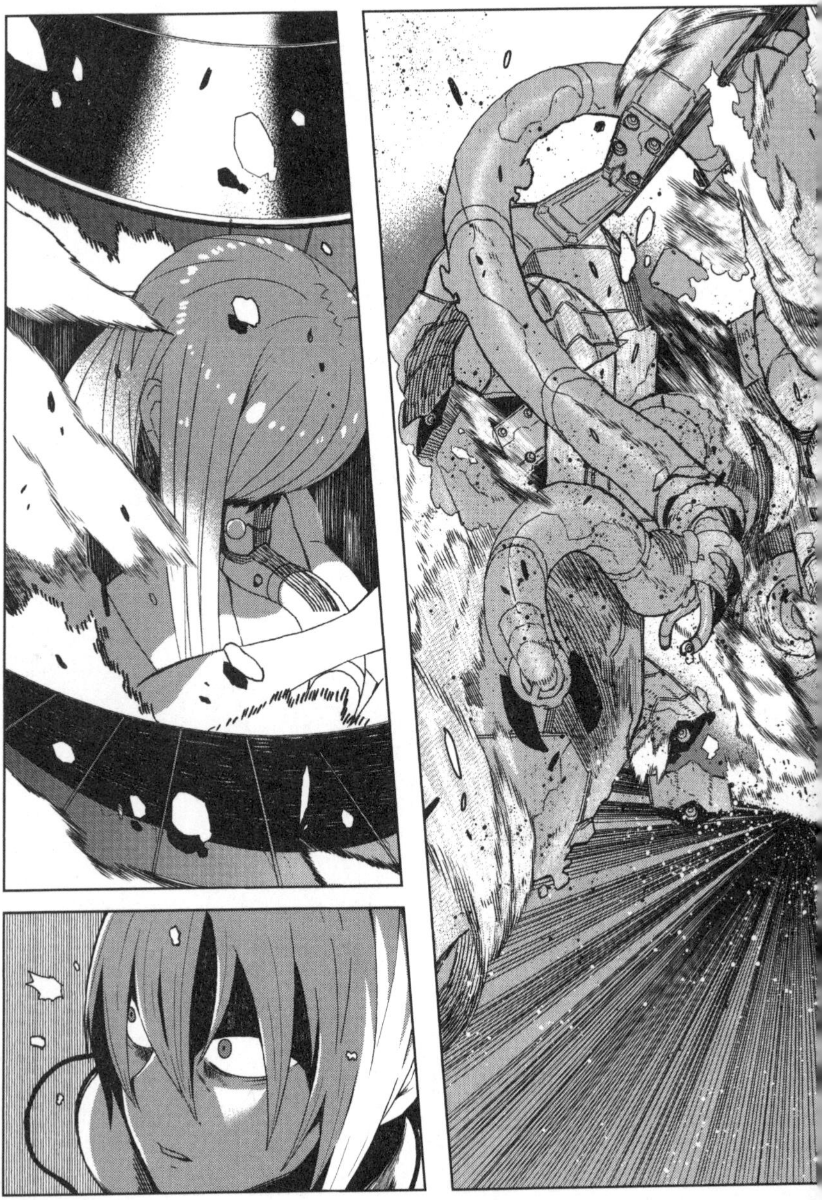

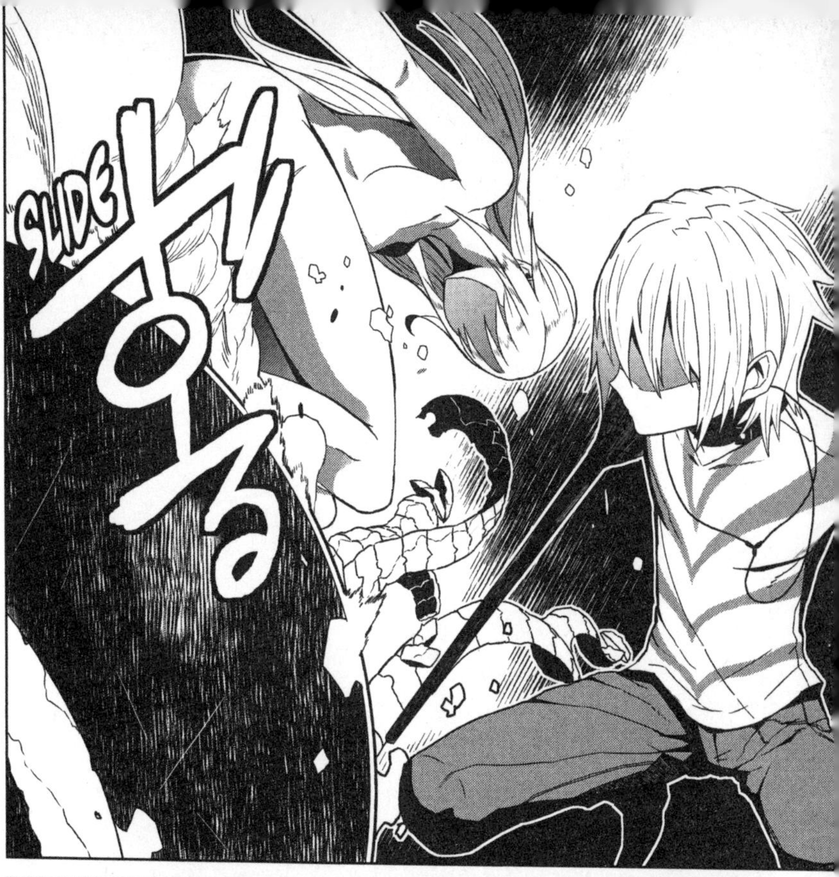
SLIDE

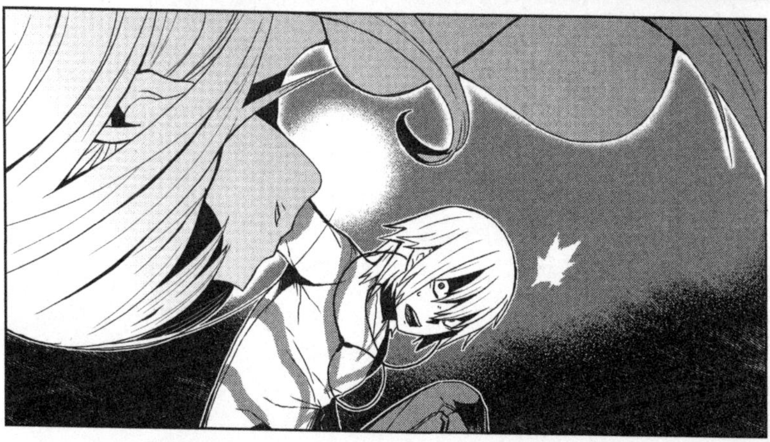

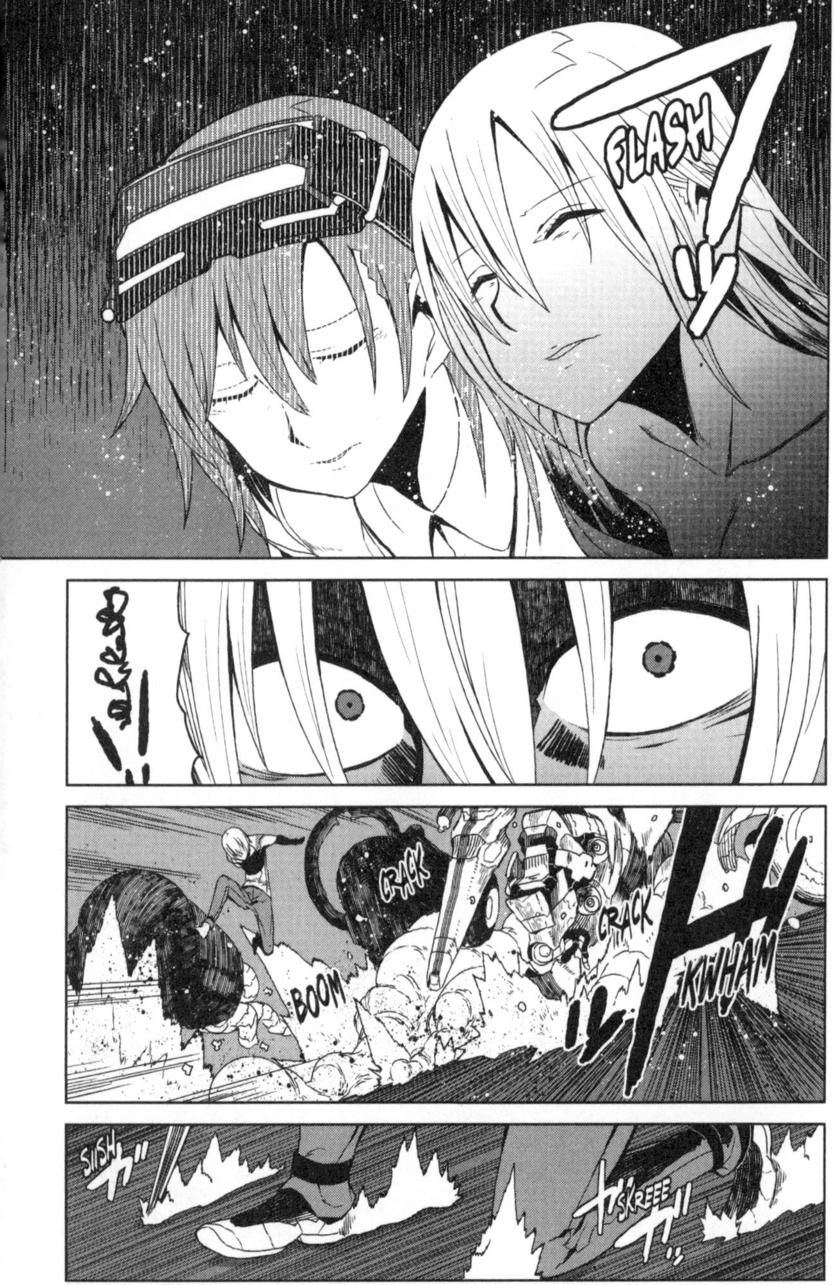
FLASH
CRACK
CRACK
KWHAM
BOOM
SIISH
SKREEE

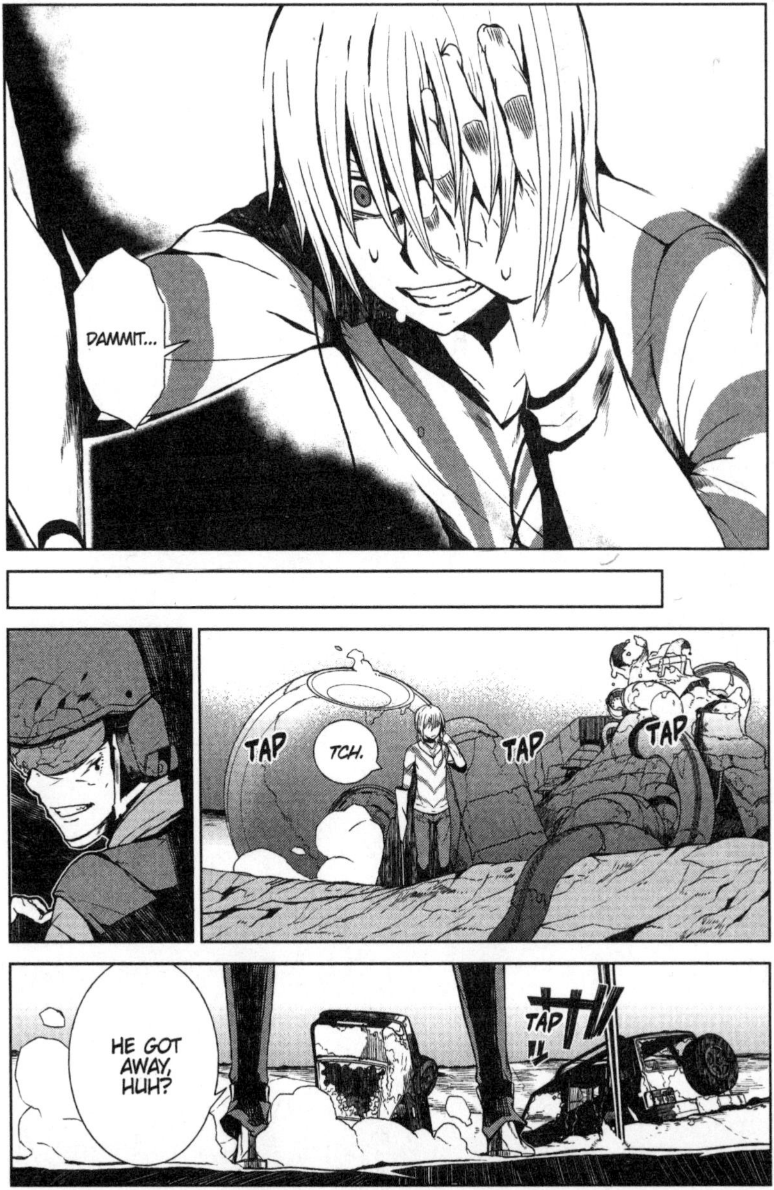
DAMMIT...
TAP
TAP
TCH.
TAP
TAP
HE GOT AWAY, HUH?

OOO-
KAY.

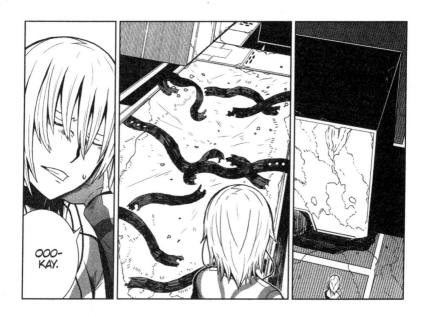

LOOM

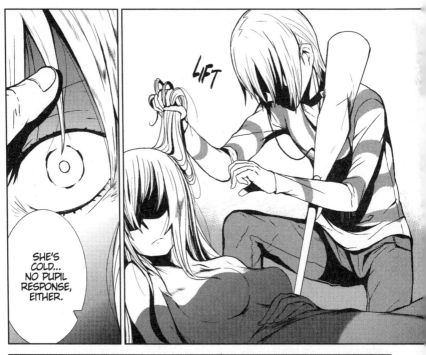

LIFT

SHE'S COLD... NO PUPIL RESPONSE, EITHER.

I GUESS THEY STUFFED A **CORPSE** INTO THAT THING.

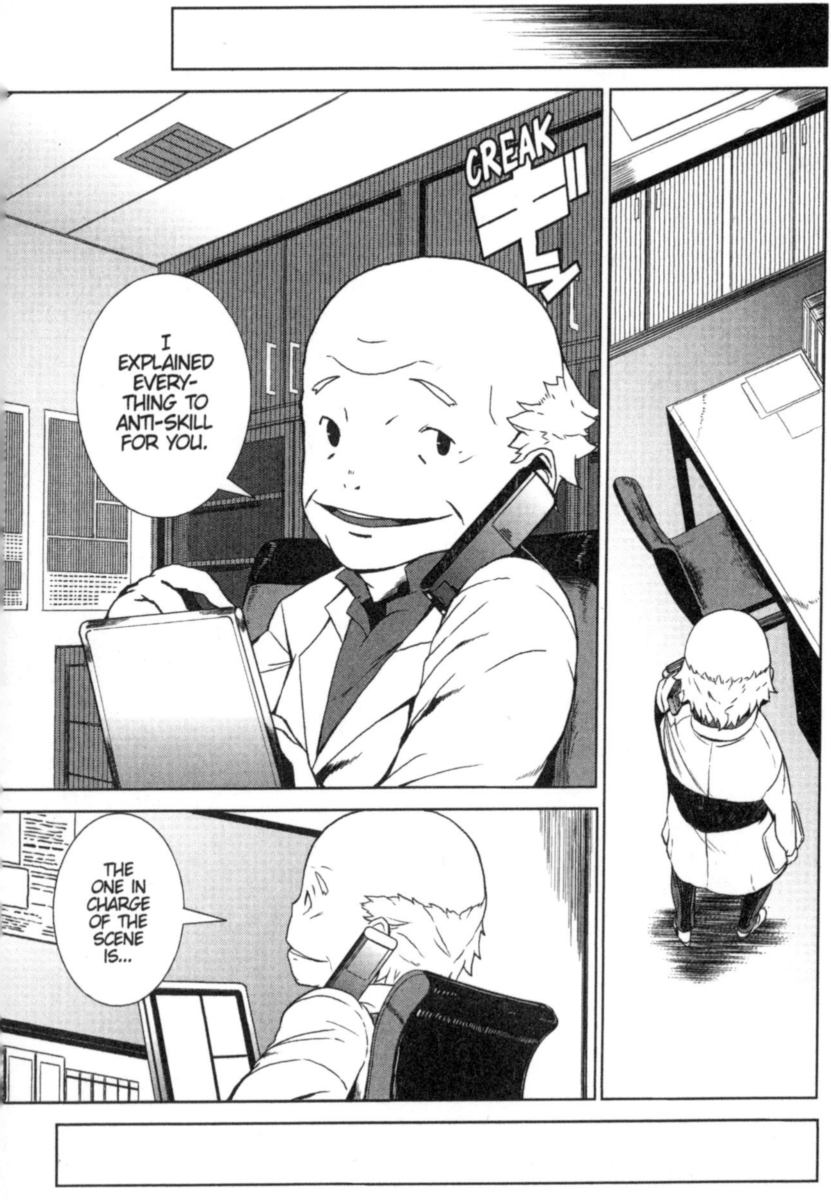
CREAK
I EXPLAINED EVERY-THING TO ANTI-SKILL FOR YOU.
THE ONE IN CHARGE OF THE SCENE IS...

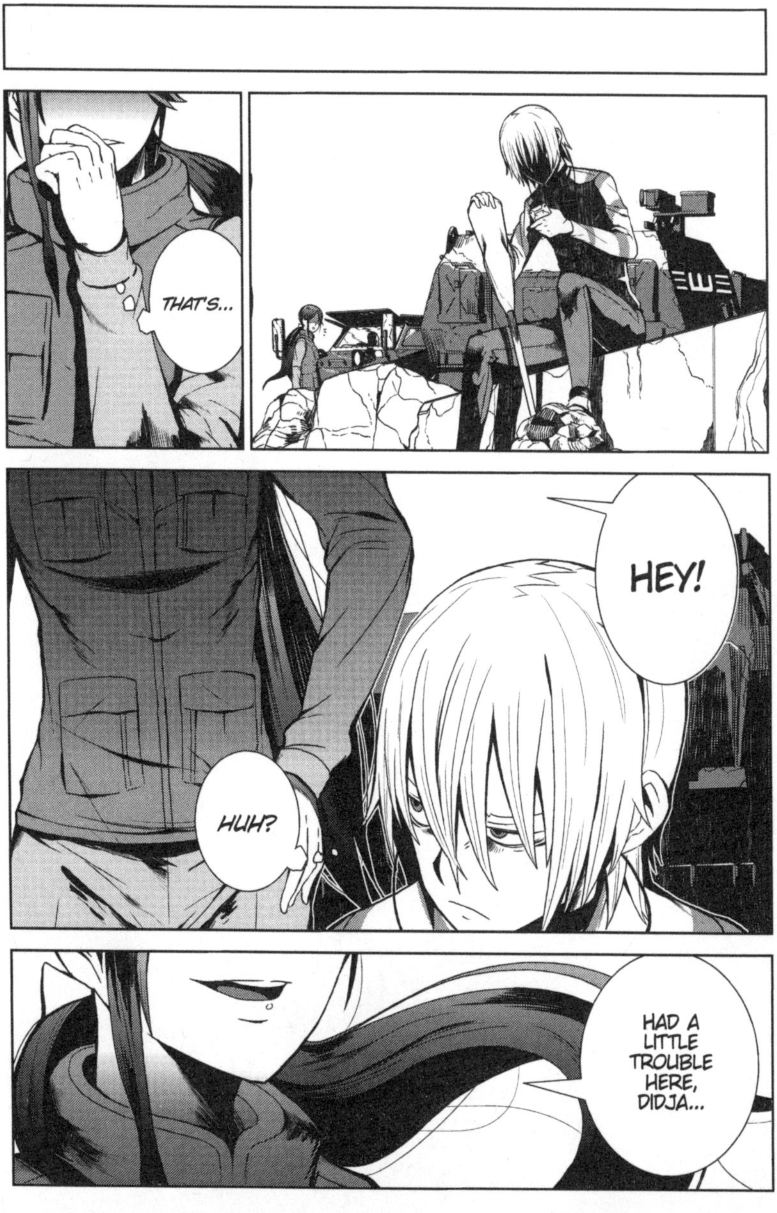
THAT'S...
HEY!
HUH?
HAD A LITTLE TROUBLE HERE, DIDJA...

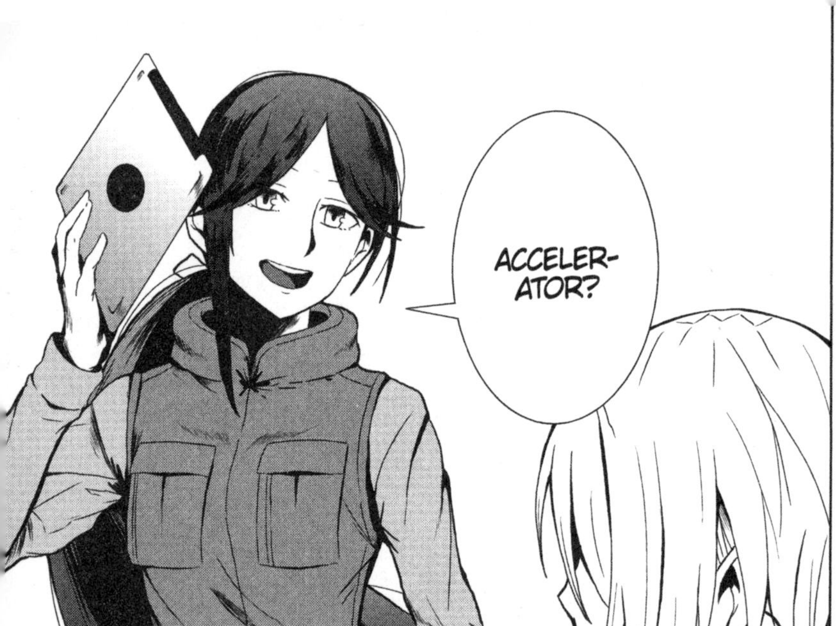
ACCELER-
ATOR?
WHO THE HELL?
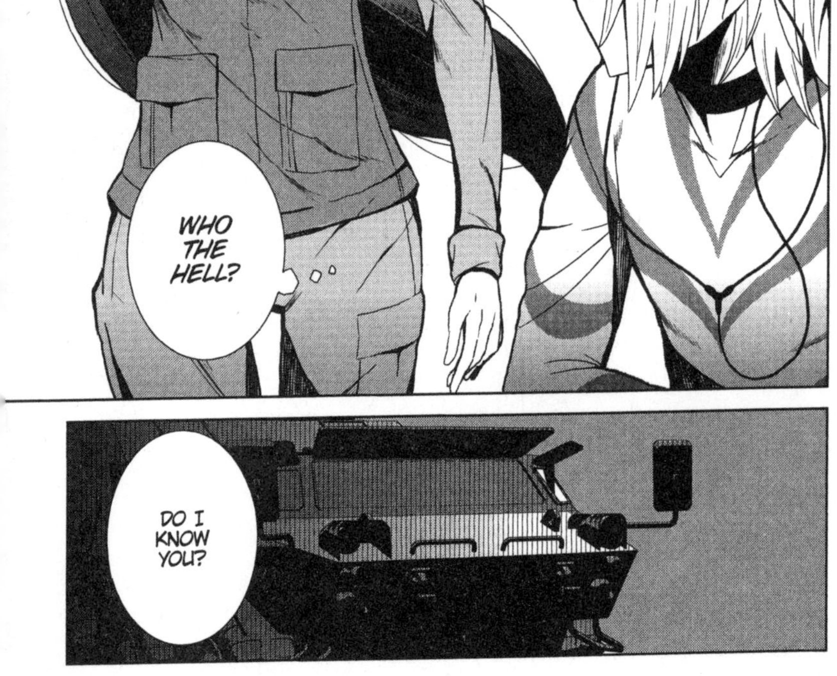
DO I KNOW YOU?

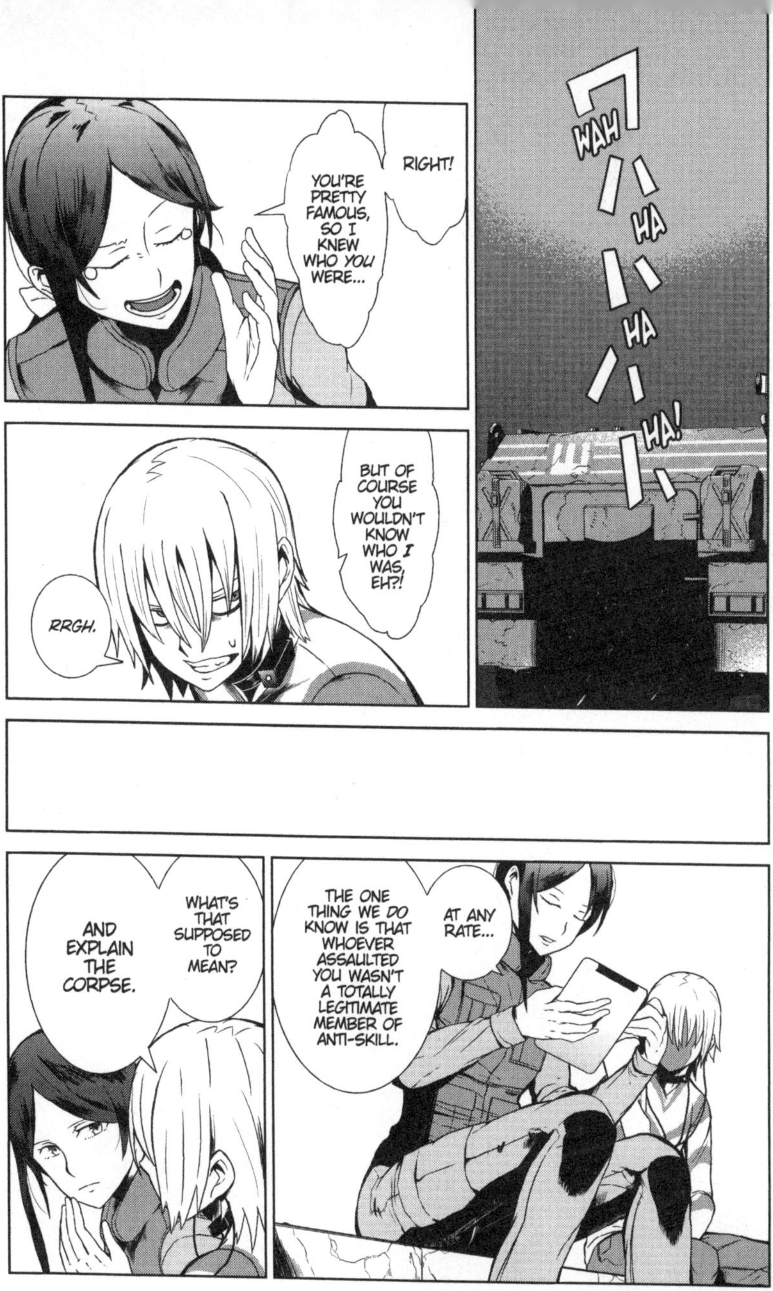
WAH HA HA HA!
RIGHT!
YOU'RE PRETTY FAMOUS, SO I KNEW WHO *YOU* WERE...
BUT OF COURSE YOU WOULDN'T KNOW WHO *I* WAS, EH?!
RRGH.
AT ANY RATE...
THE ONE THING WE *DO* KNOW IS THAT WHOEVER ASSAULTED YOU WASN'T A TOTALLY LEGITIMATE MEMBER OF ANTI-SKILL.
WHAT'S THAT SUPPOSED TO MEAN?
AND EXPLAIN THE CORPSE.

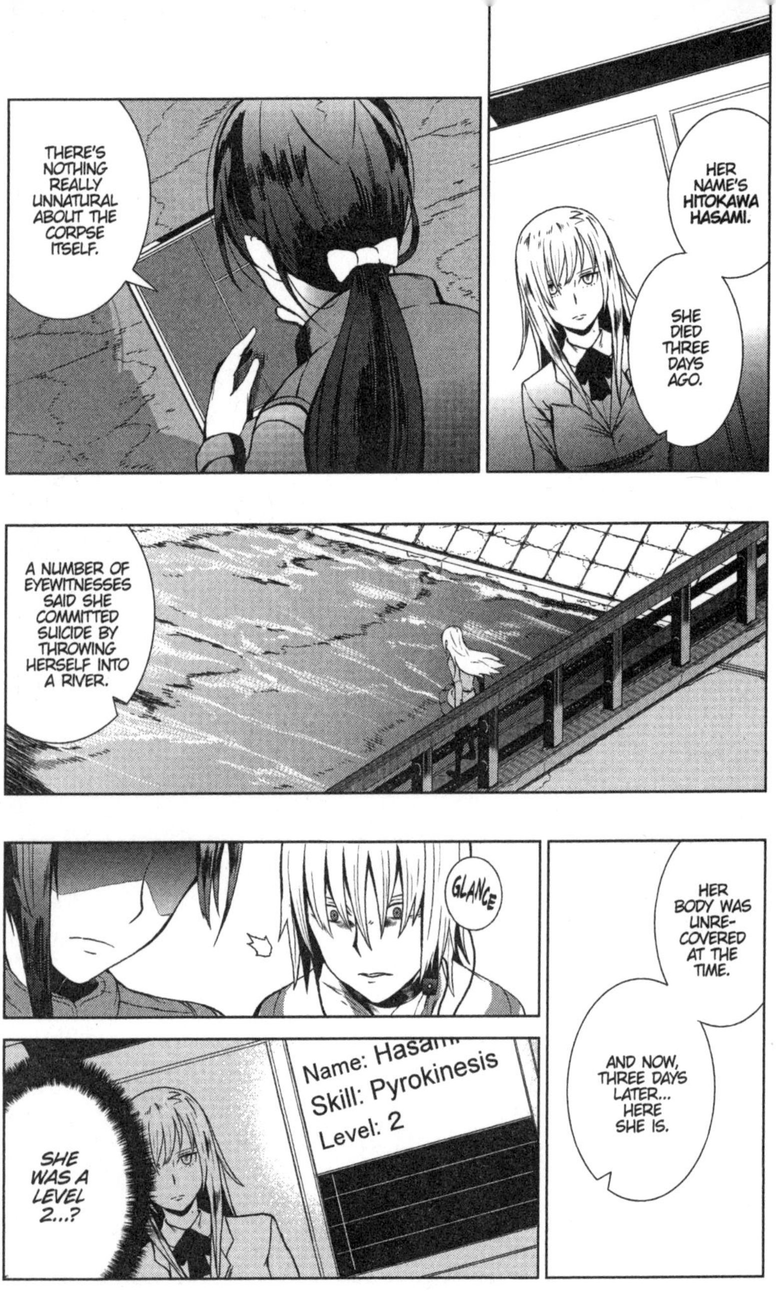
HER NAME'S HITOKAWA HASAMI.
SHE DIED THREE DAYS AGO.
THERE'S NOTHING REALLY UNNATURAL ABOUT THE CORPSE ITSELF.
A NUMBER OF EYEWITNESSES SAID SHE COMMITTED SUICIDE BY THROWING HERSELF INTO A RIVER.
HER BODY WAS UNRE-COVERED AT THE TIME.
AND NOW, THREE DAYS LATER... HERE SHE IS.
GLANCE
Name: Hasami
Skill: Pyrokinesis
Level: 2
SHE WAS A LEVEL 2...?

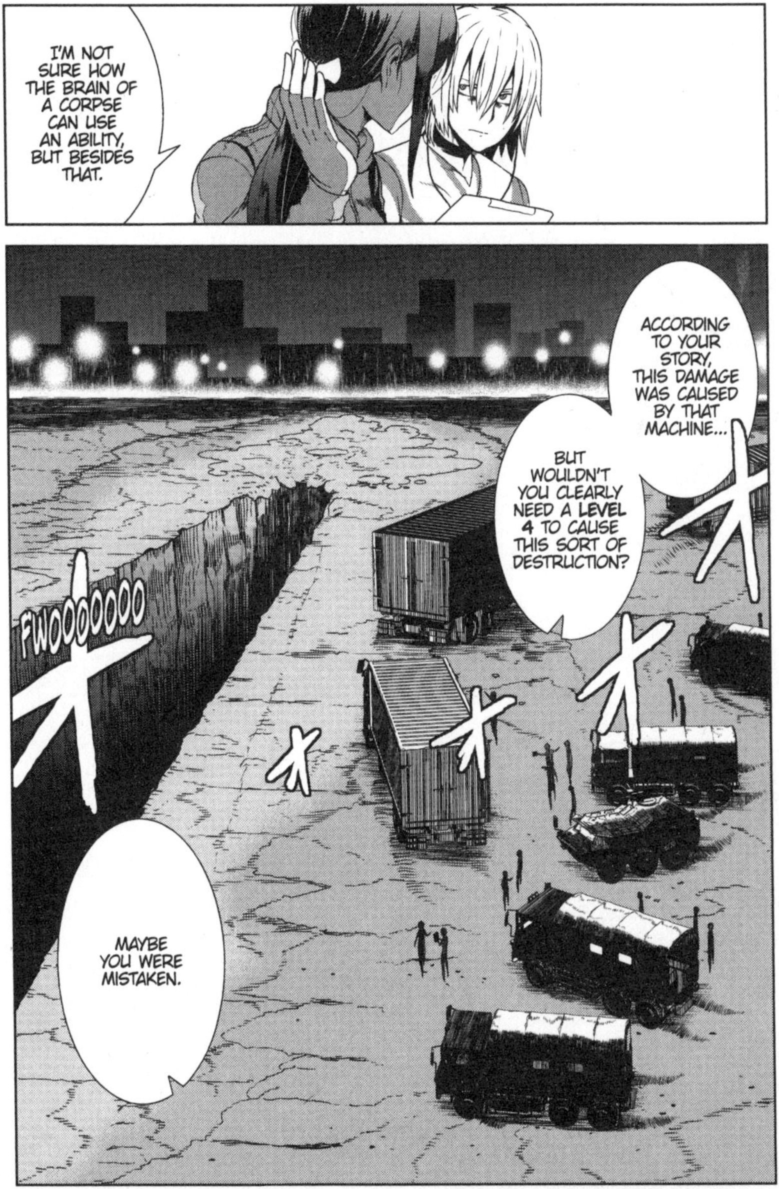
I'M NOT SURE HOW THE BRAIN OF A CORPSE CAN USE AN ABILITY, BUT BESIDES THAT.
ACCORDING TO YOUR STORY, THIS DAMAGE WAS CAUSED BY THAT MACHINE...
BUT WOULDN'T YOU CLEARLY NEED A LEVEL 4 TO CAUSE THIS SORT OF DESTRUCTION?
FWOOOOOOO
MAYBE YOU WERE MISTAKEN.

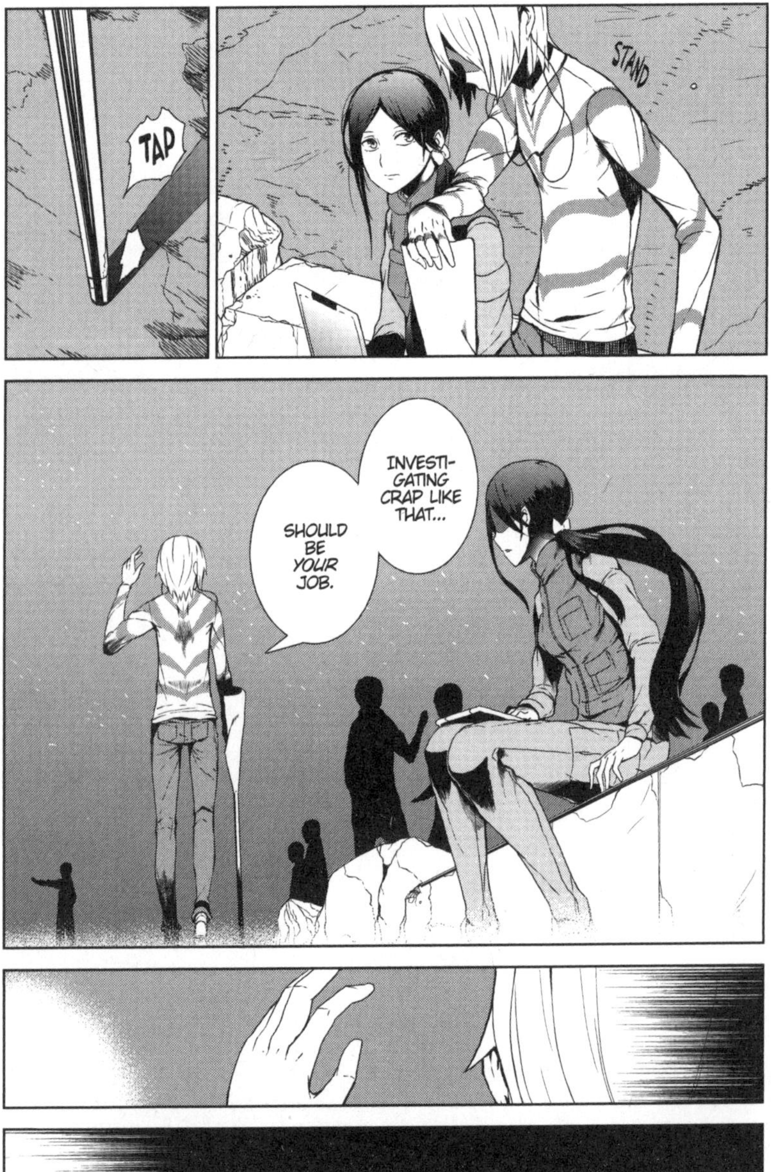
STAND
TAP
INVESTI-GATING CRAP LIKE THAT...
SHOULD BE YOUR JOB.

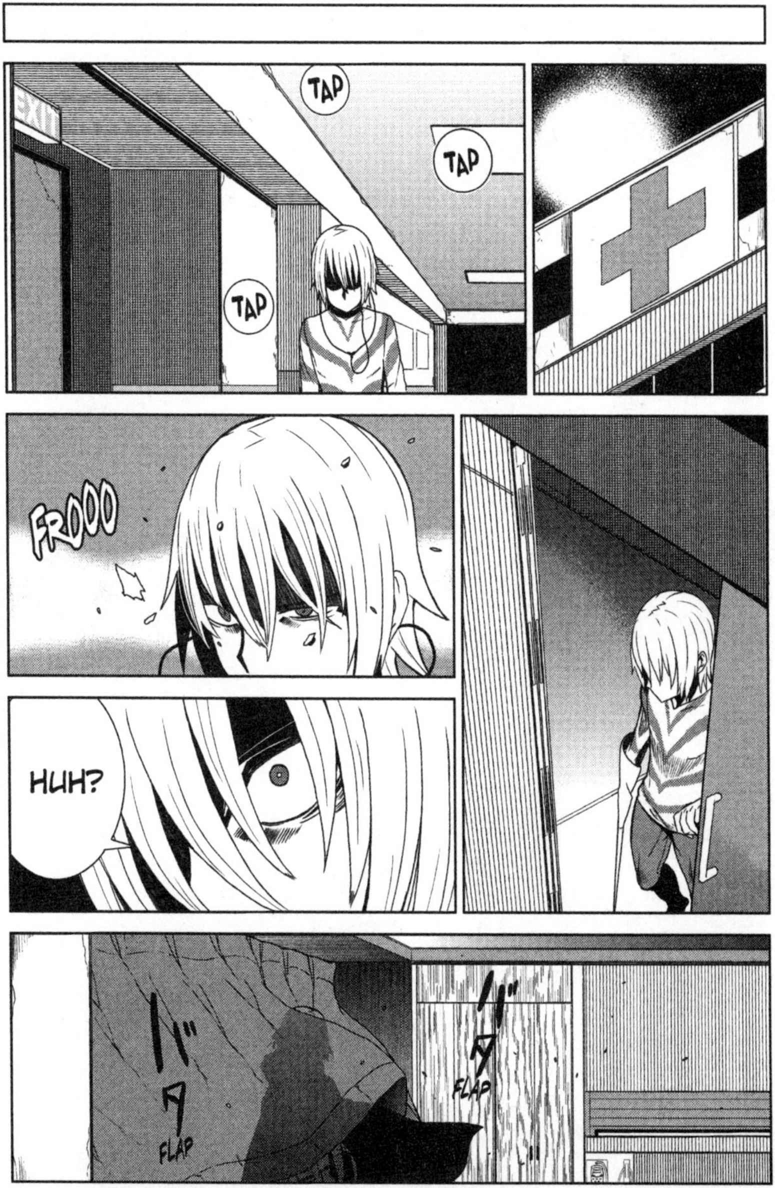
TAP
TAP
TAP
FROOO
HUH?
バタ
FLAP
バタ
FLAP

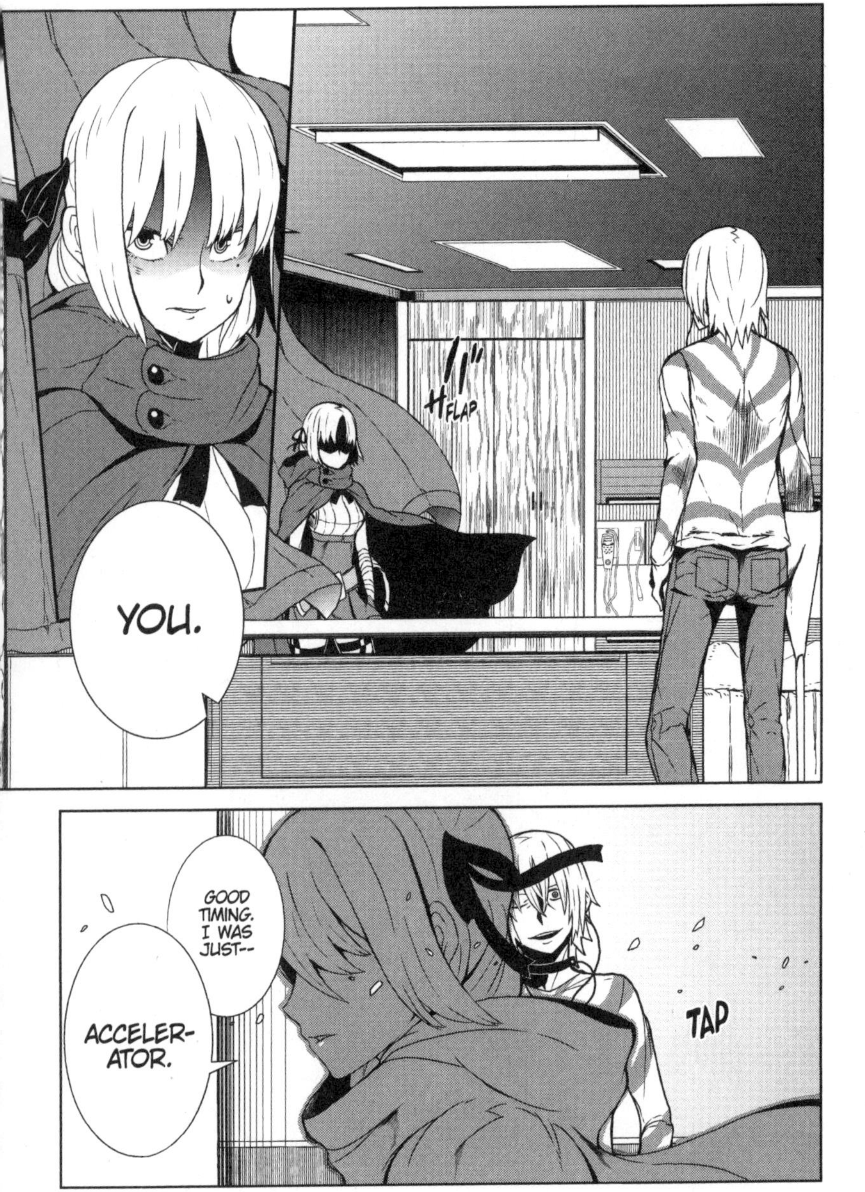
FLAP
YOU.
TAP
GOOD TIMING. I WAS JUST--
ACCELER-ATOR.

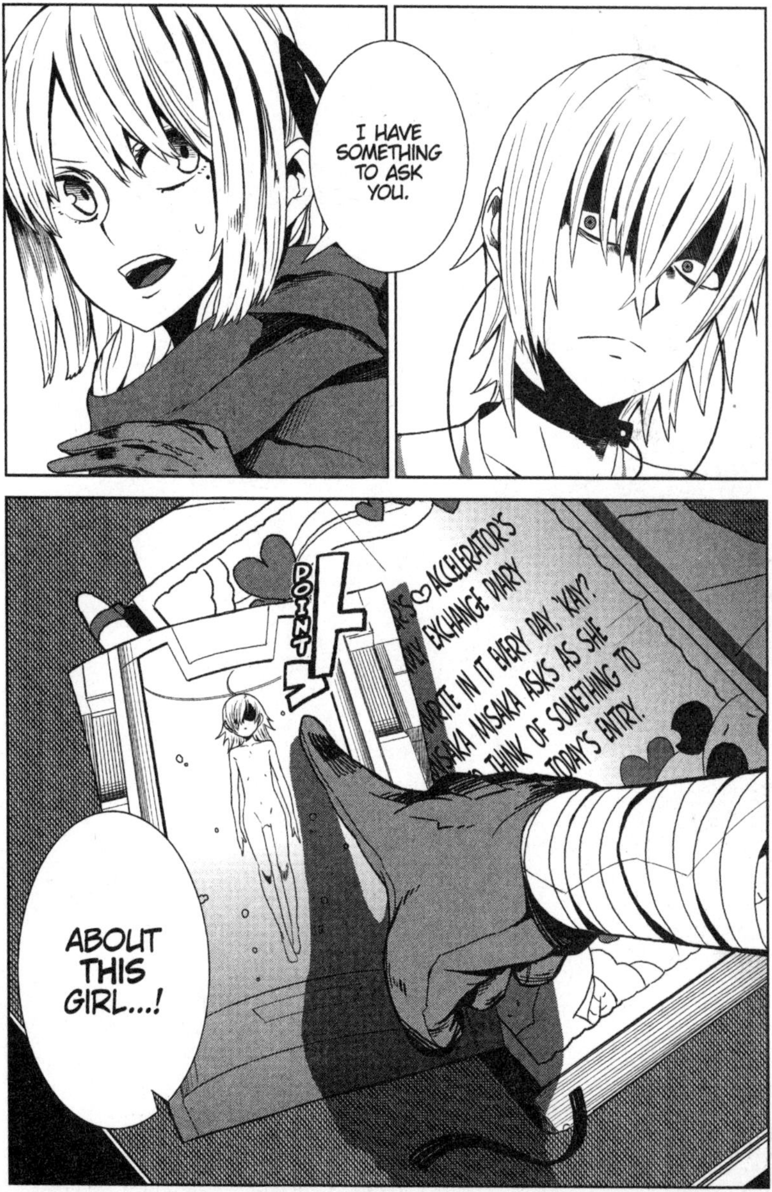
I HAVE SOMETHING TO ASK YOU.
ACCELERATOR'S EXCHANGE DIARY
POINT
ABOUT THIS GIRL...!

a certain
SCIENTIFIC
ACCELERATOR

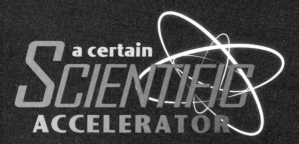

とある科学の一方通行

とある
魔術の
禁書目録
外伝

CHAPTER 2

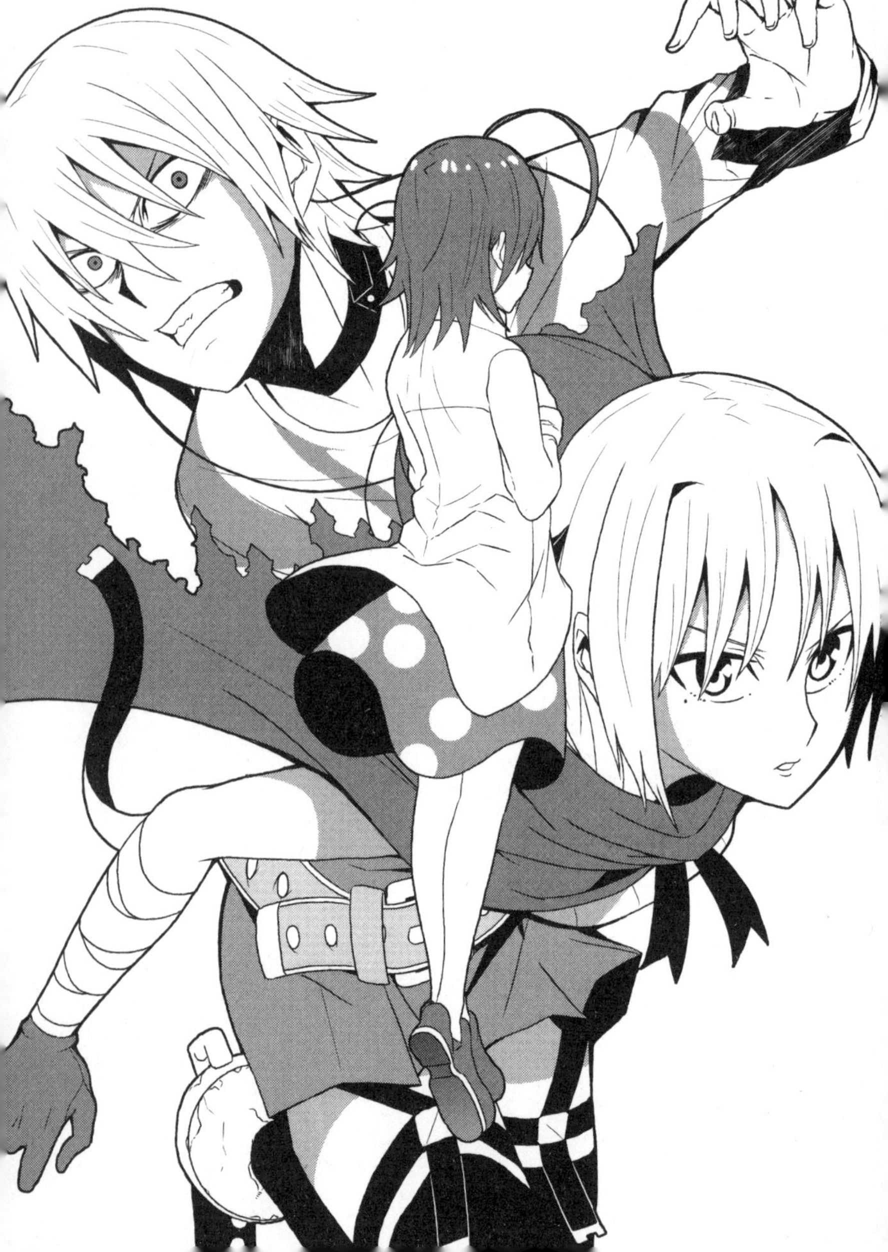

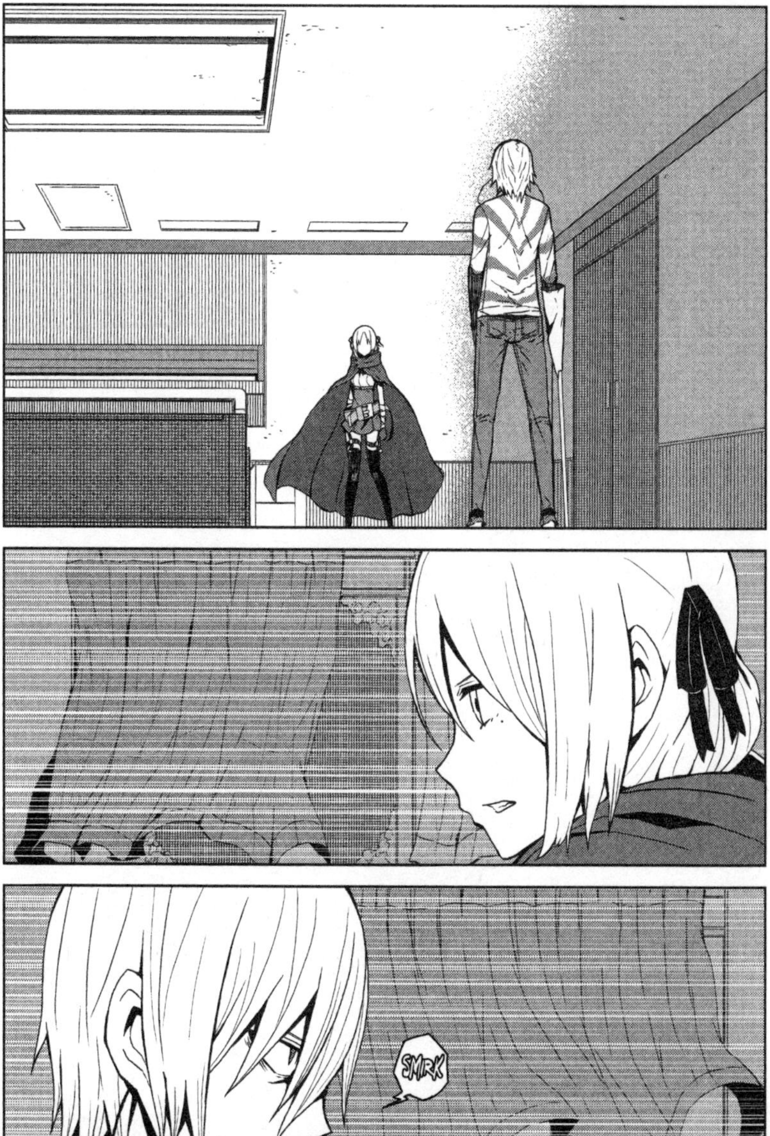
SMIRK

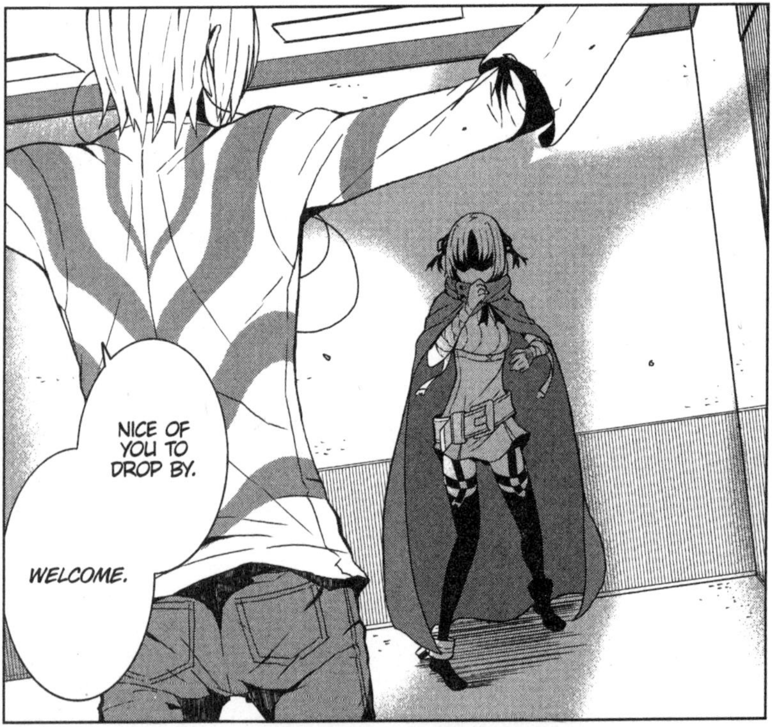
NICE OF YOU TO DROP BY.
WELCOME.
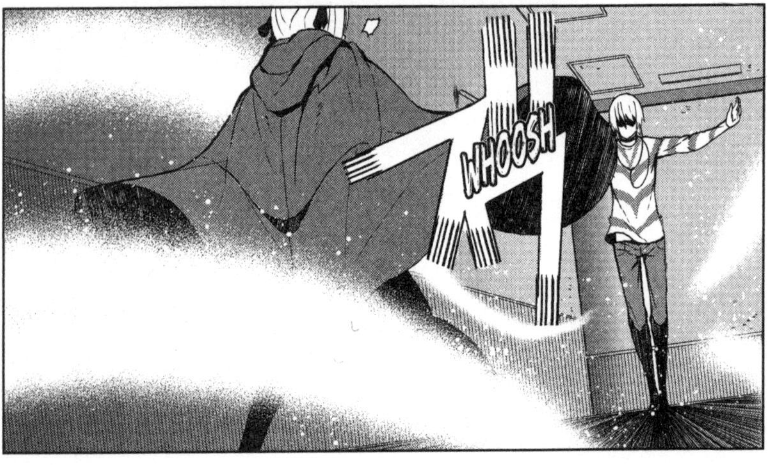
WHOOSH

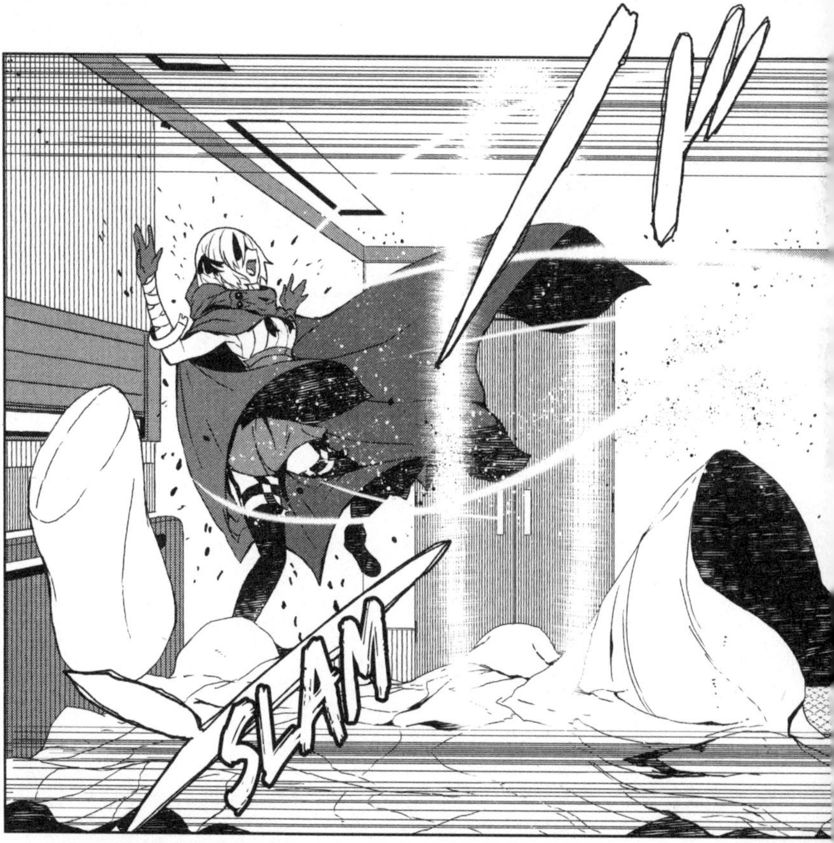
SLAM

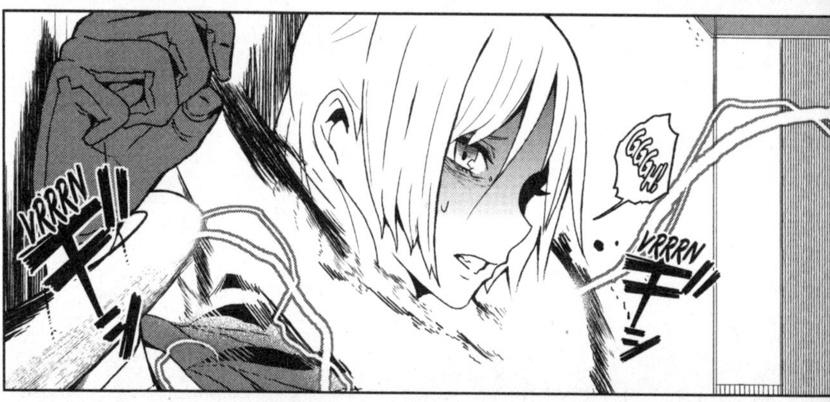
GGGH!!
VRRRN
VRRRN

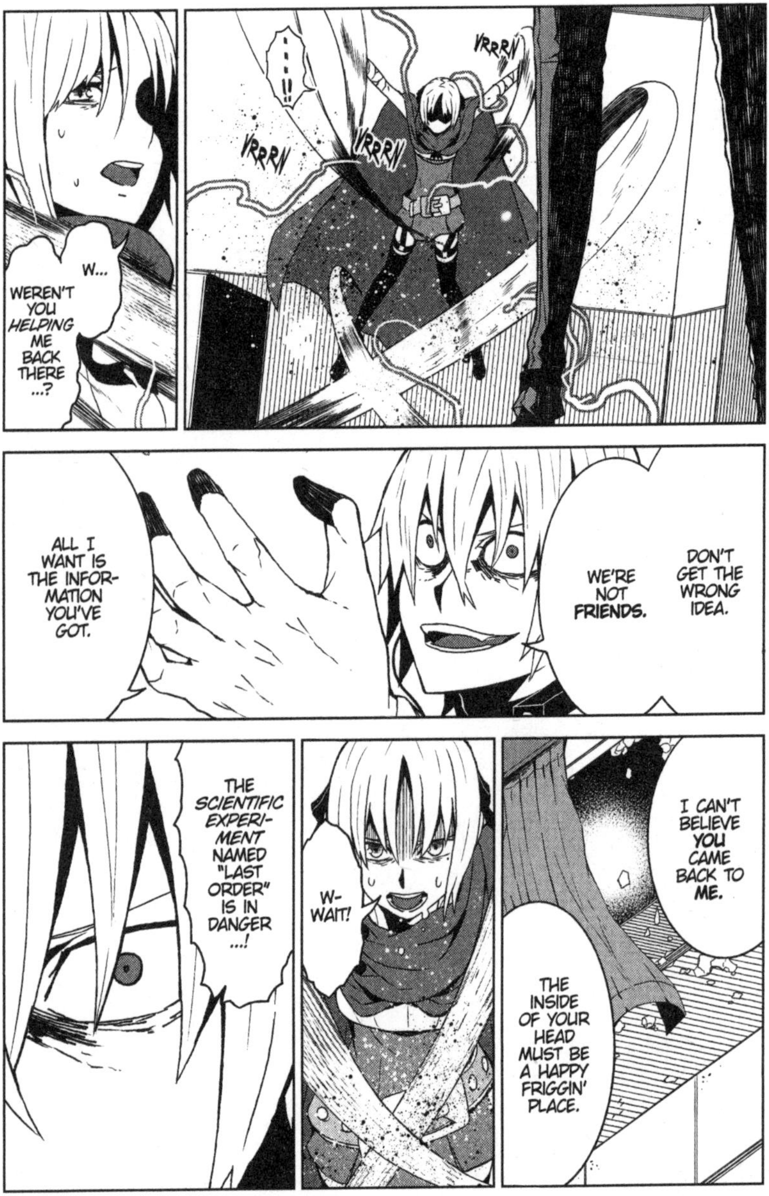

...!!
VRRRN
VRRRN
VRRRN
W...
WEREN'T YOU HELPING ME BACK THERE ...?
DON'T GET THE WRONG IDEA.
WE'RE NOT FRIENDS.
ALL I WANT IS THE INFORMATION YOU'VE GOT.
I CAN'T BELIEVE YOU CAME BACK TO ME.
THE INSIDE OF YOUR HEAD MUST BE A HAPPY FRIGGIN' PLACE.
W-WAIT!
THE SCIENTIFIC EXPERIMENT NAMED "LAST ORDER" IS IN DANGER ...!

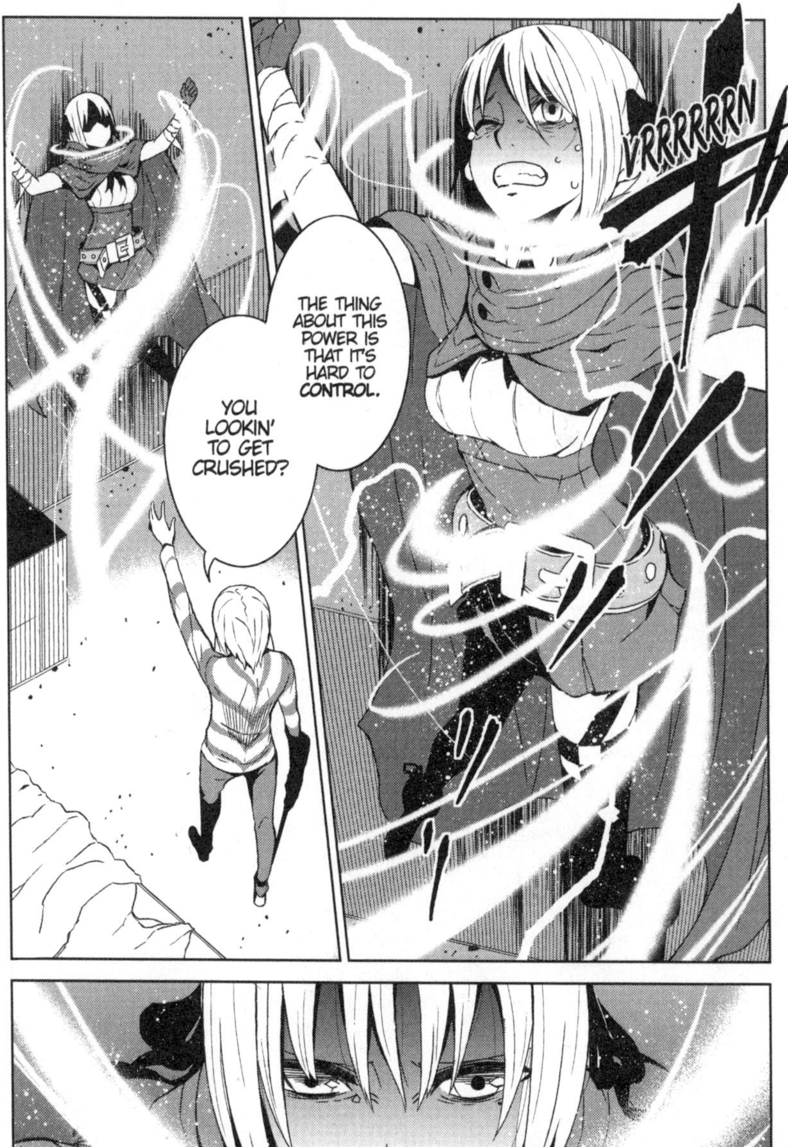
VRRRRRRN
THE THING ABOUT THIS POWER IS THAT IT'S HARD TO CONTROL.
YOU LOOKIN' TO GET CRUSHED?

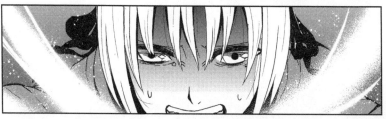

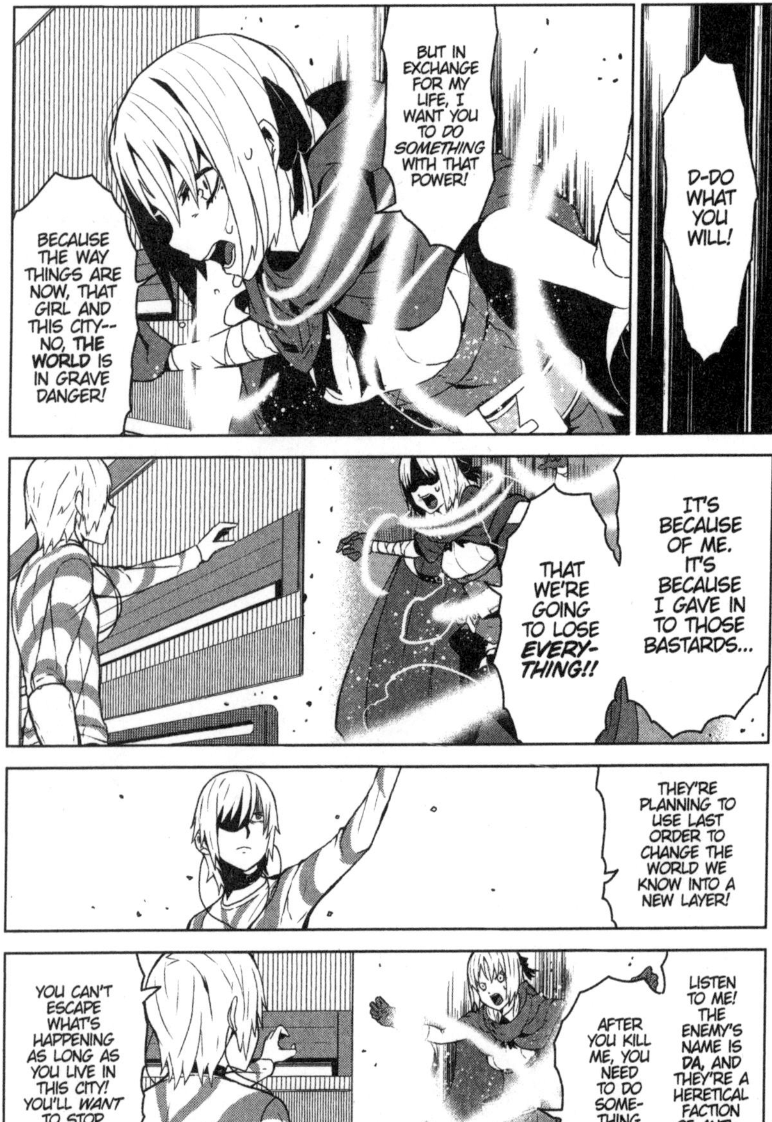
D-DO WHAT YOU WILL!
BUT IN EXCHANGE FOR MY LIFE, I WANT YOU TO *DO SOMETHING* WITH THAT POWER!
BECAUSE THE WAY THINGS ARE NOW, THAT GIRL AND THIS CITY--NO, **THE WORLD** IS IN GRAVE DANGER!
IT'S BECAUSE OF ME. IT'S BECAUSE I GAVE IN TO THOSE BASTARDS...
THAT WE'RE GOING TO LOSE ***EVERYTHING!!***
THEY'RE PLANNING TO USE LAST ORDER TO CHANGE THE WORLD WE KNOW INTO A NEW LAYER!
LISTEN TO ME! THE ENEMY'S NAME IS **DA**, AND THEY'RE A HERETICAL FACTION OF ANTI-SKILL...
AFTER YOU KILL ME, YOU NEED TO DO SOMETHING ABOUT THEM!
YOU CAN'T ESCAPE WHAT'S HAPPENING AS LONG AS YOU LIVE IN THIS CITY! YOU'LL *WANT* TO STOP THEM--AND FAST!

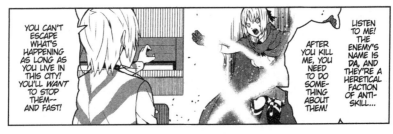

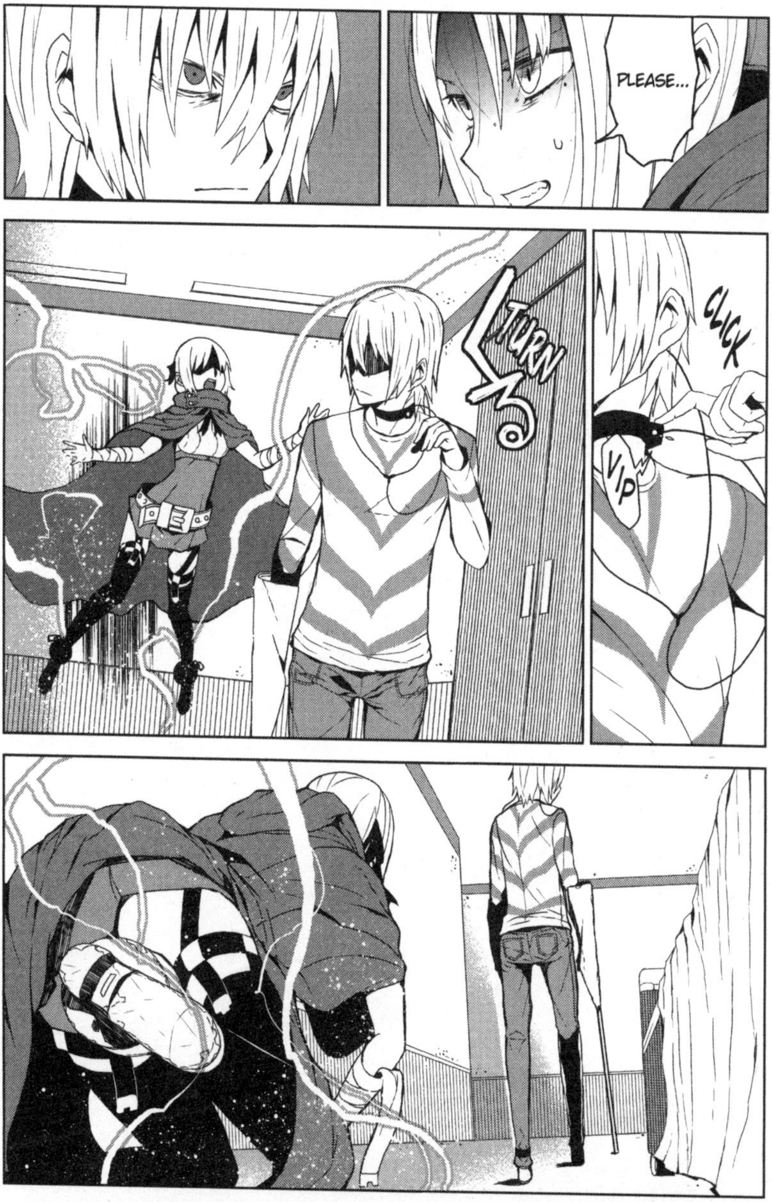
PLEASE...
CLICK
VIP
TURN

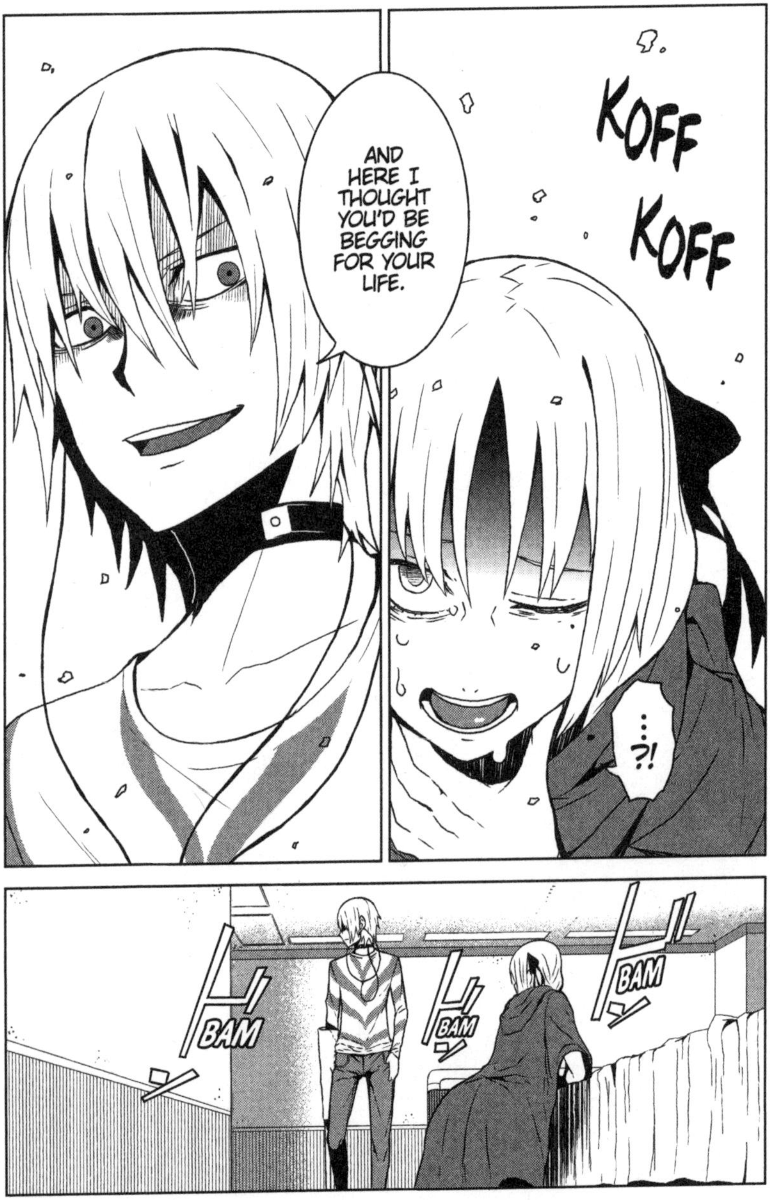
KOFF KOFF
...?!
AND HERE I THOUGHT YOU'D BE BEGGING FOR YOUR LIFE.
BAM
BAM
BAM

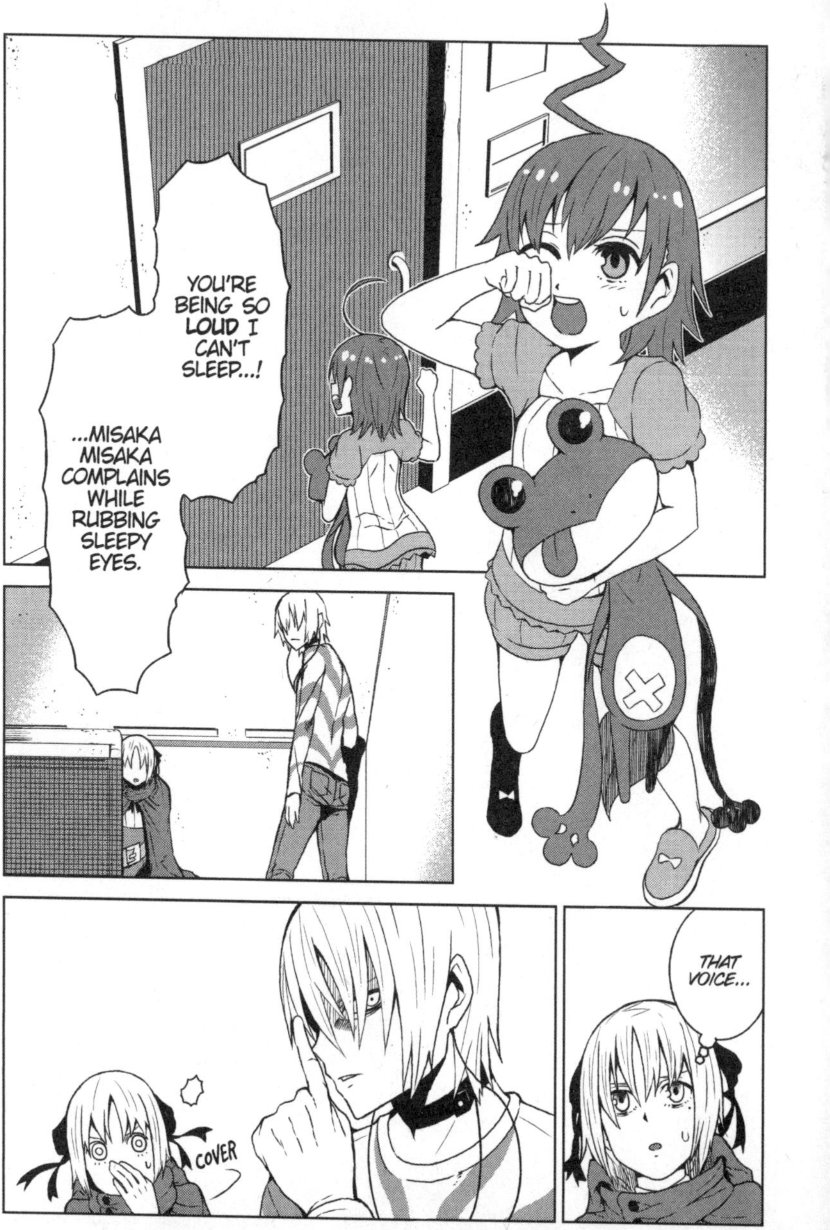
YOU'RE BEING SO **LOUD** I CAN'T SLEEP...!
...MISAKA MISAKA COMPLAINS WHILE RUBBING SLEEPY EYES.
THAT VOICE...
COVER

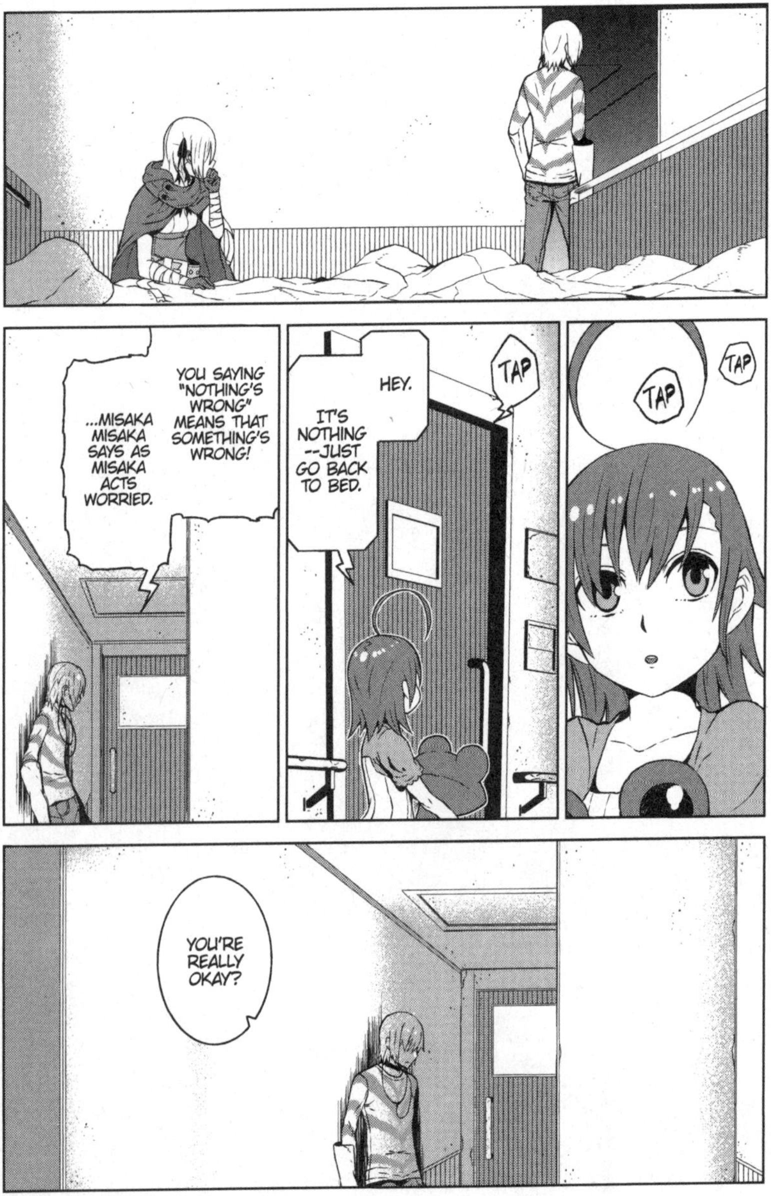
TAP
TAP
TAP
TAP
HEY.
IT'S NOTHING --JUST GO BACK TO BED.
YOU SAYING "NOTHING'S WRONG" MEANS THAT SOMETHING'S WRONG!
...MISAKA MISAKA SAYS AS MISAKA ACTS WORRIED.
YOU'RE REALLY OKAY?

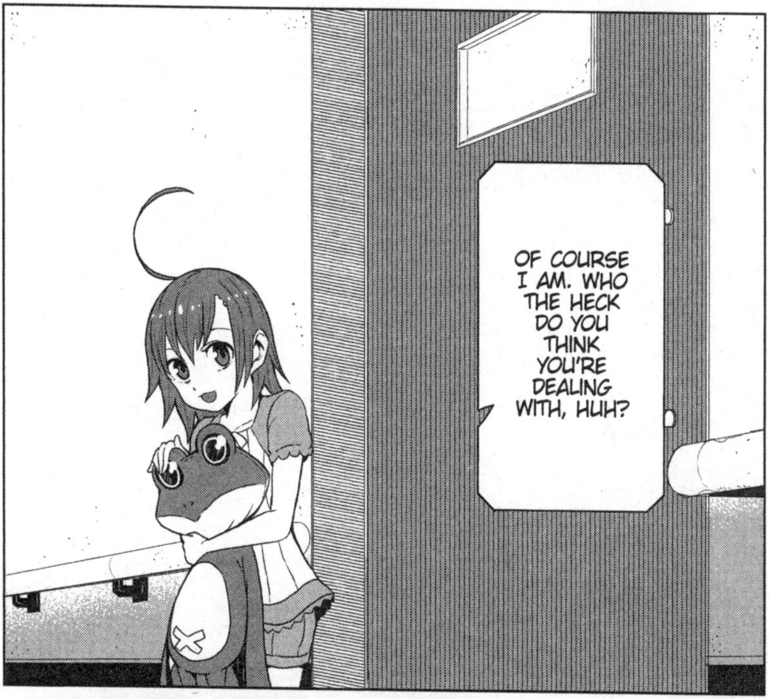
OF COURSE I AM. WHO THE HECK DO YOU THINK YOU'RE DEALING WITH, HUH?
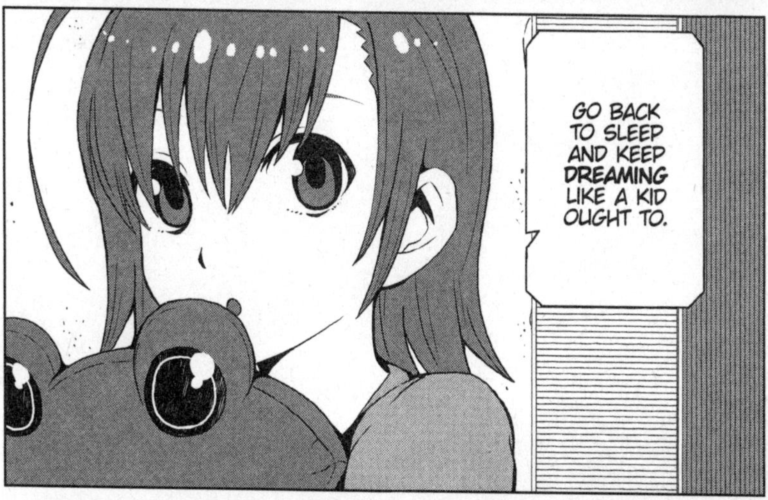
GO BACK TO SLEEP AND KEEP **DREAMING** LIKE A KID OUGHT TO.

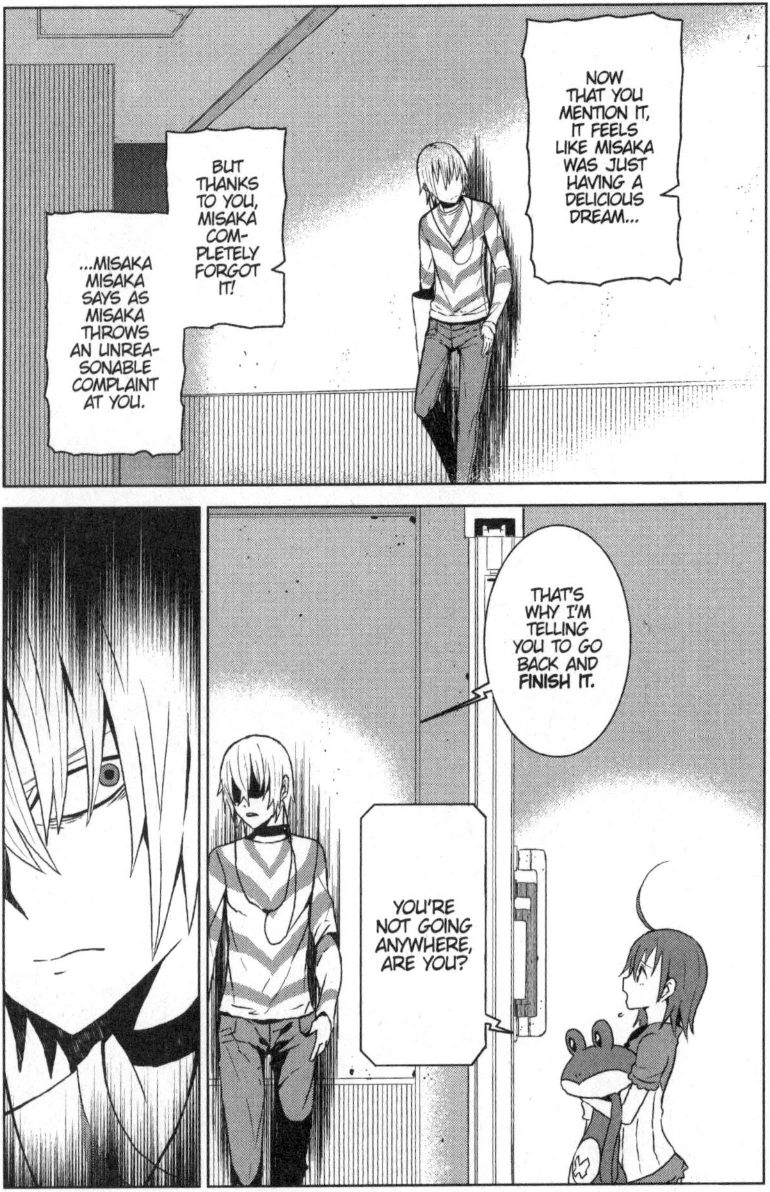
NOW THAT YOU MENTION IT, IT FEELS LIKE MISAKA WAS JUST HAVING A DELICIOUS DREAM...
BUT THANKS TO YOU, MISAKA COMPLETELY FORGOT IT!
...MISAKA MISAKA SAYS AS MISAKA THROWS AN UNREASONABLE COMPLAINT AT YOU.
THAT'S WHY I'M TELLING YOU TO GO BACK AND FINISH IT.
YOU'RE NOT GOING ANYWHERE, ARE YOU?

NO.

I'LL BE HERE.

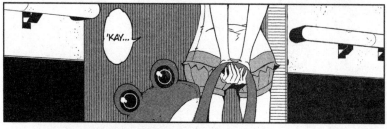

'KAY...

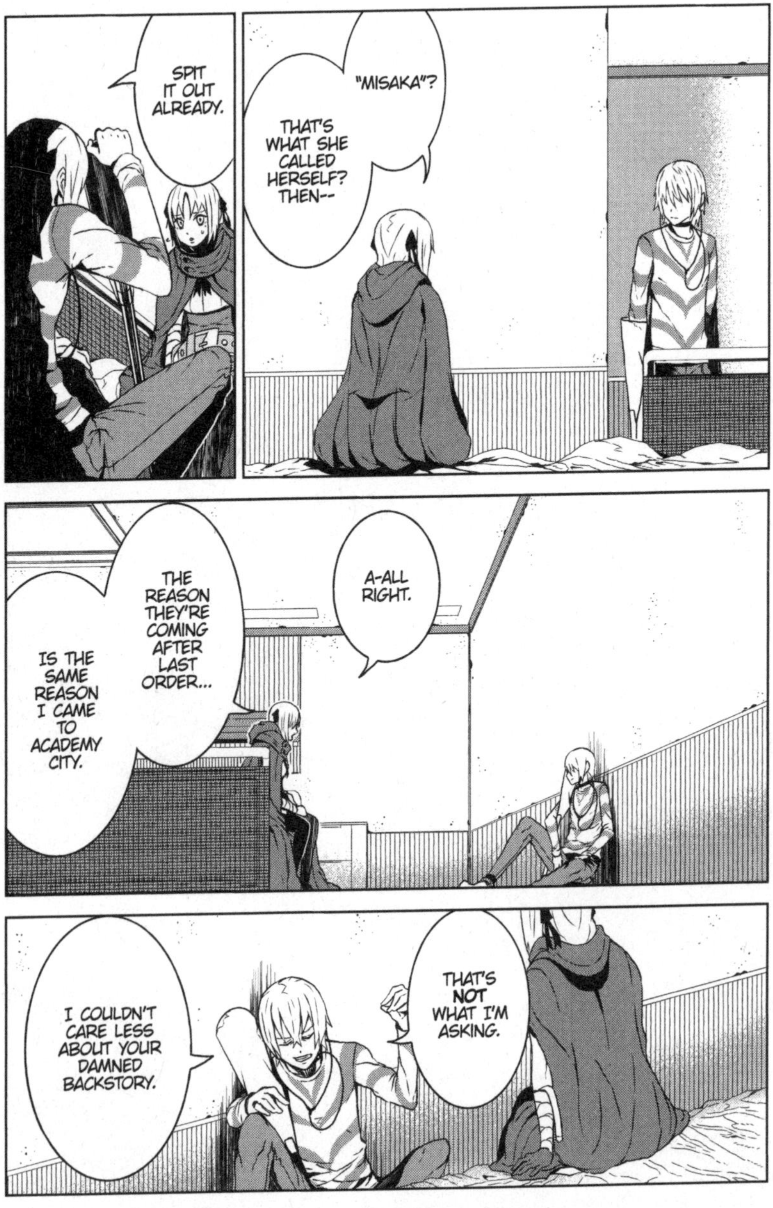
"MISAKA"?
THAT'S WHAT SHE CALLED HERSELF? THEN--
SPIT IT OUT ALREADY.
A-ALL RIGHT.
THE REASON THEY'RE COMING AFTER LAST ORDER...
IS THE SAME REASON I CAME TO ACADEMY CITY.
THAT'S **NOT** WHAT I'M ASKING.
I COULDN'T CARE LESS ABOUT YOUR DAMNED BACKSTORY.

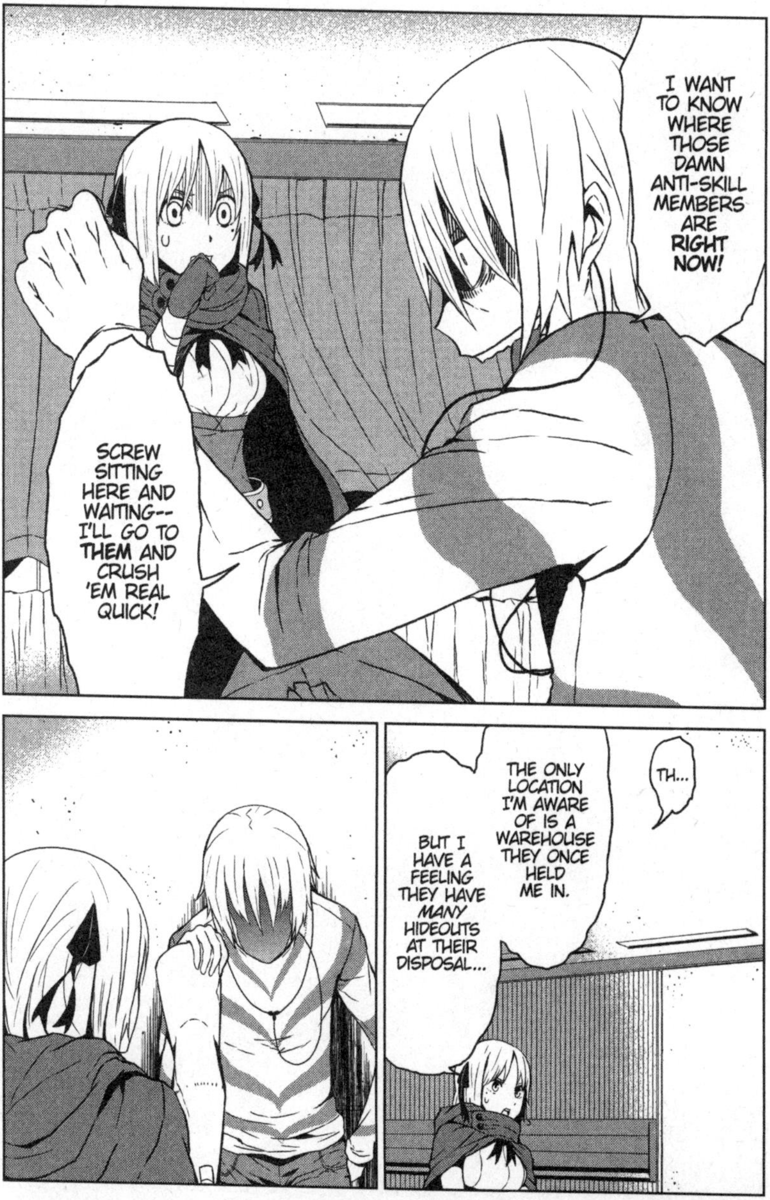
I WANT TO KNOW WHERE THOSE DAMN ANTI-SKILL MEMBERS ARE **RIGHT NOW!**
SCREW SITTING HERE AND WAITING-- I'LL GO TO **THEM** AND CRUSH 'EM REAL QUICK!
TH...
THE ONLY LOCATION I'M AWARE OF IS A WAREHOUSE THEY ONCE HELD ME IN.
BUT I HAVE A FEELING THEY HAVE *MANY* HIDEOUTS AT THEIR DISPOSAL...

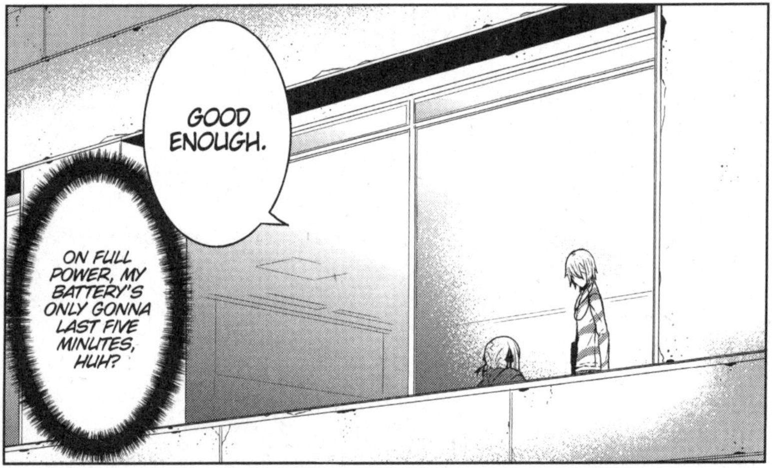
GOOD ENOUGH.
ON FULL POWER, MY BATTERY'S ONLY GONNA LAST FIVE MINUTES, HUH?

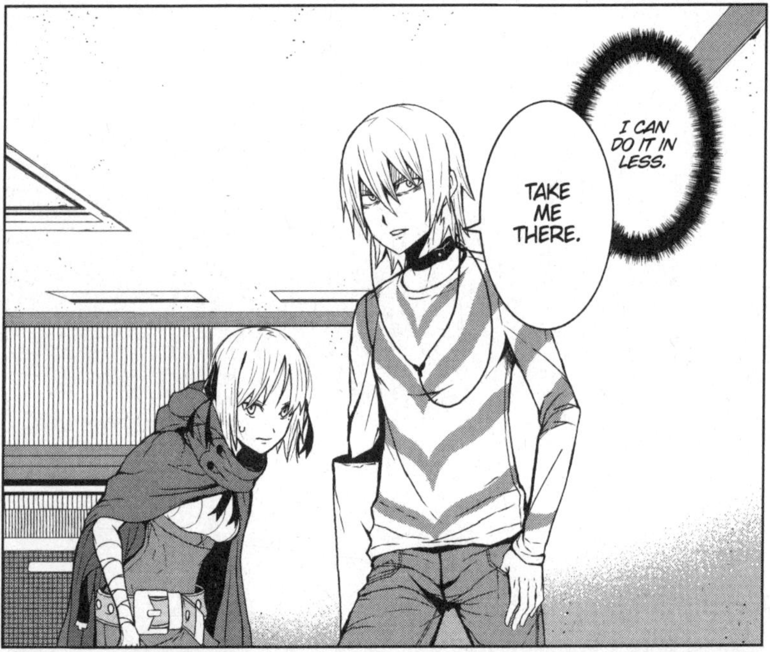
I CAN DO IT IN LESS.
TAKE ME THERE.

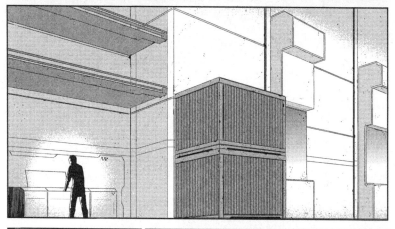

SO, I HEAR YOU WENT UP AGAINST ACCELERATOR.

SOUND ONLY
User 02

ONLINE

I-IT WAS LIGHT CONTACT, AT MOST.

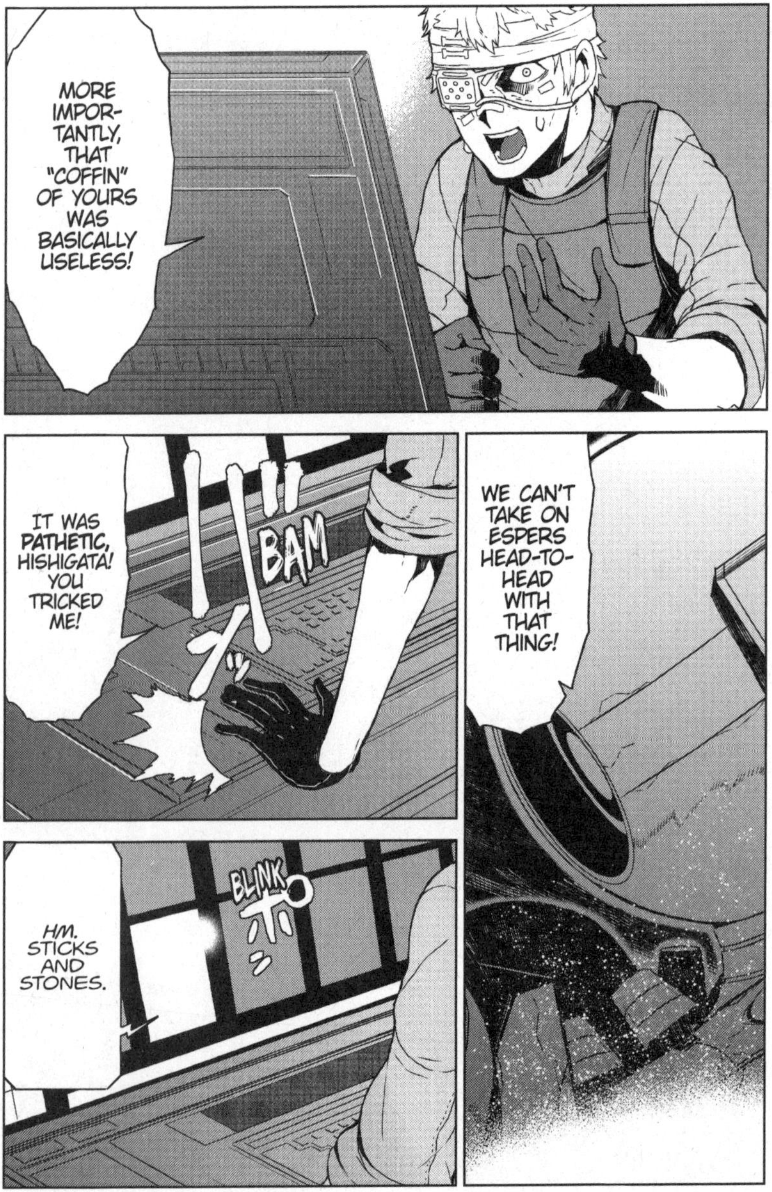
MORE IMPOR-TANTLY, THAT "COFFIN" OF YOURS WAS BASICALLY USELESS!
WE CAN'T TAKE ON ESPERS HEAD-TO-HEAD WITH THAT THING!
IT WAS PATHETIC, HISHIGATA! YOU TRICKED ME!
BAM
BLINK
HM. STICKS AND STONES.

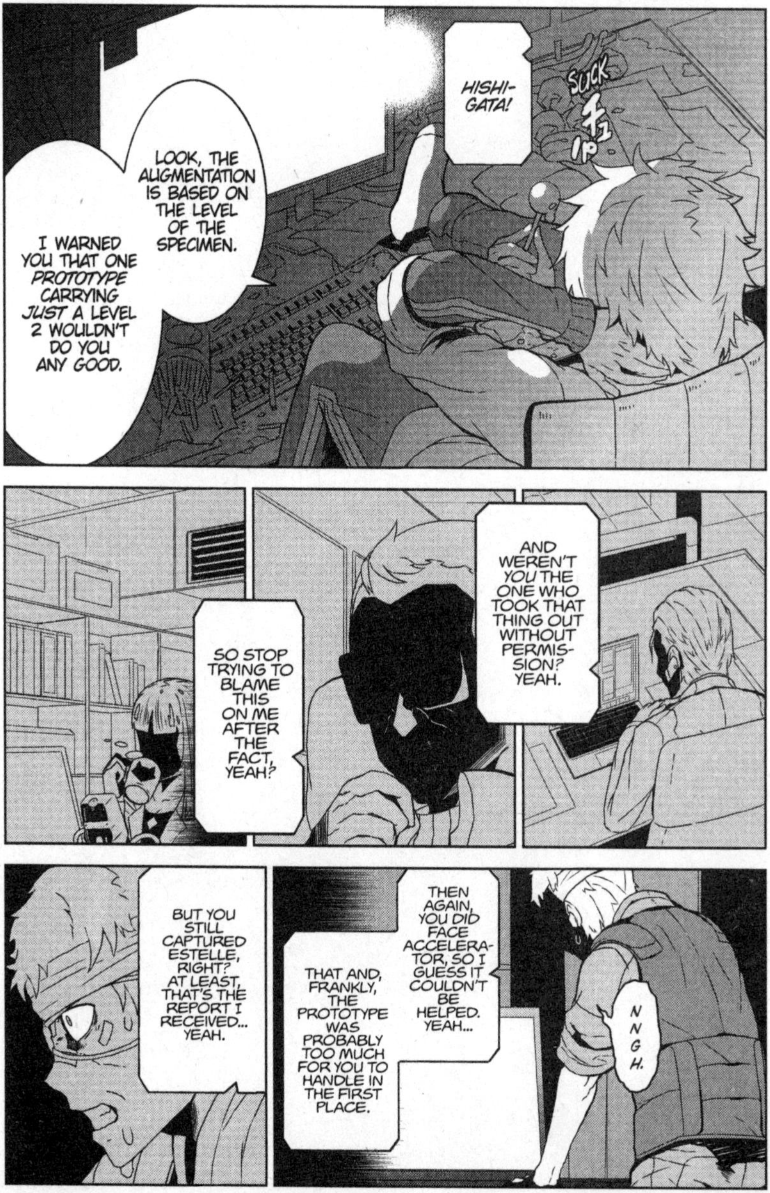
HISHI-GATA!
SUCK
LOOK, THE AUGMENTATION IS BASED ON THE LEVEL OF THE SPECIMEN.
I WARNED YOU THAT ONE *PROTOTYPE* CARRYING *JUST* A LEVEL 2 WOULDN'T DO YOU ANY *GOOD*.
AND WEREN'T *YOU* THE ONE WHO TOOK THAT THING OUT WITHOUT PERMIS-SION? YEAH.
SO STOP TRYING TO BLAME THIS ON ME AFTER THE FACT, YEAH?
THEN AGAIN, YOU *DID* FACE ACCELERA-TOR, SO I GUESS IT COULDN'T BE HELPED. YEAH...
THAT AND, FRANKLY, THE PROTOTYPE WAS PROBABLY TOO MUCH FOR YOU TO HANDLE IN THE FIRST PLACE.
NNGH.
BUT YOU STILL CAPTURED ESTELLE, RIGHT? AT LEAST, THAT'S THE REPORT I RECEIVED... YEAH.

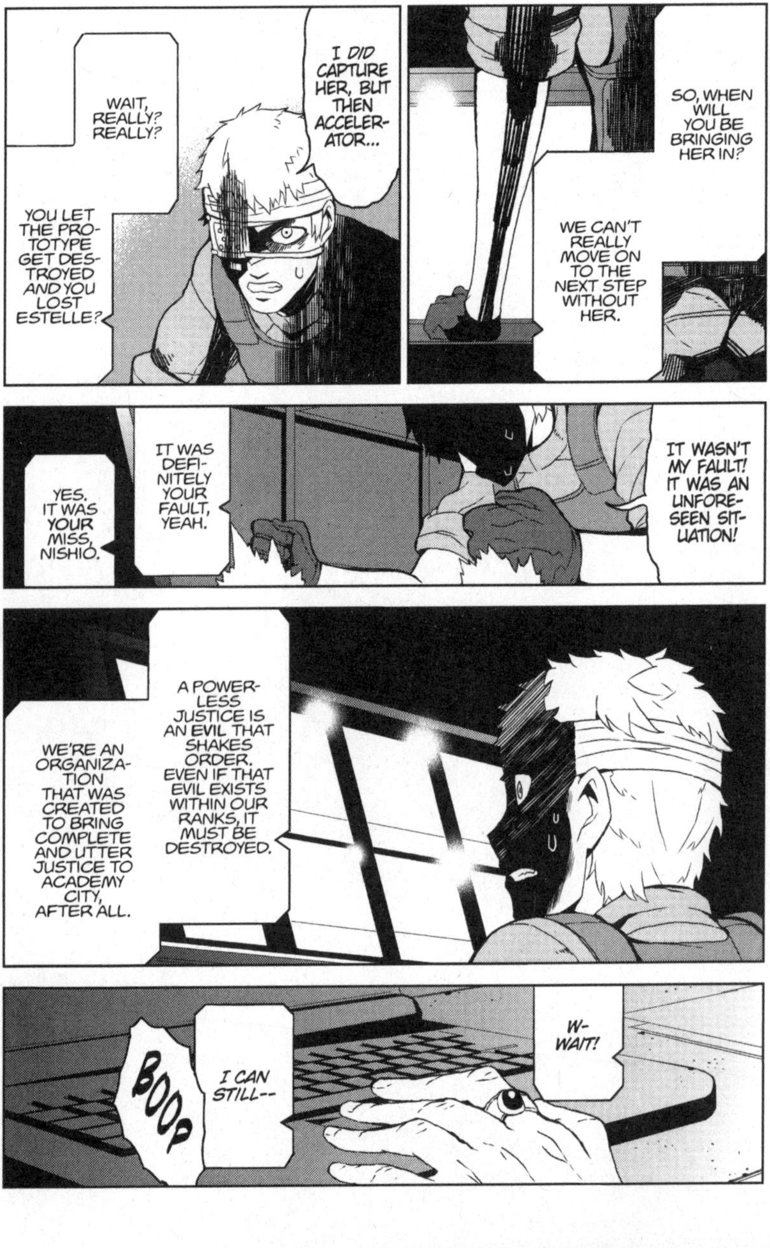
SO, WHEN WILL YOU BE BRINGING HER IN?
WE CAN'T REALLY MOVE ON TO THE NEXT STEP WITHOUT HER.
I *DID* CAPTURE HER, BUT THEN ACCELERATOR...
WAIT, REALLY? REALLY?
YOU LET THE PROTOTYPE GET DESTROYED AND YOU LOST ESTELLE?
IT WASN'T MY FAULT! IT WAS AN UNFORESEEN SITUATION!
IT WAS DEFINITELY YOUR FAULT, YEAH.
YES. IT WAS **YOUR** MISS, NISHIO.
A POWERLESS JUSTICE IS AN **EVIL** THAT SHAKES ORDER. EVEN IF THAT EVIL EXISTS WITHIN OUR RANKS, IT MUST BE DESTROYED.
WE'RE AN ORGANIZATION THAT WAS CREATED TO BRING COMPLETE AND UTTER JUSTICE TO ACADEMY CITY, AFTER ALL.
W-WAIT!
I CAN STILL--
BOOP

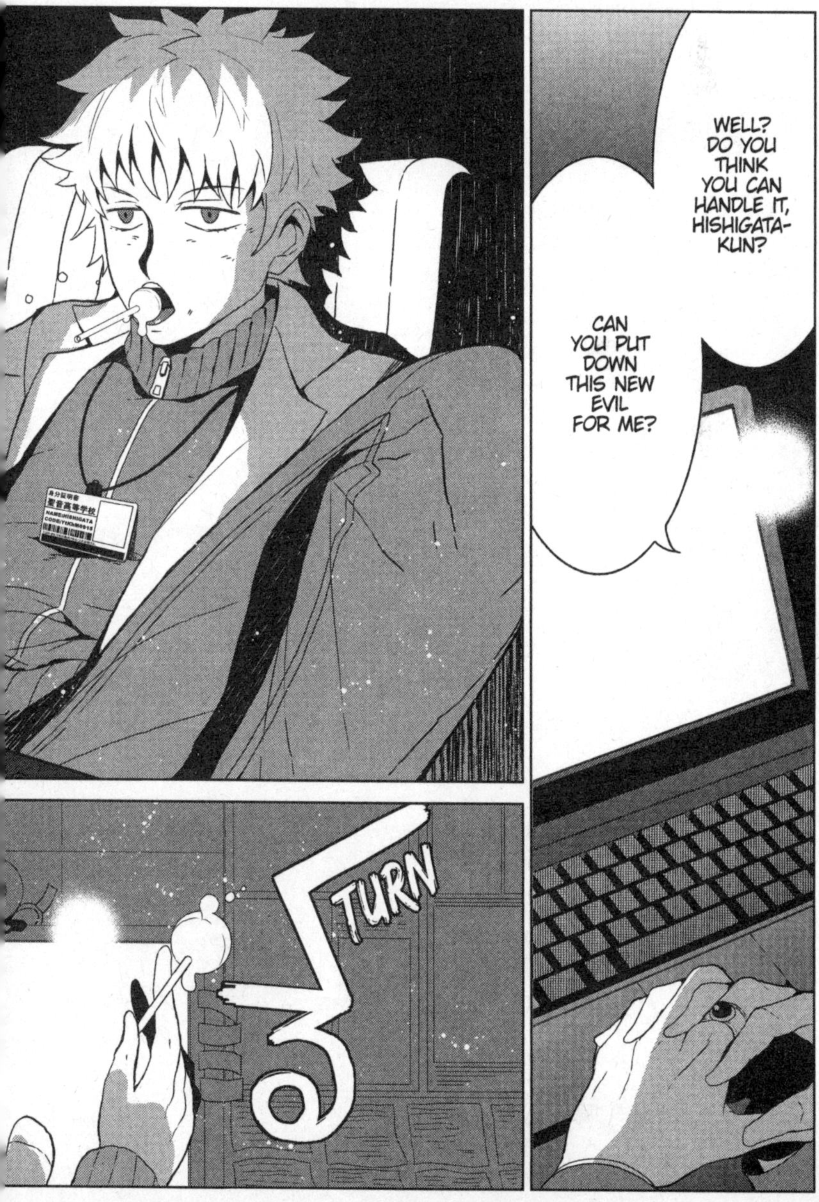
WELL? DO YOU THINK YOU CAN HANDLE IT, HISHIGATA-KUN?
CAN YOU PUT DOWN THIS NEW EVIL FOR ME?
TURN

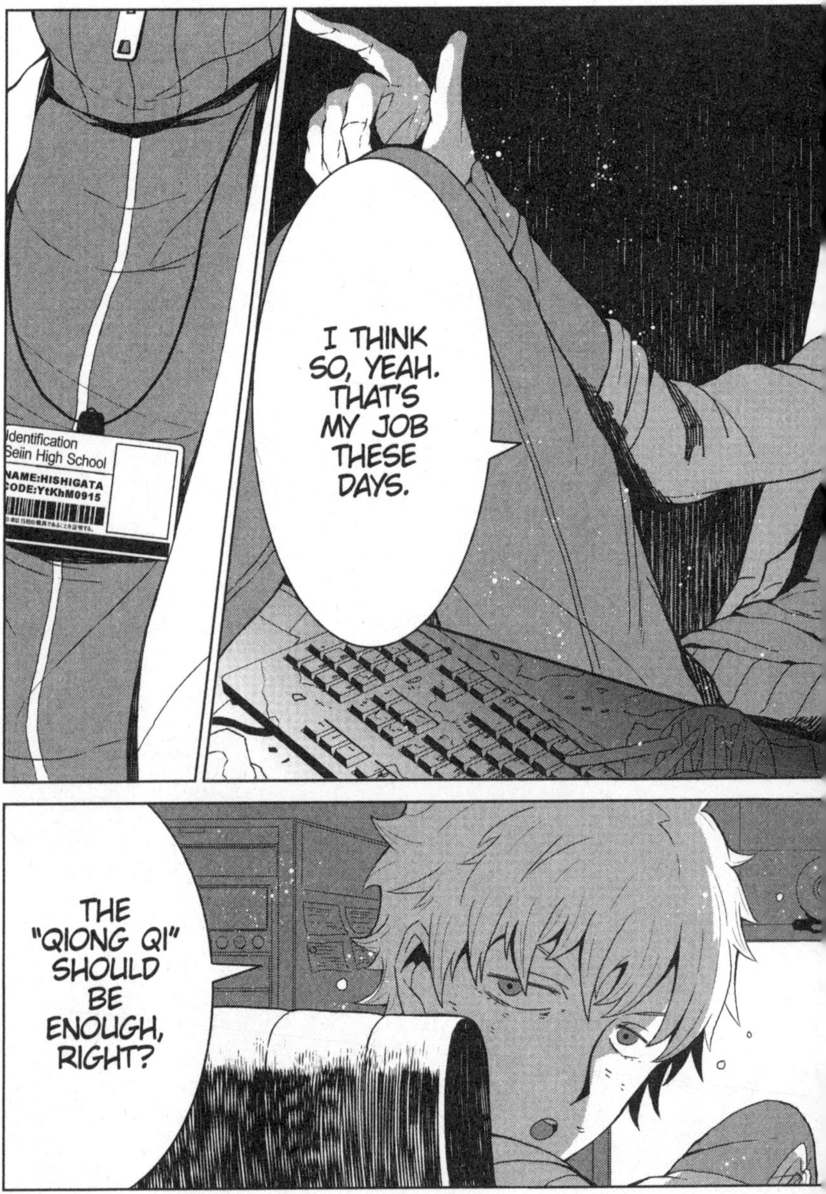
I THINK SO, YEAH. THAT'S MY JOB THESE DAYS.
Identification
Seiin High School
NAME:HISHIGATA
CODE:YtKhM0915
THE "QIONG QI" SHOULD BE ENOUGH, RIGHT?

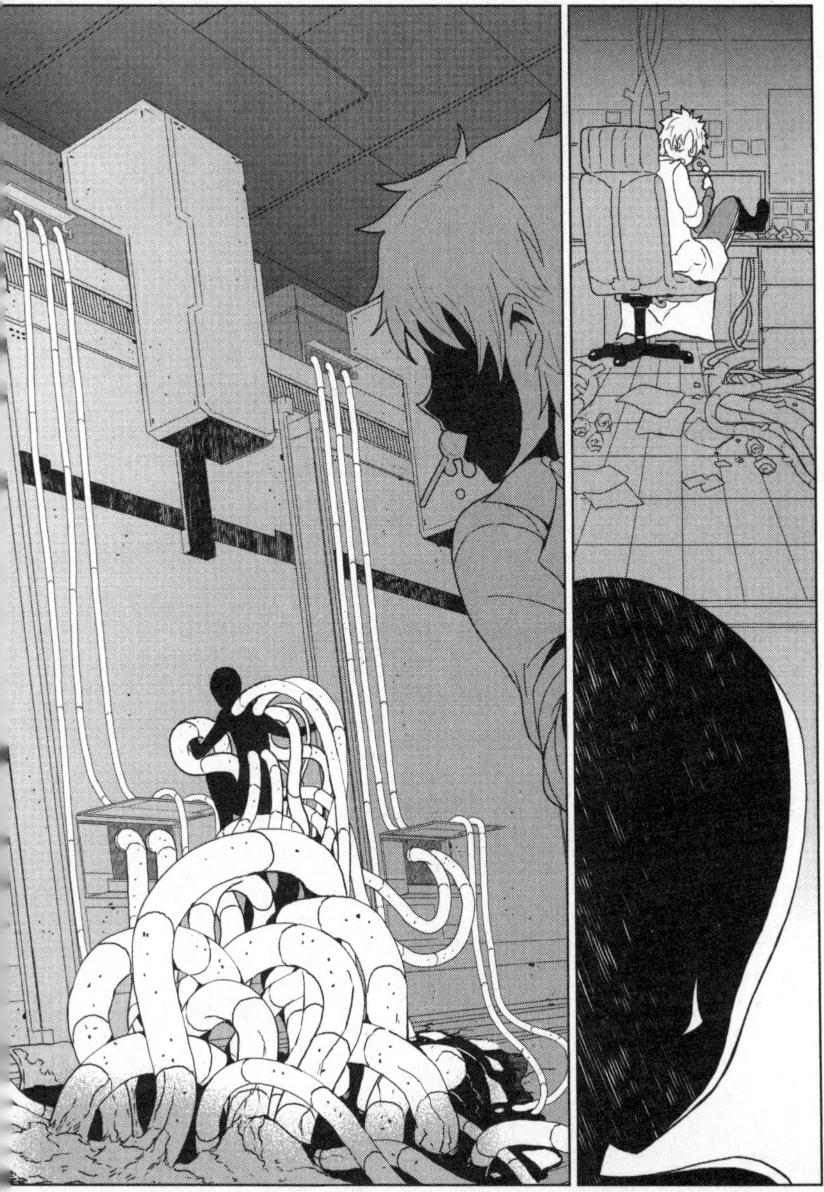

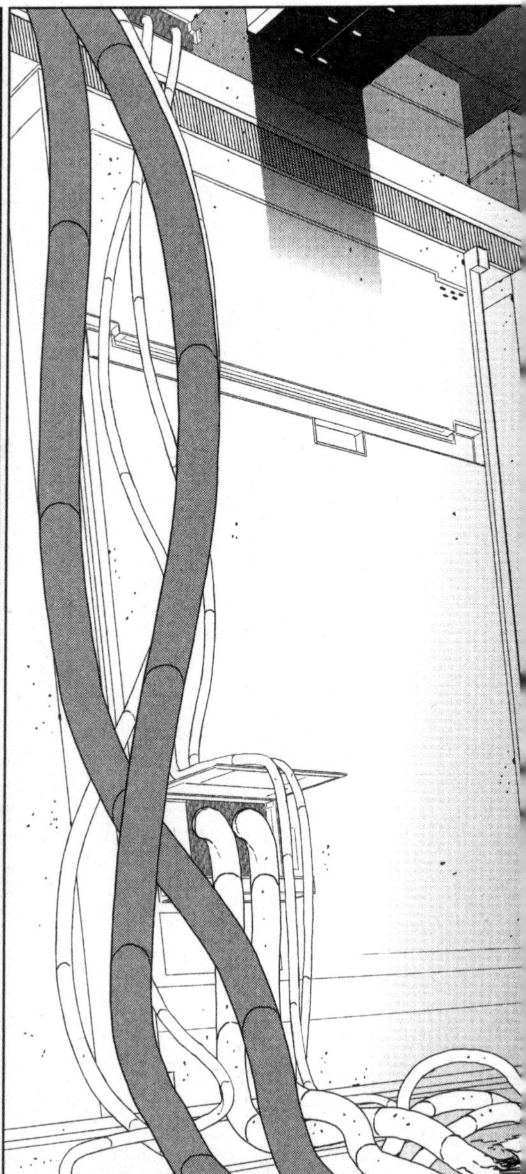

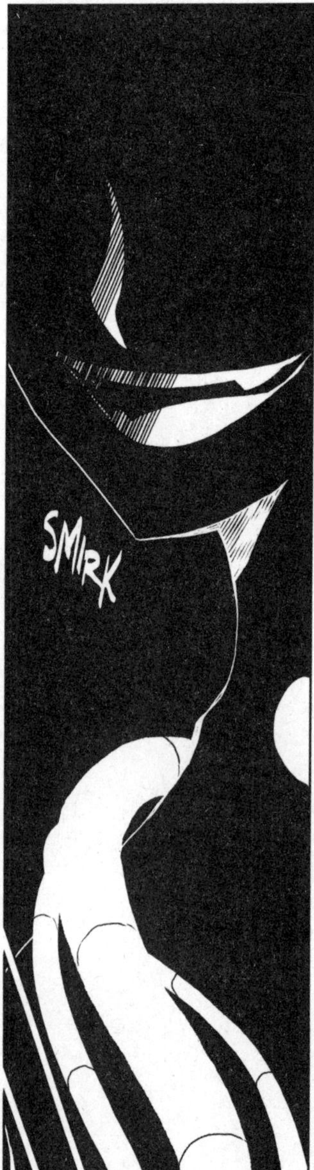
SMIRK

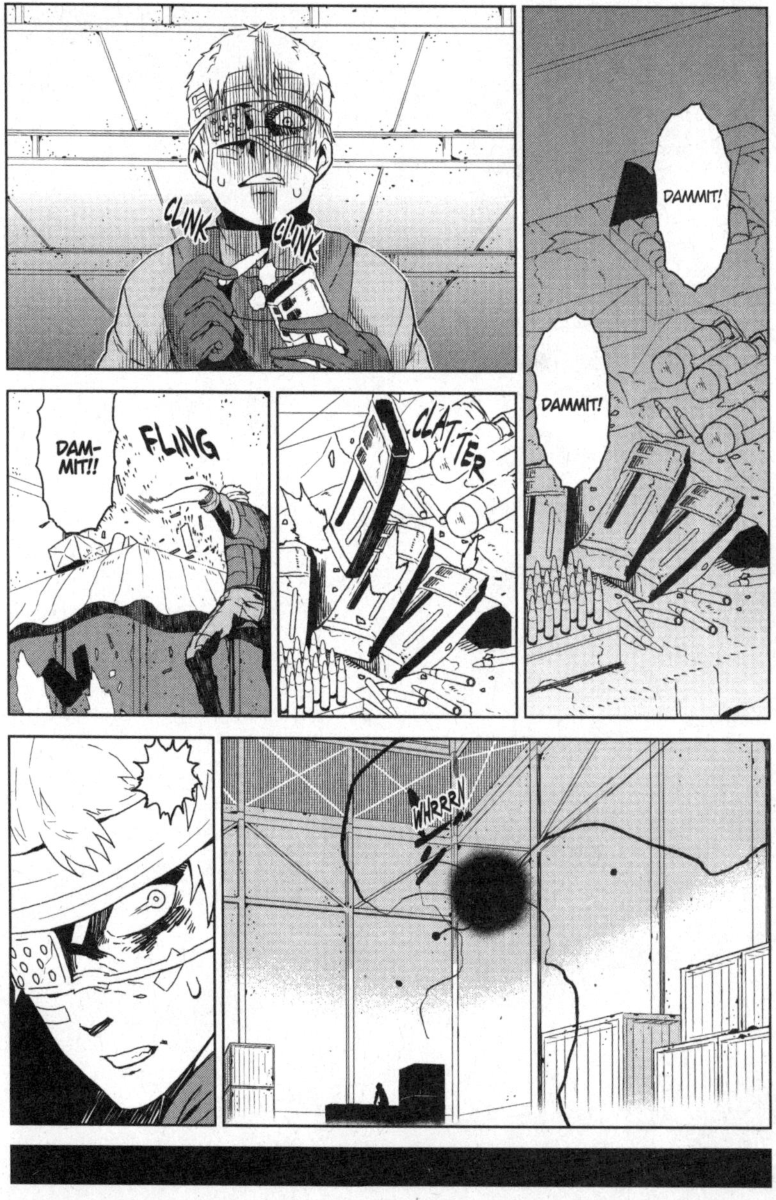
DAMMIT!
DAMMIT!
CLINK
CLINK
CLATTER
DAM-MIT!!
FLING
WHRRRN

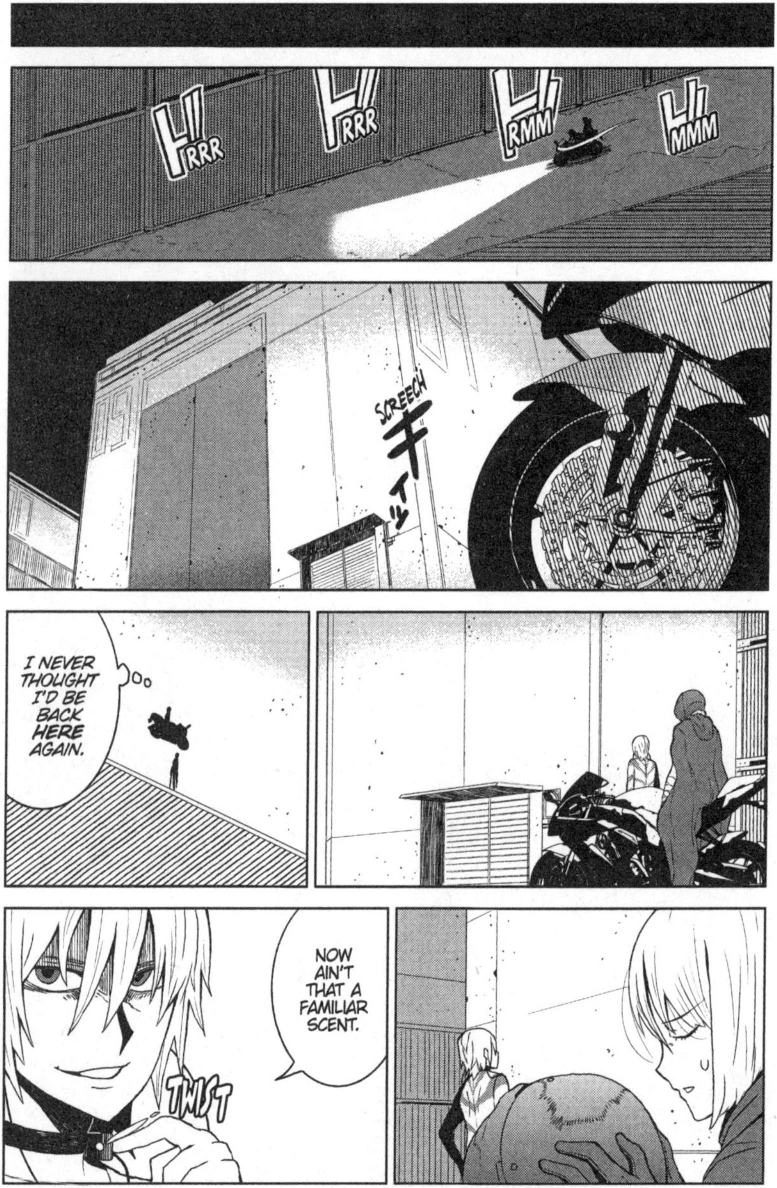
RRR
RRR
RMM
MMM
SCREECH
I NEVER THOUGHT I'D BE BACK HERE AGAIN.
NOW AIN'T THAT A FAMILIAR SCENT.
TWIST

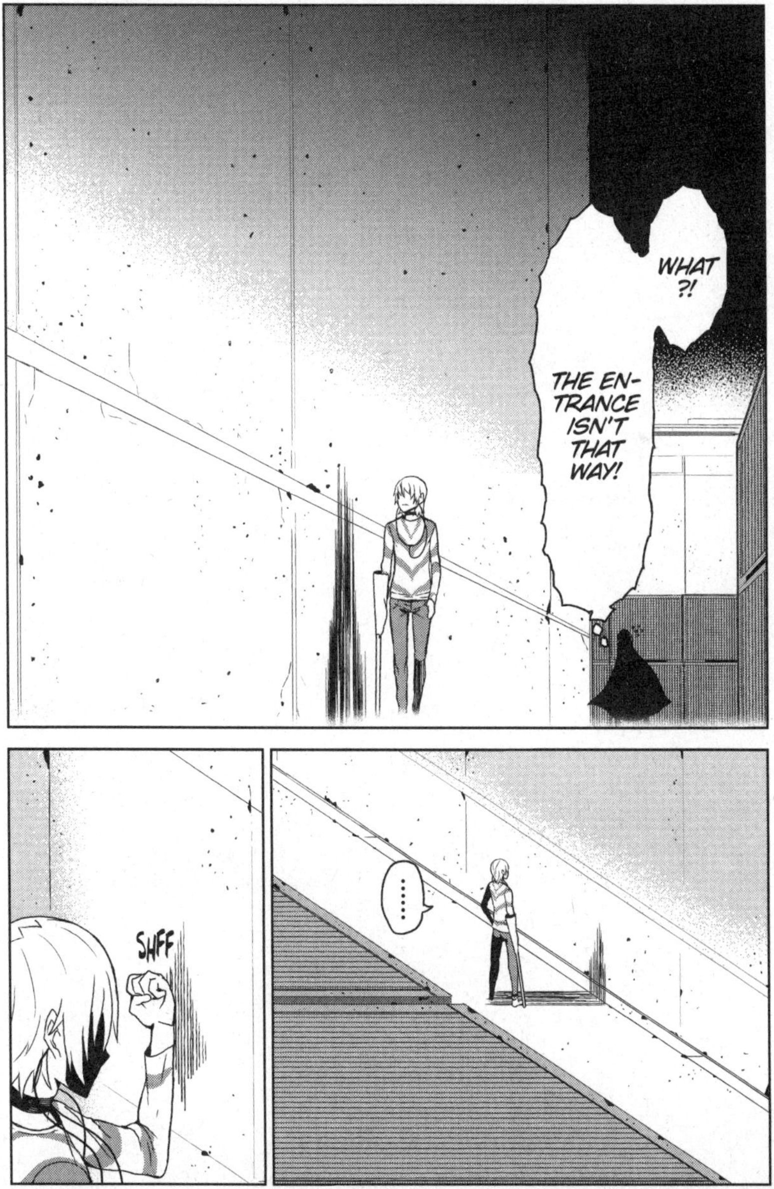
WHAT ?!
THE EN-TRANCE ISN'T THAT WAY!
......
SHFF

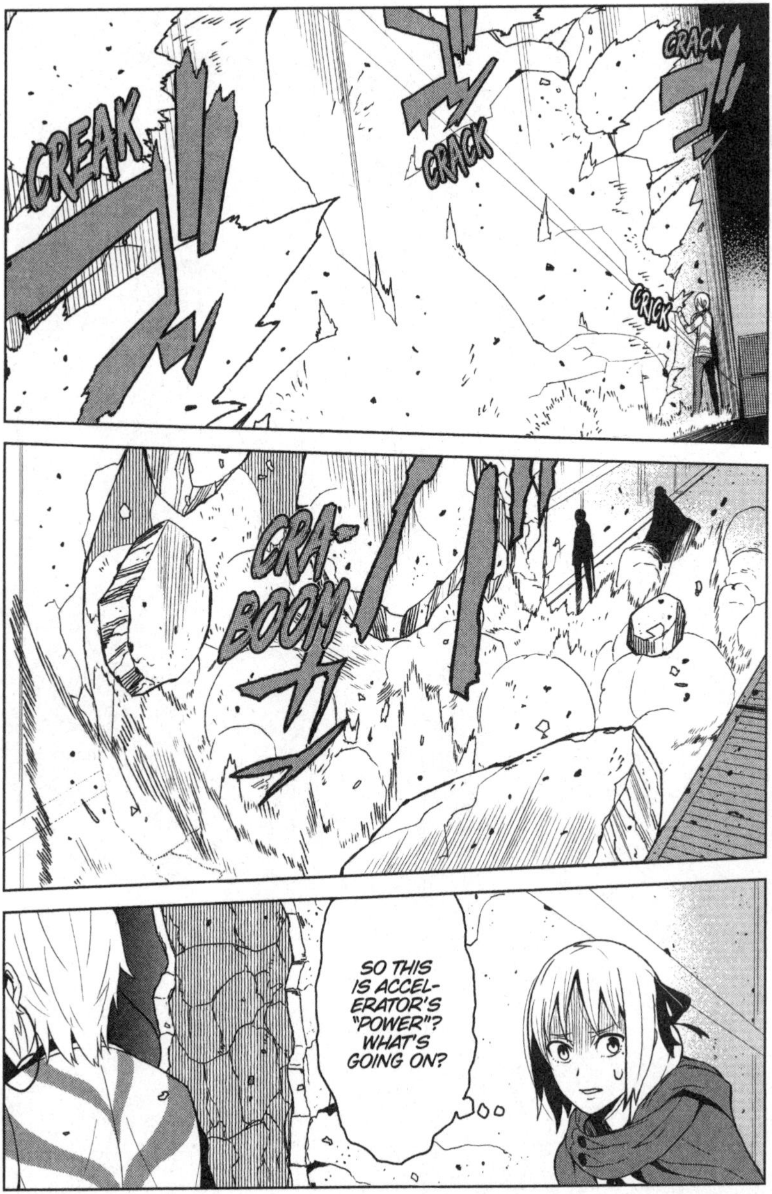
CRACK
CRACK
CREAK
CRICK
CRA-BOOM
SO THIS IS ACCEL-ERATOR'S "POWER"? WHAT'S GOING ON?

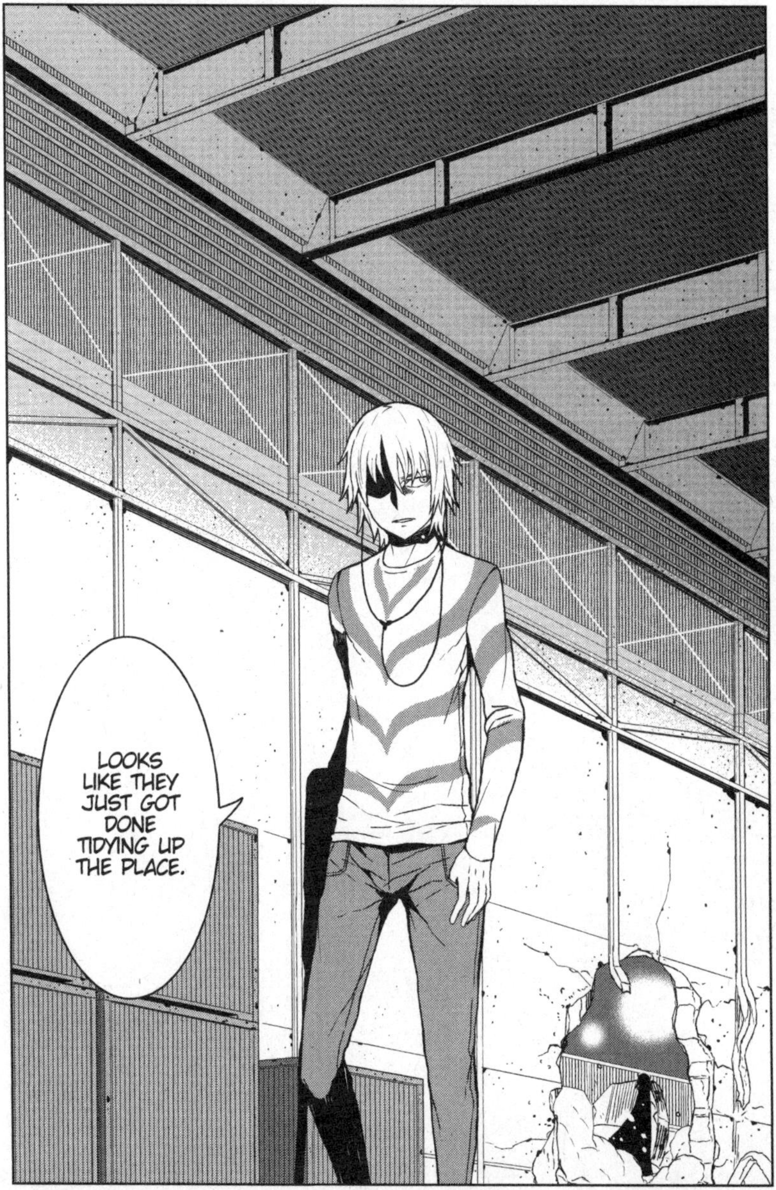
LOOKS LIKE THEY JUST GOT DONE TIDYING UP THE PLACE.

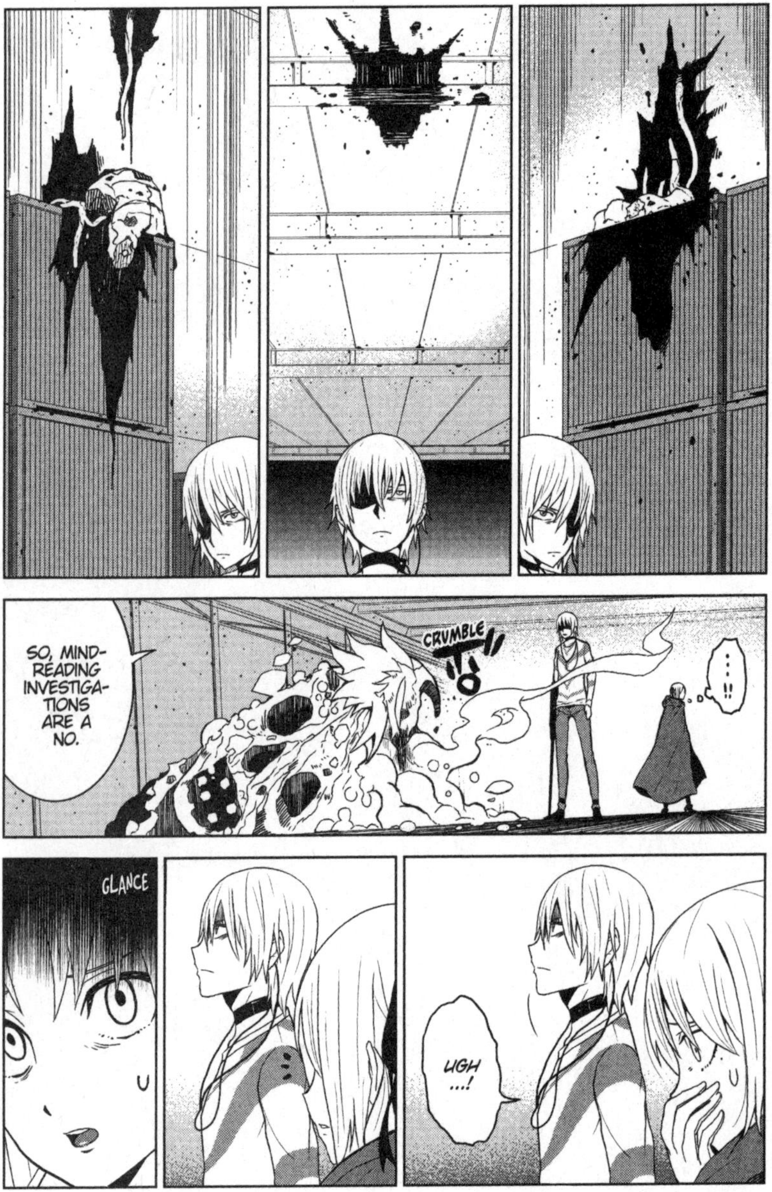

...!!
CRUMBLE
SO, MIND-READING INVESTIGATIONS ARE A NO.
UGH ...!
GLANCE

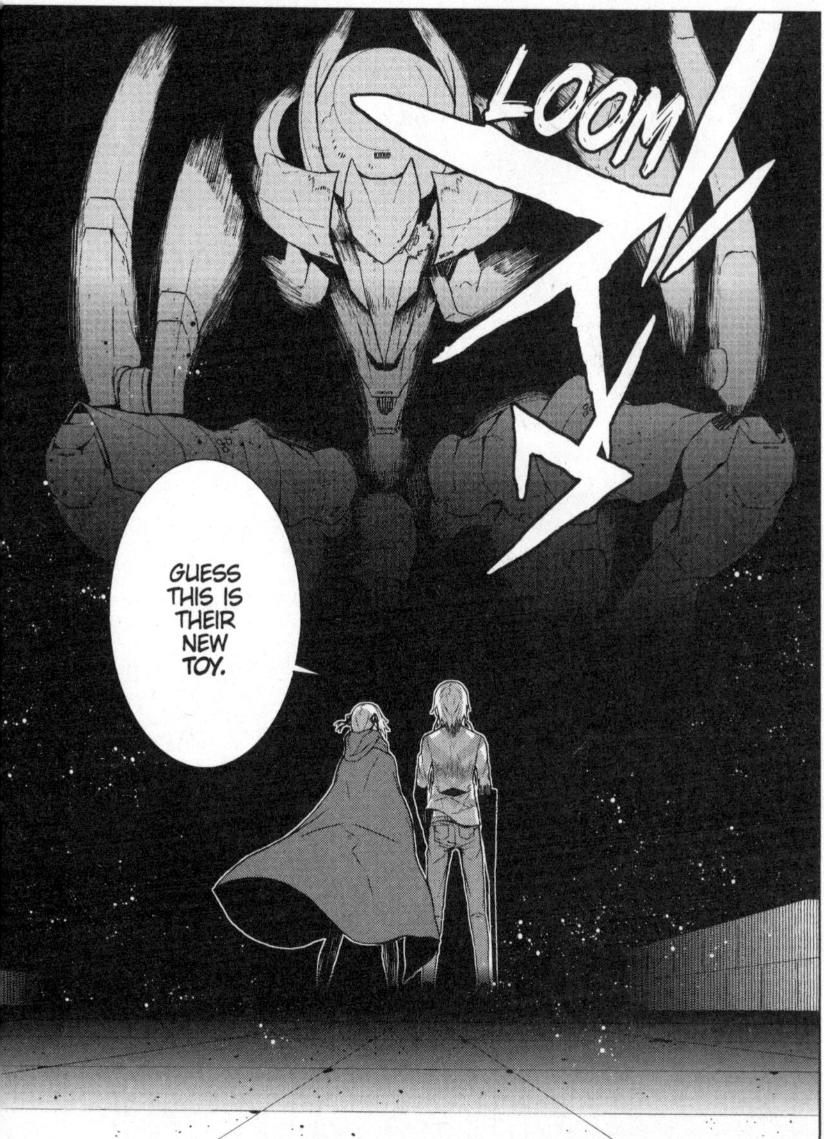
LOOM
GUESS THIS IS THEIR NEW TOY.

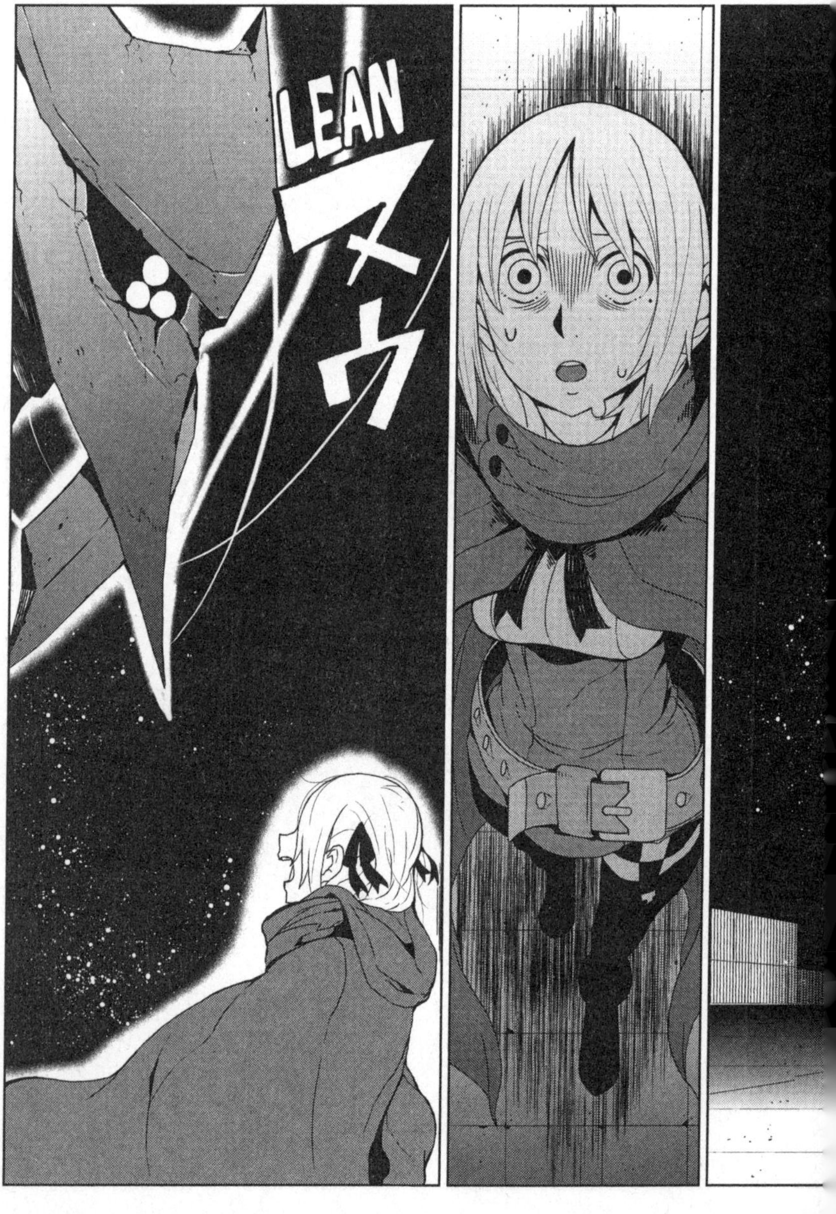
LEAN
ヌゥ

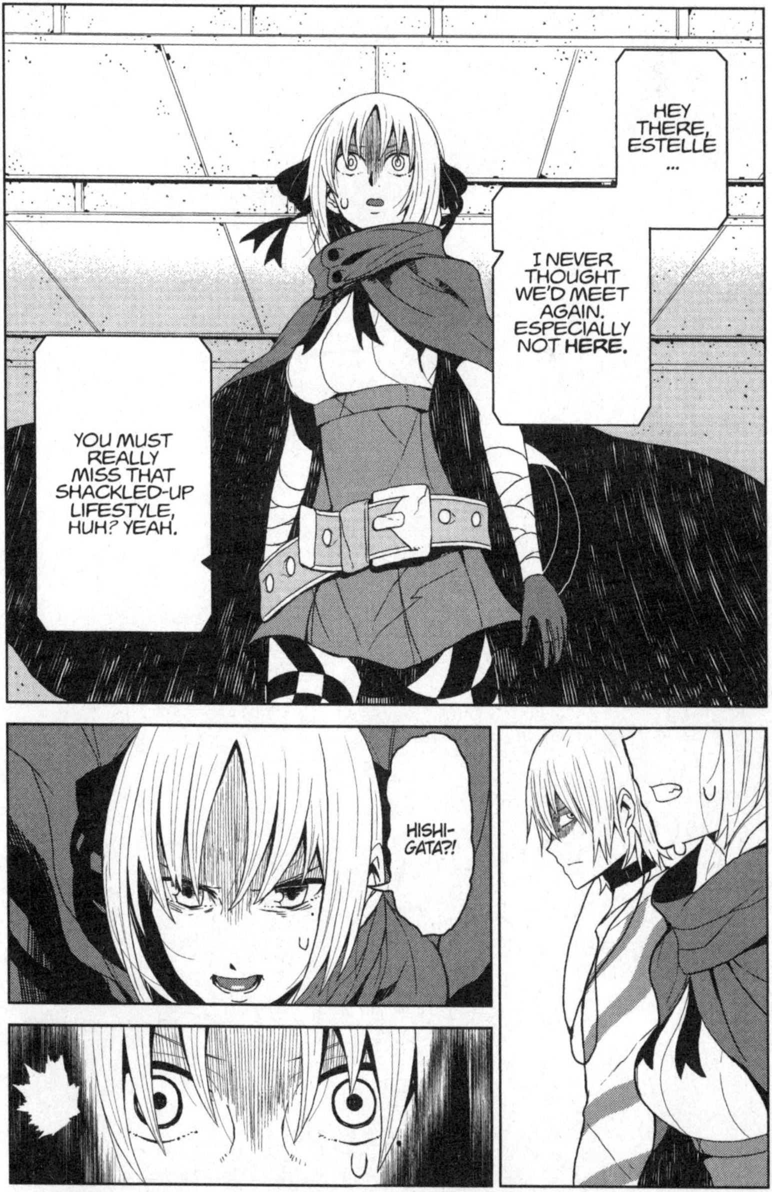
HEY THERE, ESTELLE ...
I NEVER THOUGHT WE'D MEET AGAIN. ESPECIALLY NOT HERE.
YOU MUST REALLY MISS THAT SHACKLED-UP LIFESTYLE, HUH? YEAH.
HISHI-GATA?!

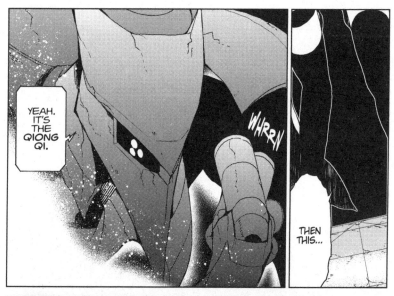

YEAH. IT'S THE QIONG QI.

WHRRN

THEN THIS...

YOU COM- PLETED IT?!

IT'S HERE, SO YEAH.

BY THE WAY-- THIS ISN'T A PROTO- TYPE.

SO, HARUMI IS PLANNING TO START IT, THEN.

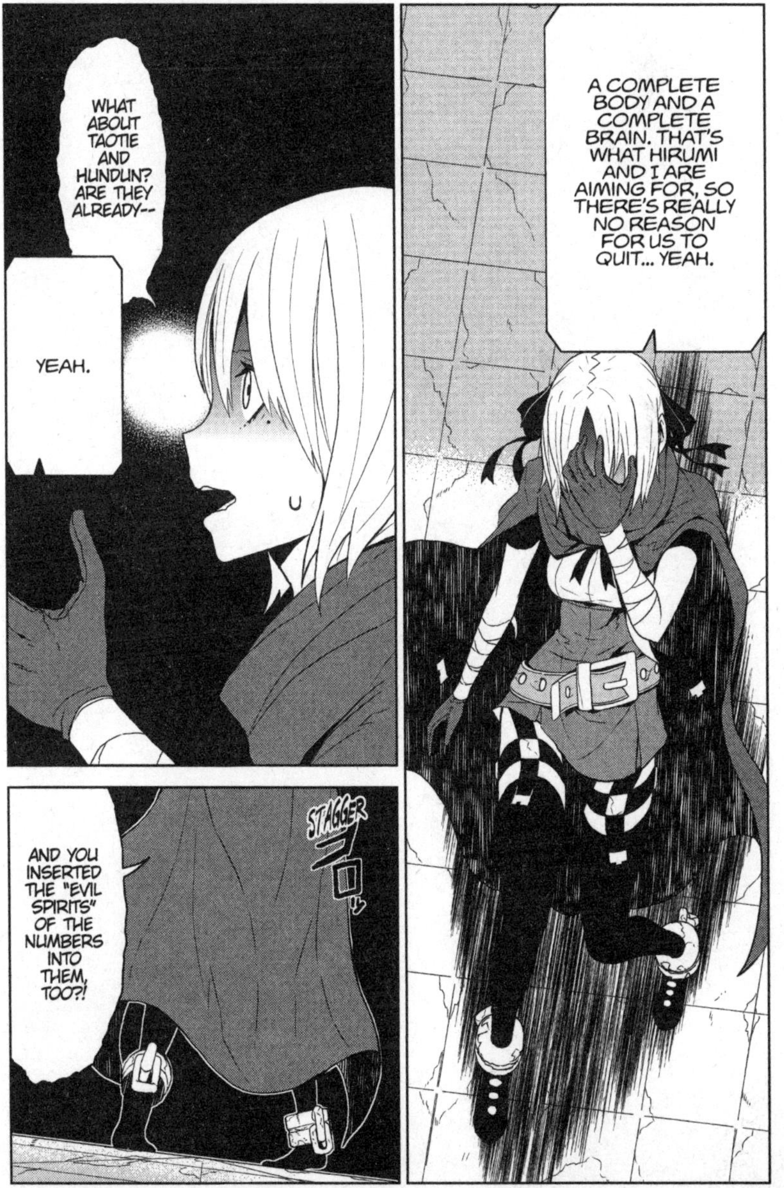
A COMPLETE BODY AND A COMPLETE BRAIN. THAT'S WHAT HIRUMI AND I ARE AIMING FOR, SO THERE'S REALLY NO REASON FOR US TO QUIT... YEAH.
WHAT ABOUT TAOTIE AND HUNDUN? ARE THEY ALREADY--
YEAH.
STAGGER
AND YOU INSERTED THE "EVIL SPIRITS" OF THE NUMBERS INTO THEM, TOO?!

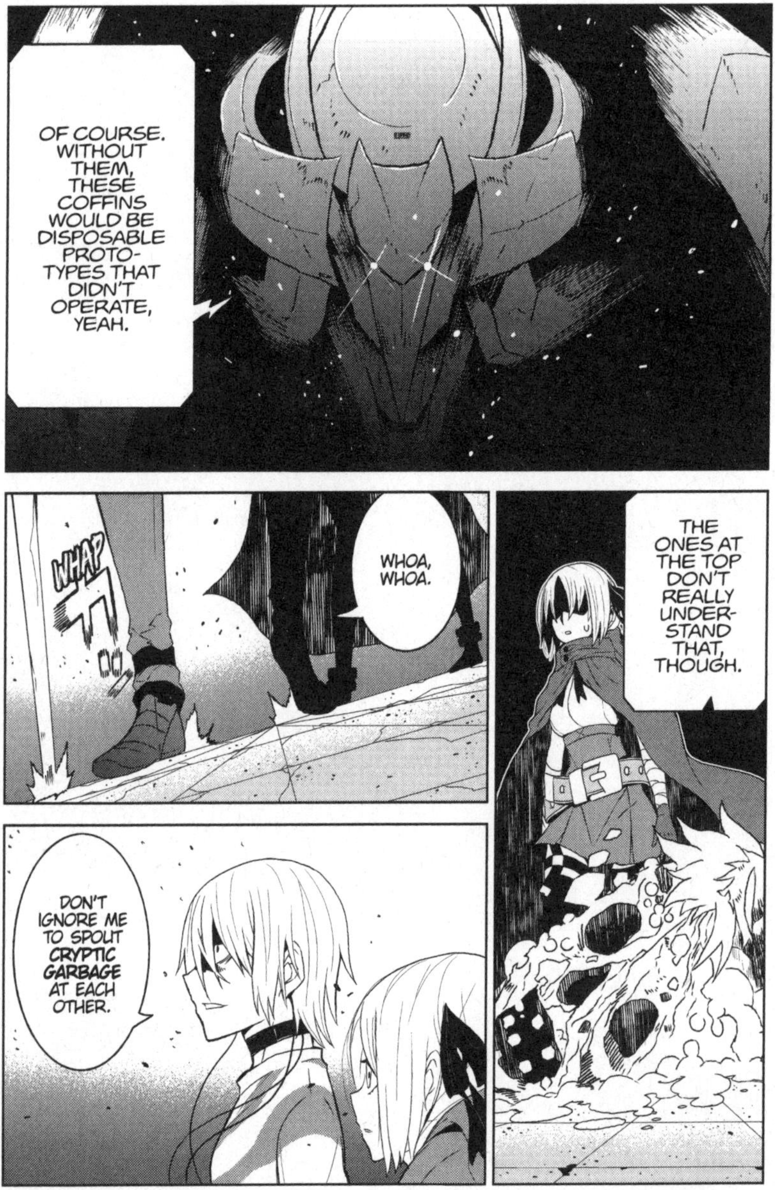
OF COURSE. WITHOUT THEM, THESE COFFINS WOULD BE DISPOSABLE PROTO-TYPES THAT DIDN'T OPERATE, YEAH.
THE ONES AT THE TOP DON'T REALLY UNDER-STAND THAT, THOUGH.
WHAP
WHOA, WHOA.
DON'T IGNORE ME TO SPOUT CRYPTIC GARBAGE AT EACH OTHER.

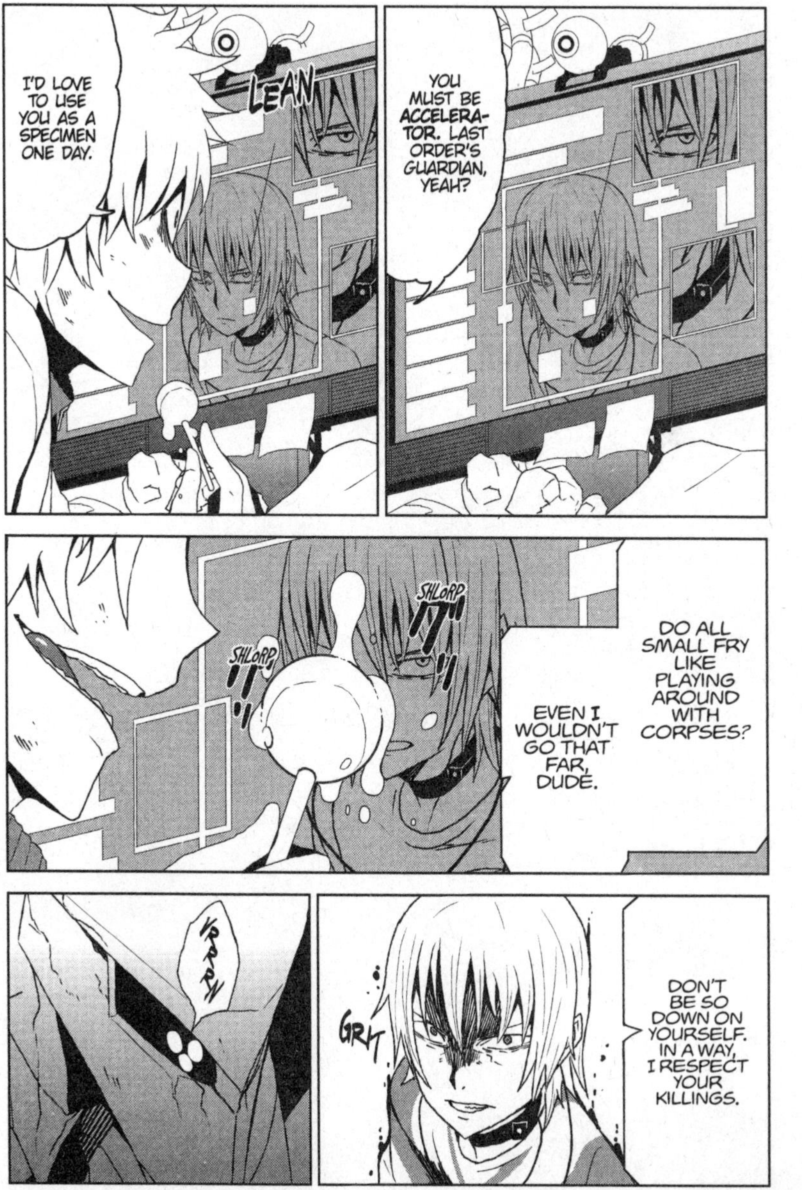
YOU MUST BE ACCELERATOR. LAST ORDER'S GUARDIAN, YEAH?
LEAN
I'D LOVE TO USE YOU AS A SPECIMEN ONE DAY.
DO ALL SMALL FRY LIKE PLAYING AROUND WITH CORPSES?
EVEN I WOULDN'T GO THAT FAR, DUDE.
SHLORP
SHLORP
DON'T BE SO DOWN ON YOURSELF. IN A WAY, I RESPECT YOUR KILLINGS.
GRIT
VRRRN

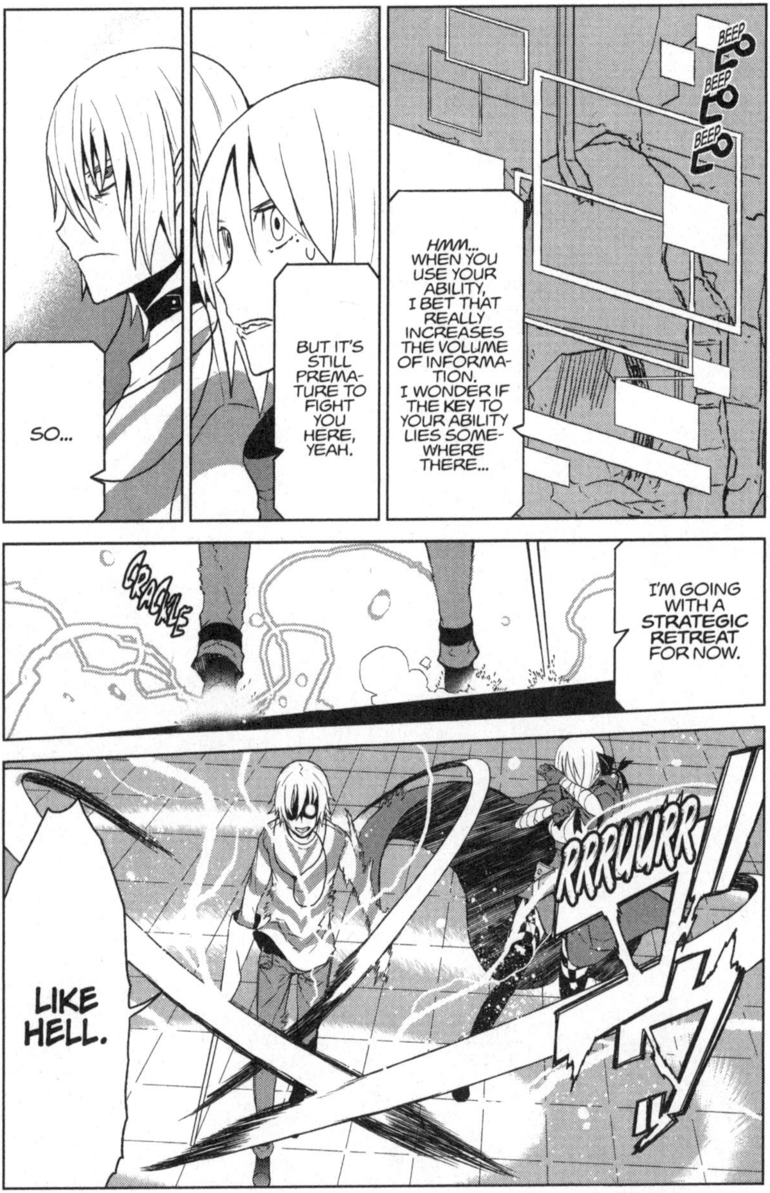
BEEP
BEEP
BEEP
HMM... WHEN YOU USE YOUR ABILITY, I BET THAT REALLY INCREASES THE VOLUME OF INFORMATION. I WONDER IF THE KEY TO YOUR ABILITY LIES SOMEWHERE THERE...
BUT IT'S STILL PREMATURE TO FIGHT YOU HERE, YEAH.
SO...
I'M GOING WITH A STRATEGIC RETREAT FOR NOW.
CRACKLE
RRRUUURR
LIKE HELL.

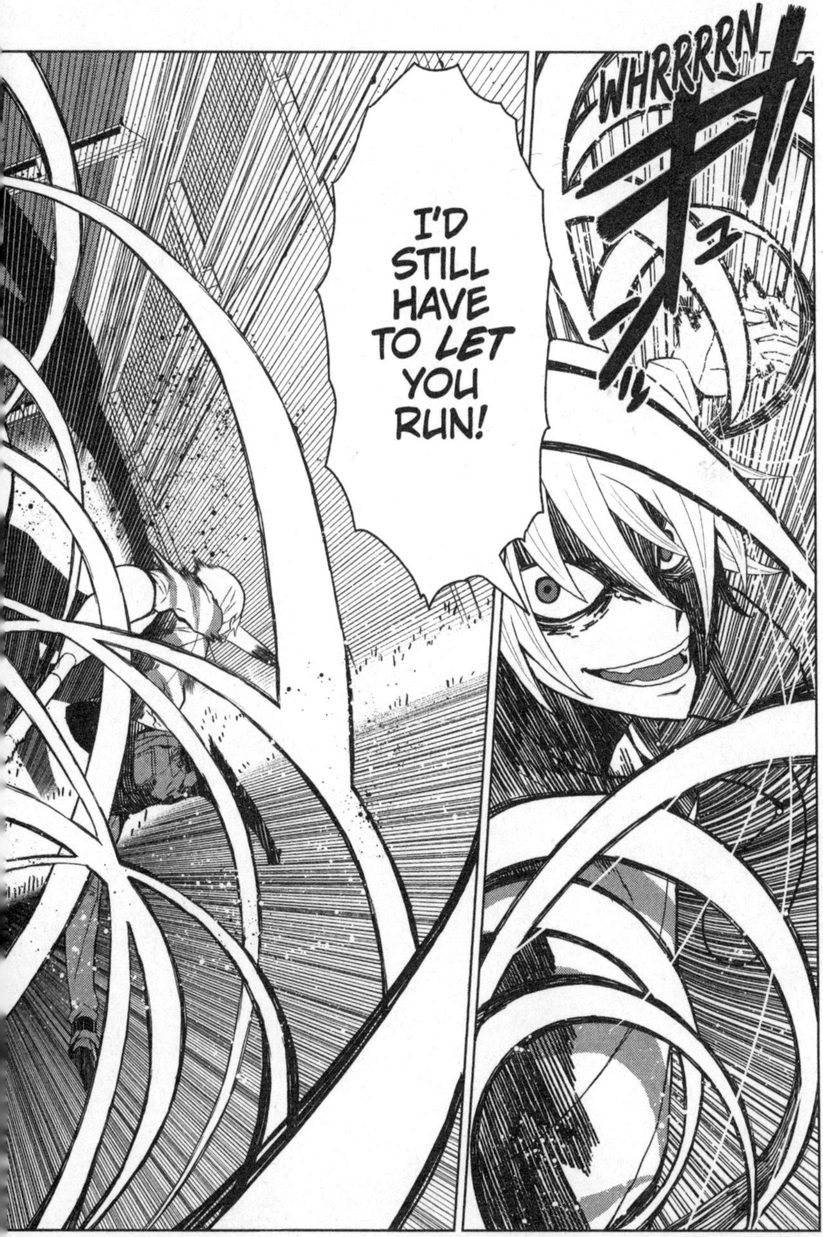
WHRRRRN
I'D STILL HAVE TO LET YOU RUN!

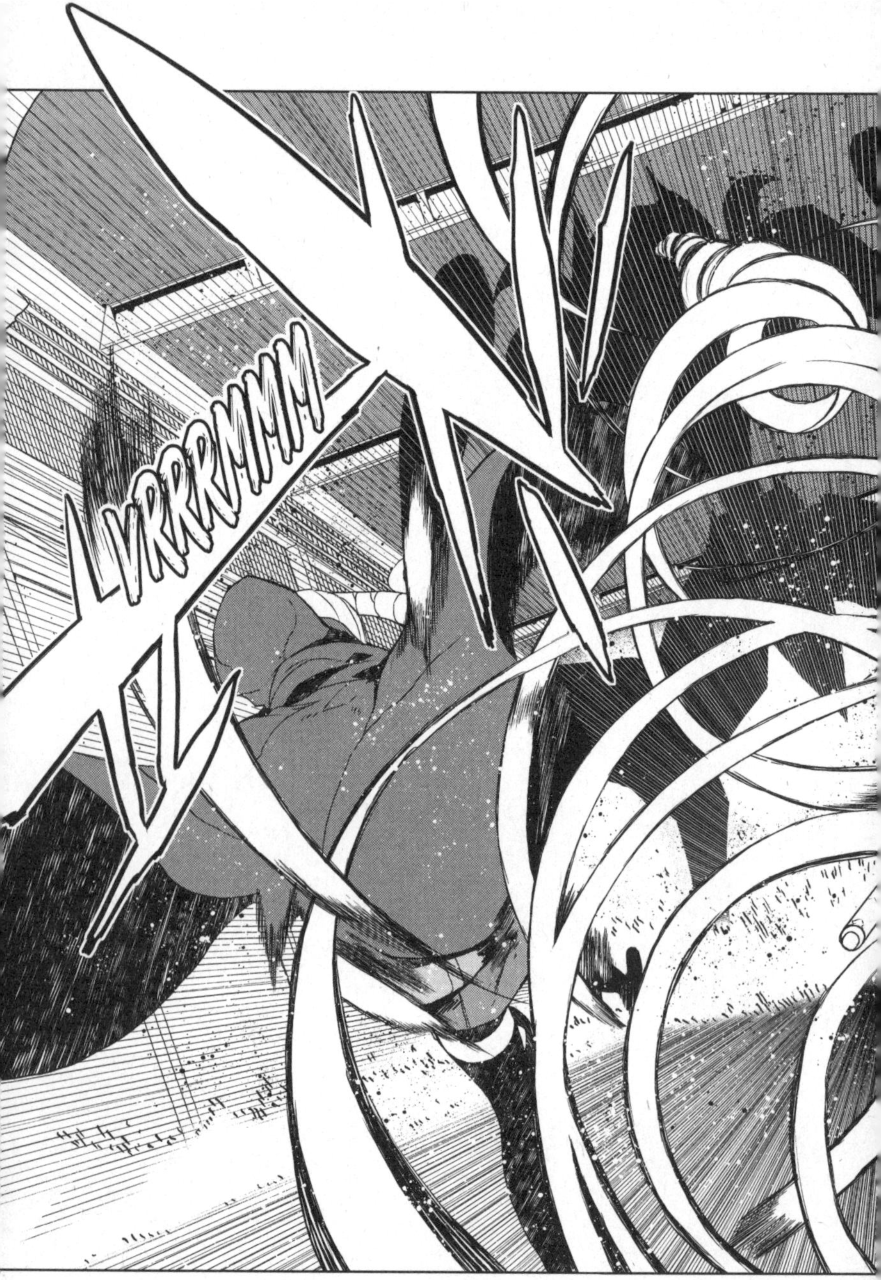
VRRRMMM

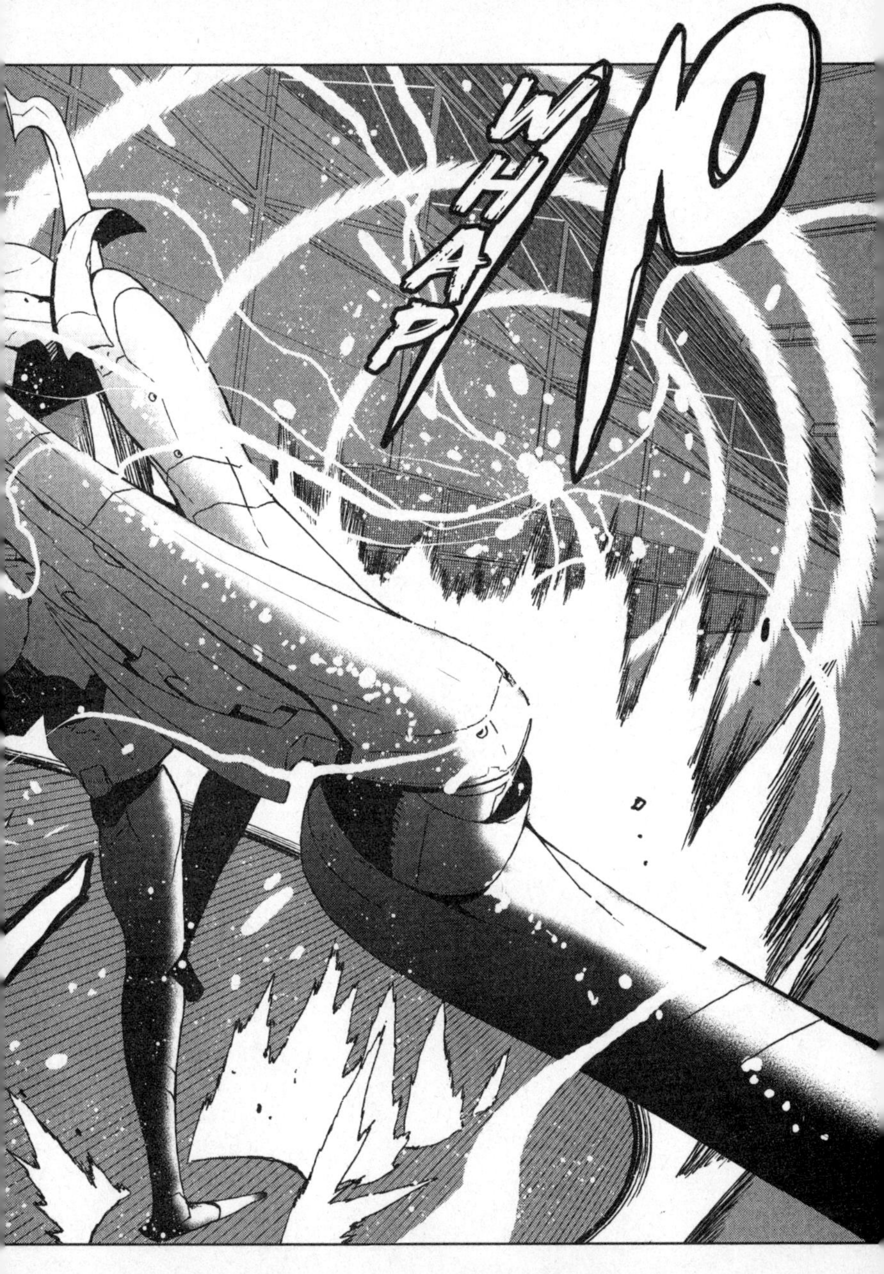
WHAP

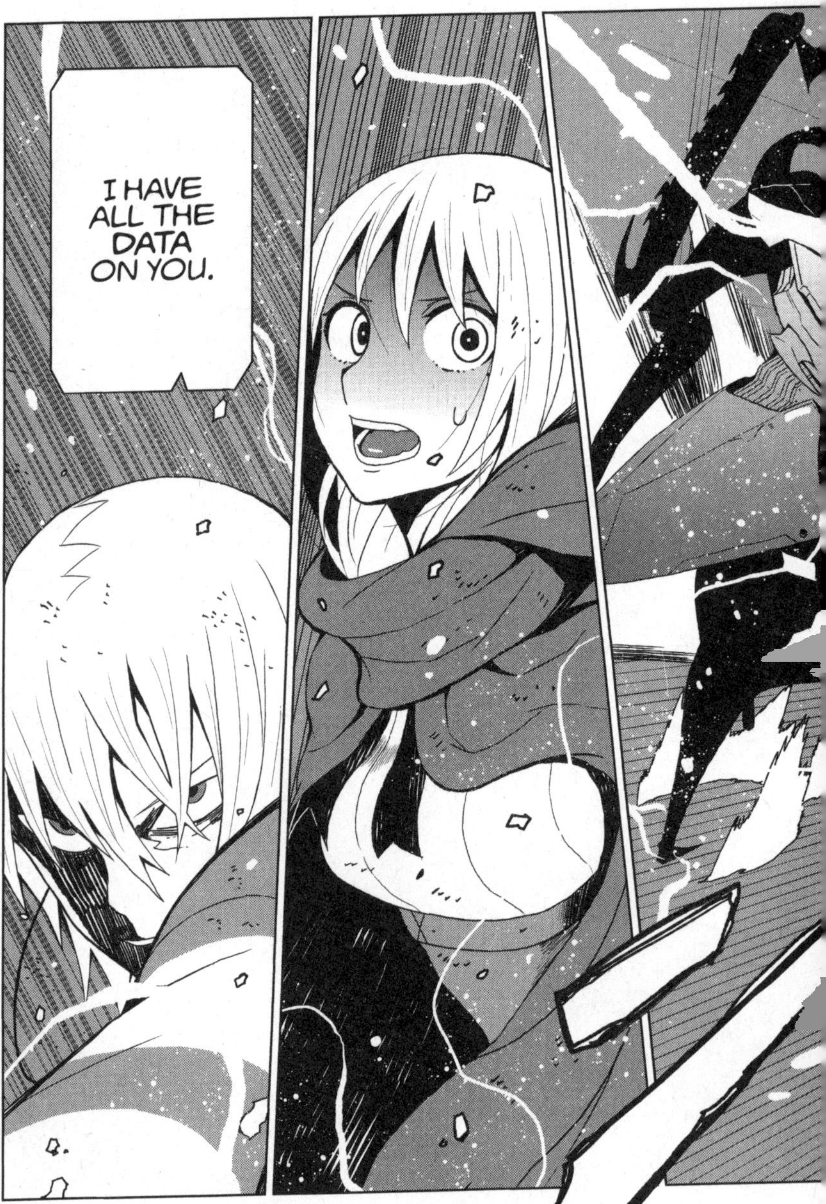
I HAVE ALL THE DATA ON YOU.

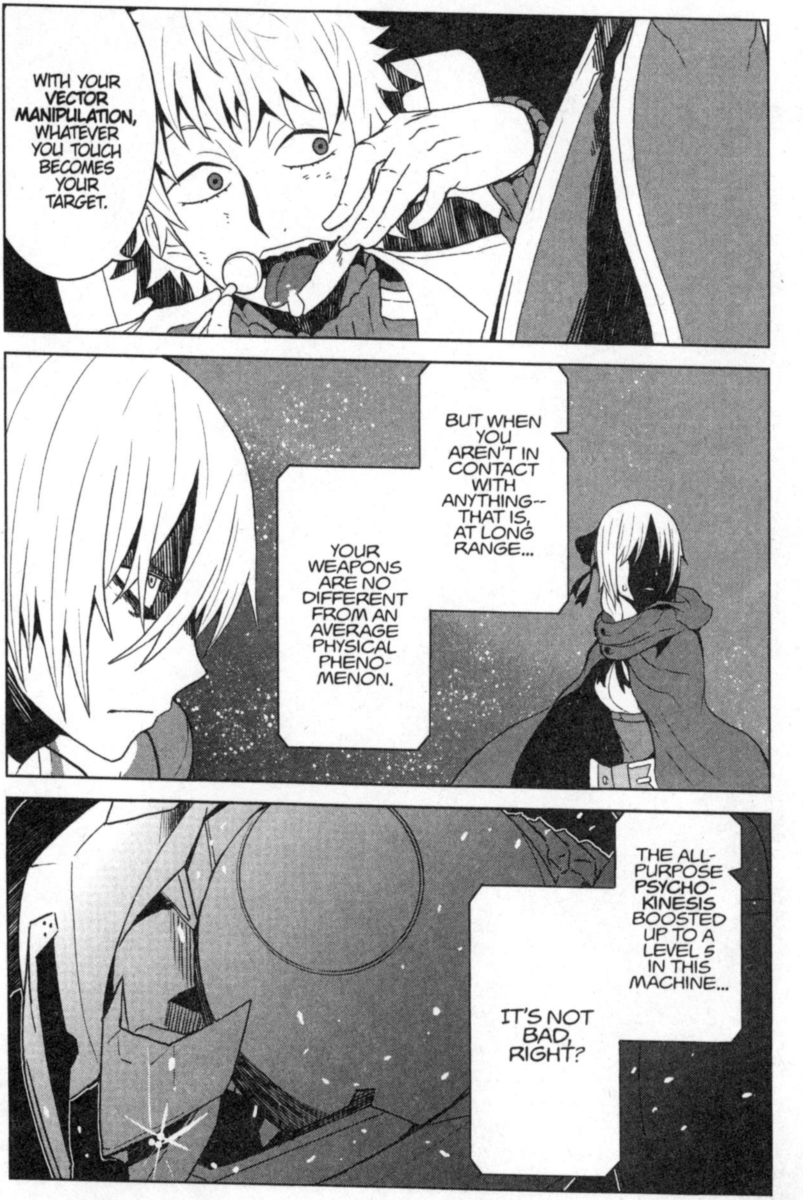
WITH YOUR VECTOR MANIPULATION, WHATEVER YOU TOUCH BECOMES YOUR TARGET.
BUT WHEN YOU AREN'T IN CONTACT WITH ANYTHING--THAT IS, AT LONG RANGE...
YOUR WEAPONS ARE NO DIFFERENT FROM AN AVERAGE PHYSICAL PHENO-MENON.
THE ALL-PURPOSE PSYCHO-KINESIS BOOSTED UP TO A LEVEL 5 IN THIS MACHINE...
IT'S NOT BAD, RIGHT?

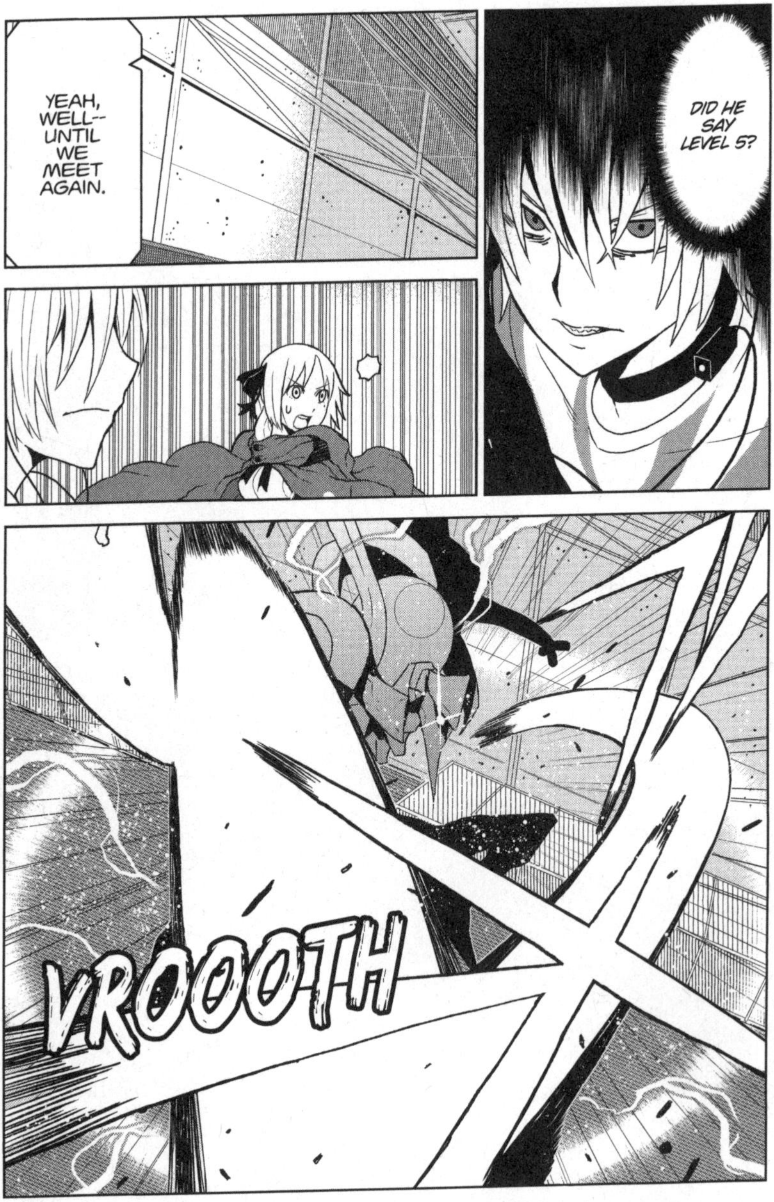
DID HE SAY LEVEL 5?
YEAH, WELL-- UNTIL WE MEET AGAIN.
VROOOTH

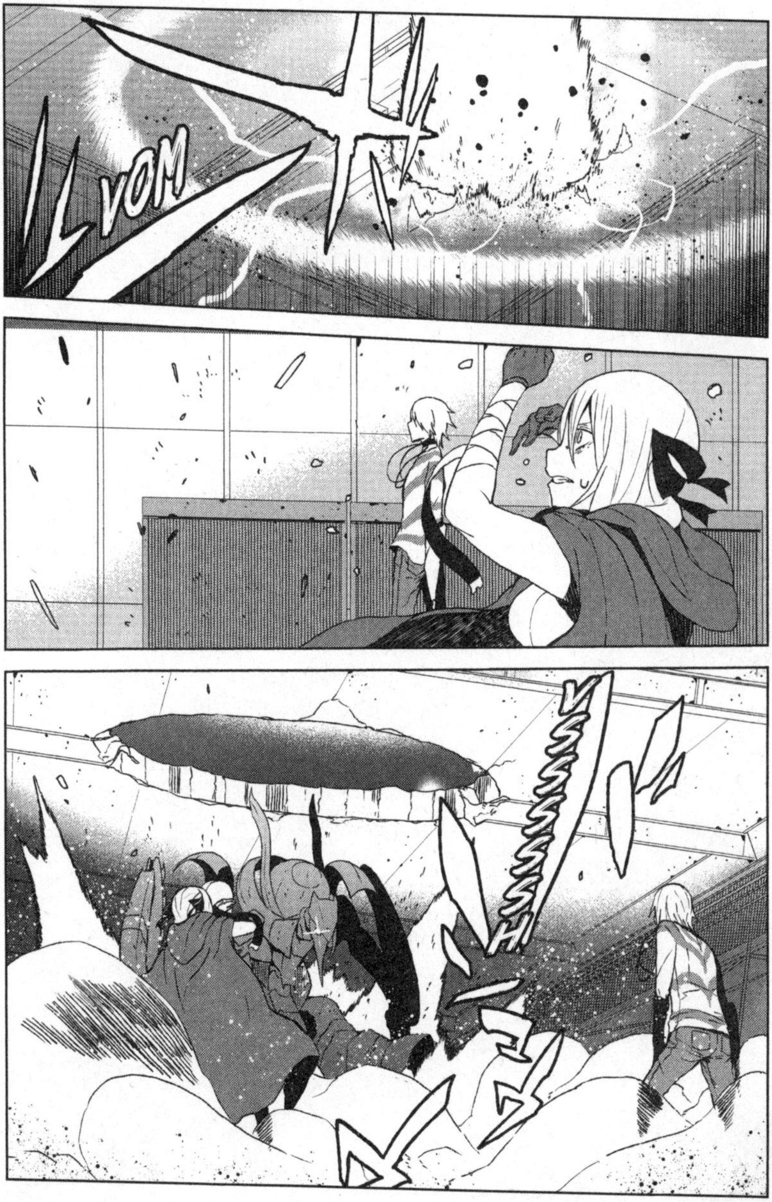
VOM
VSSSSSSSH

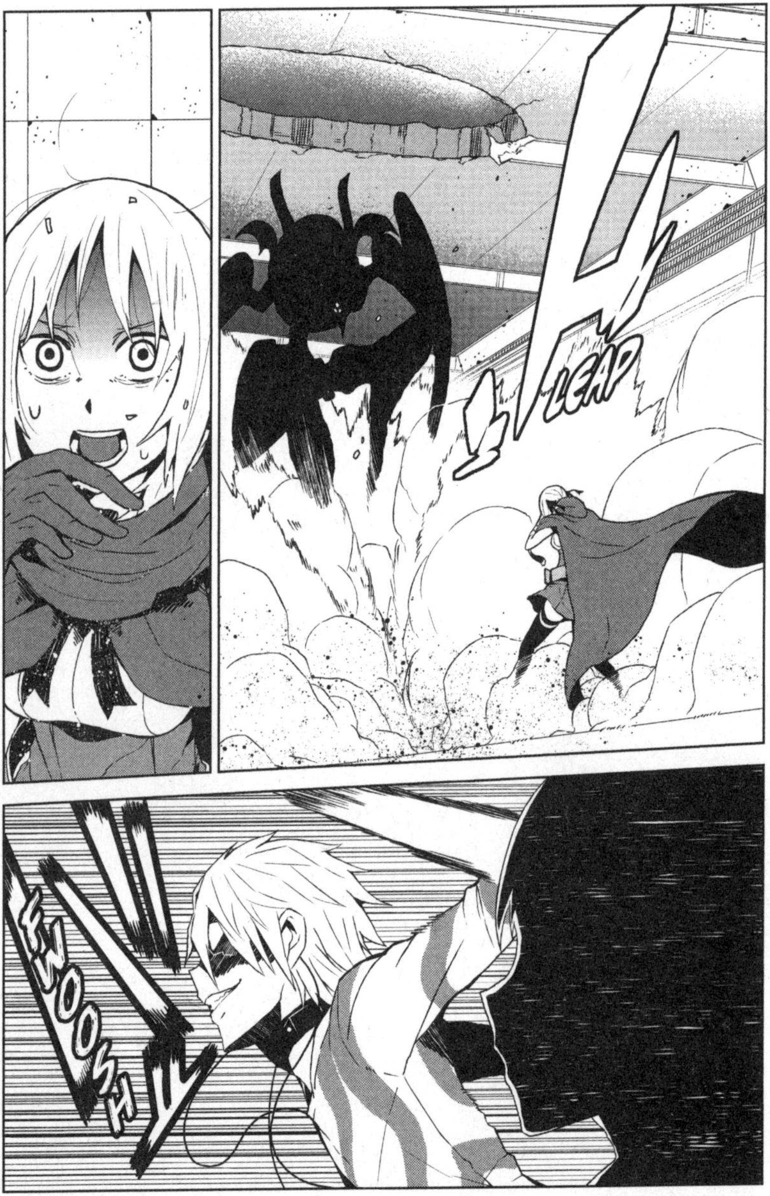
LEAP
FWOOSH!!

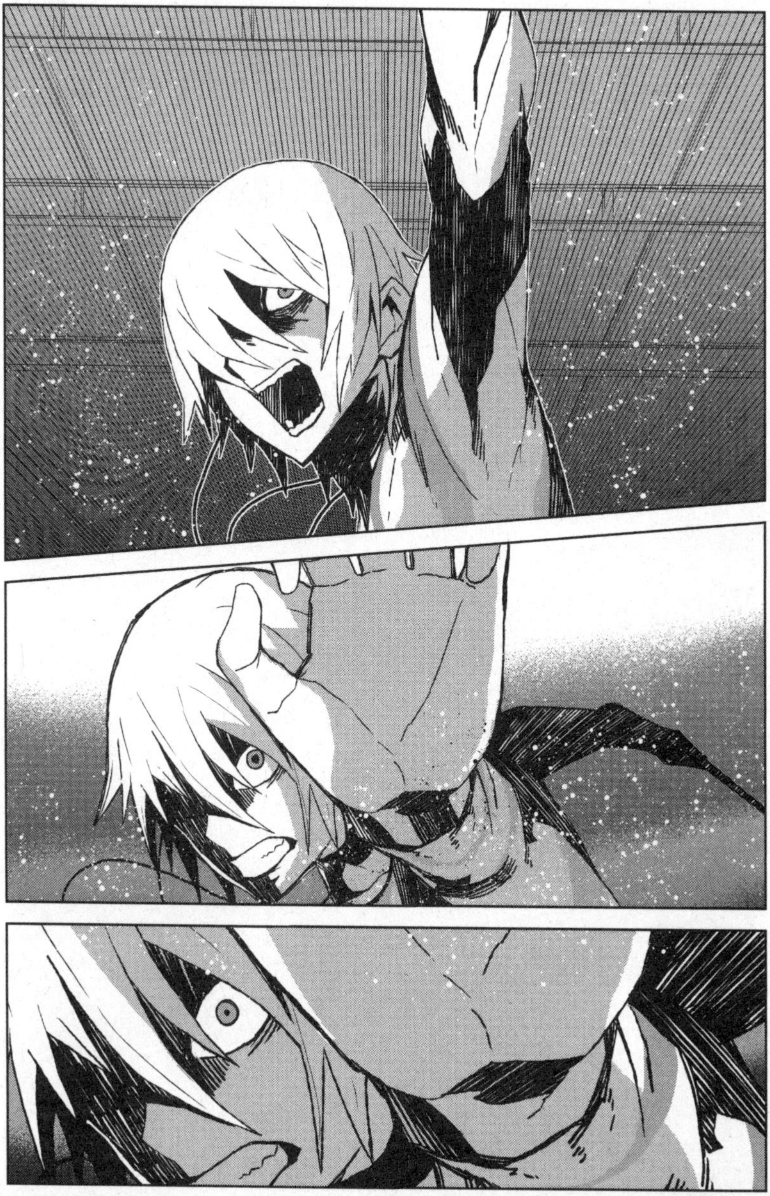

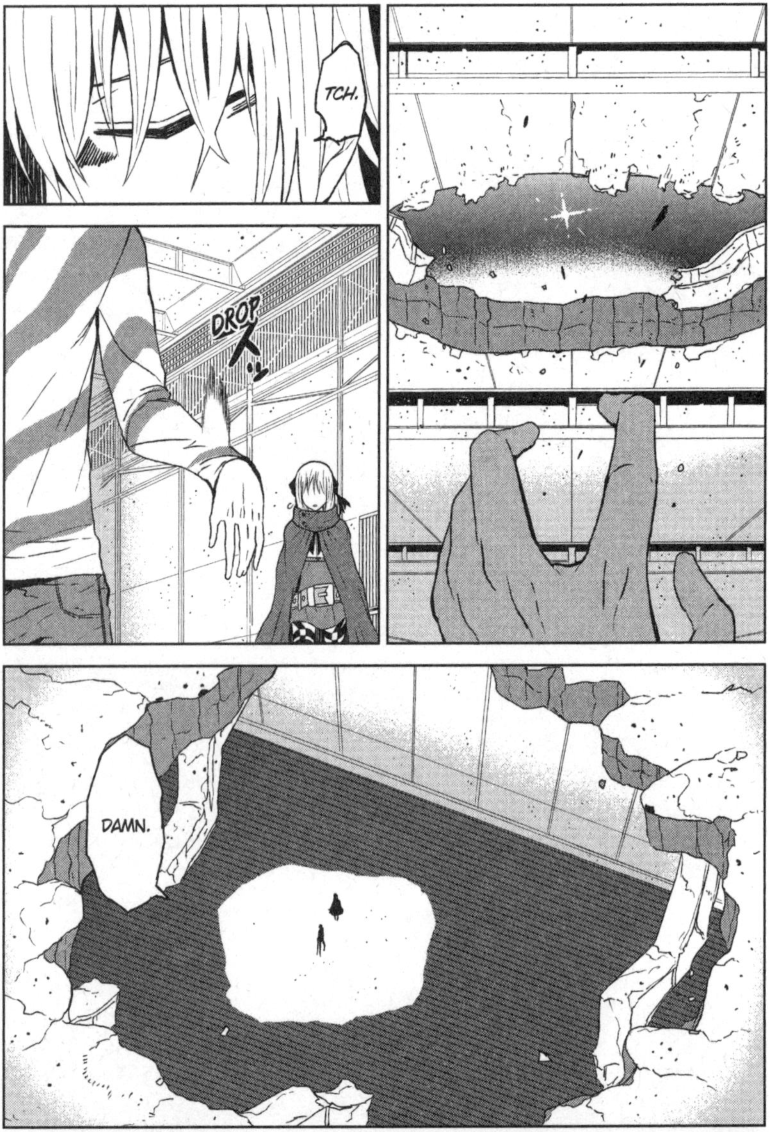
TCH.
DROP
DAMN.

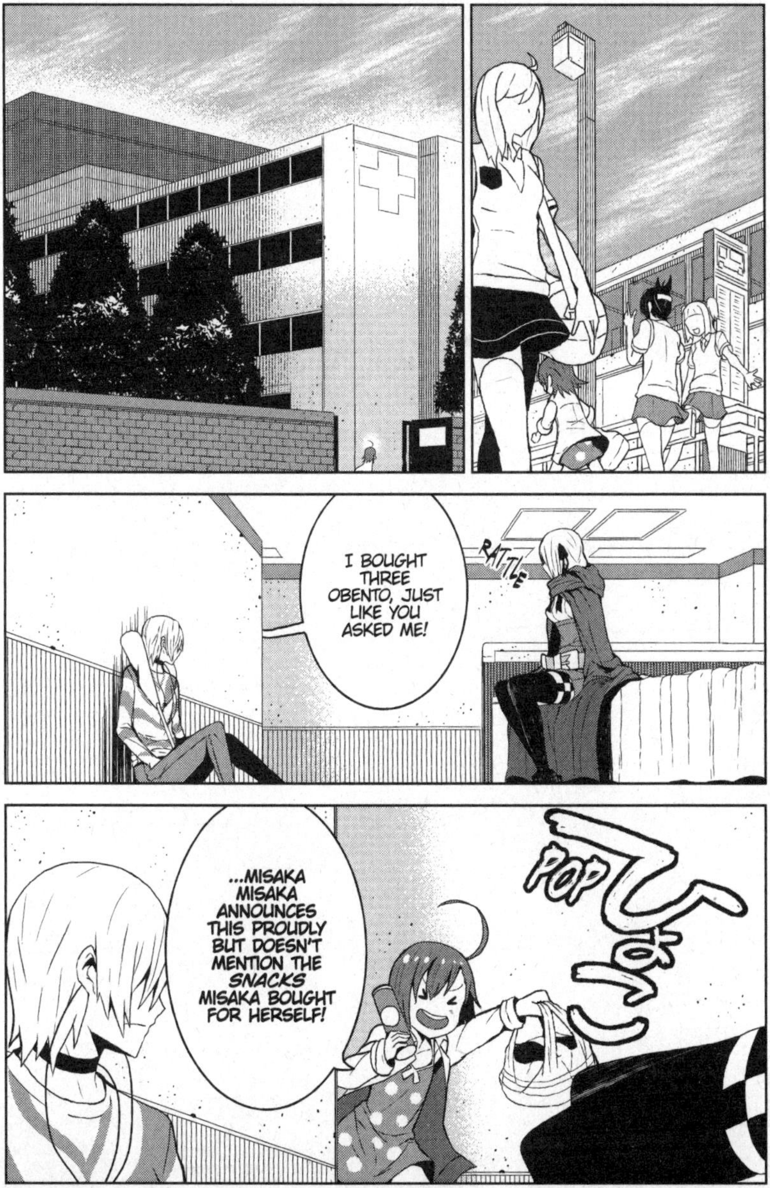
RATTLE
I BOUGHT THREE OBENTO, JUST LIKE YOU ASKED ME!
POP
...MISAKA MISAKA ANNOUNCES THIS PROUDLY BUT DOESN'T MENTION THE *SNACKS* MISAKA BOUGHT FOR HERSELF!

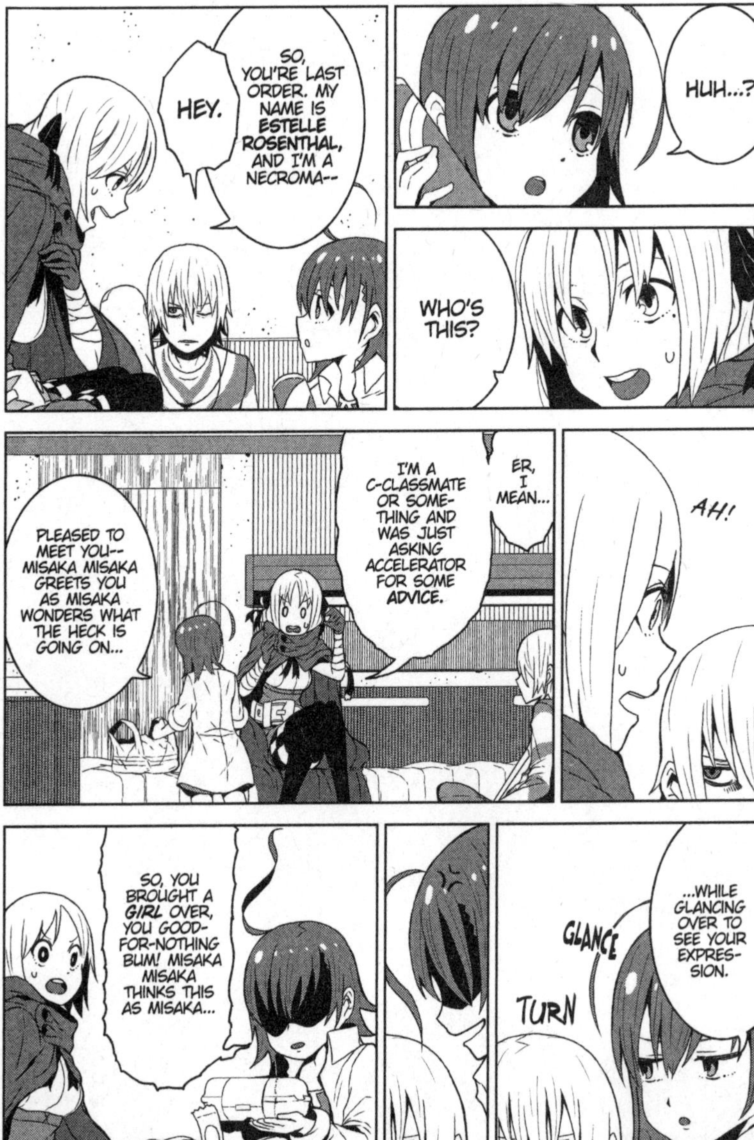
HUH...?
WHO'S THIS?
HEY.
SO, YOU'RE LAST ORDER. MY NAME IS ESTELLE ROSENTHAL, AND I'M A NECROMA--
AH!
ER, I MEAN...
I'M A C-CLASSMATE OR SOME-THING AND WAS JUST ASKING ACCELERATOR FOR SOME ADVICE.
PLEASED TO MEET YOU-- MISAKA MISAKA GREETS YOU AS MISAKA WONDERS WHAT THE HECK IS GOING ON...
...WHILE GLANCING OVER TO SEE YOUR EXPRES-SION.
GLANCE
TURN
SO, YOU BROUGHT A GIRL OVER, YOU GOOD-FOR-NOTHING BUM! MISAKA MISAKA THINKS THIS AS MISAKA...

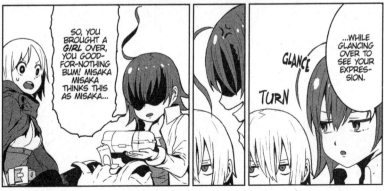

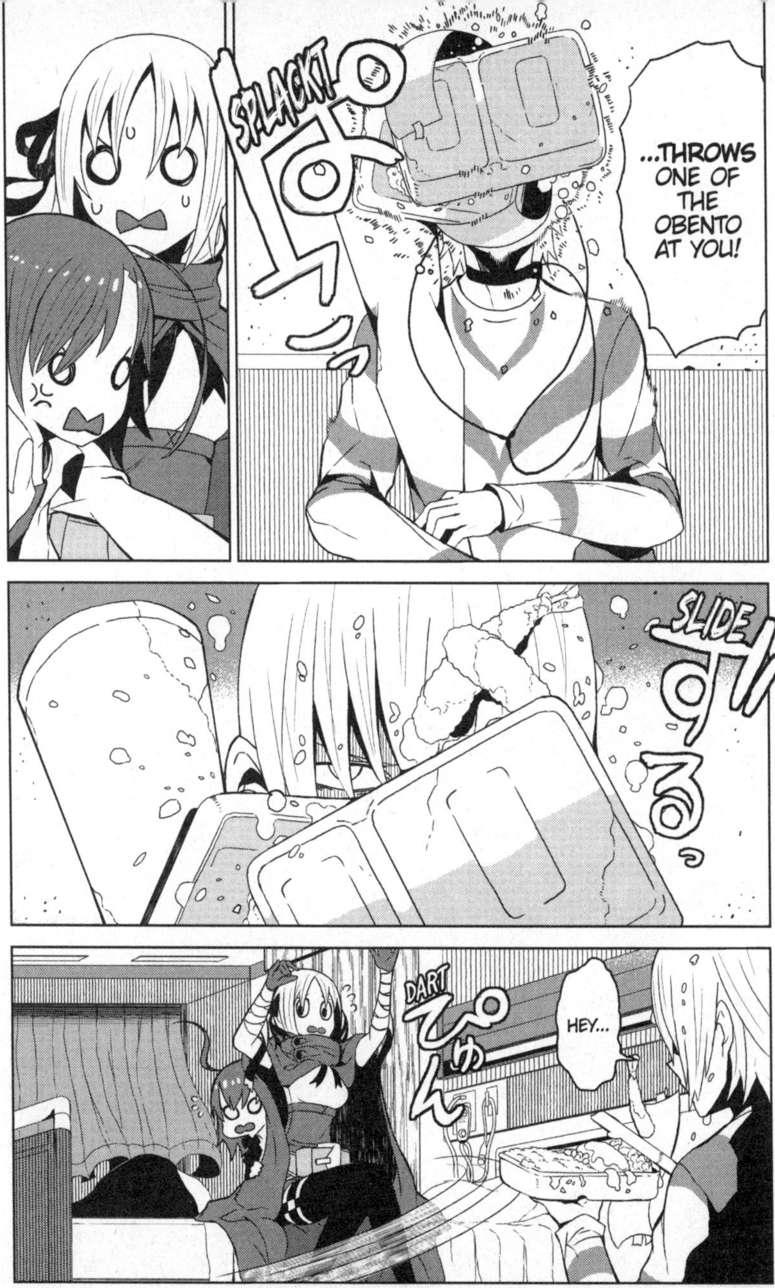
...THROWS ONE OF THE OBENTO AT YOU!
SPLACK!
SLIDE
する
HEY...
DART
ぴゅん

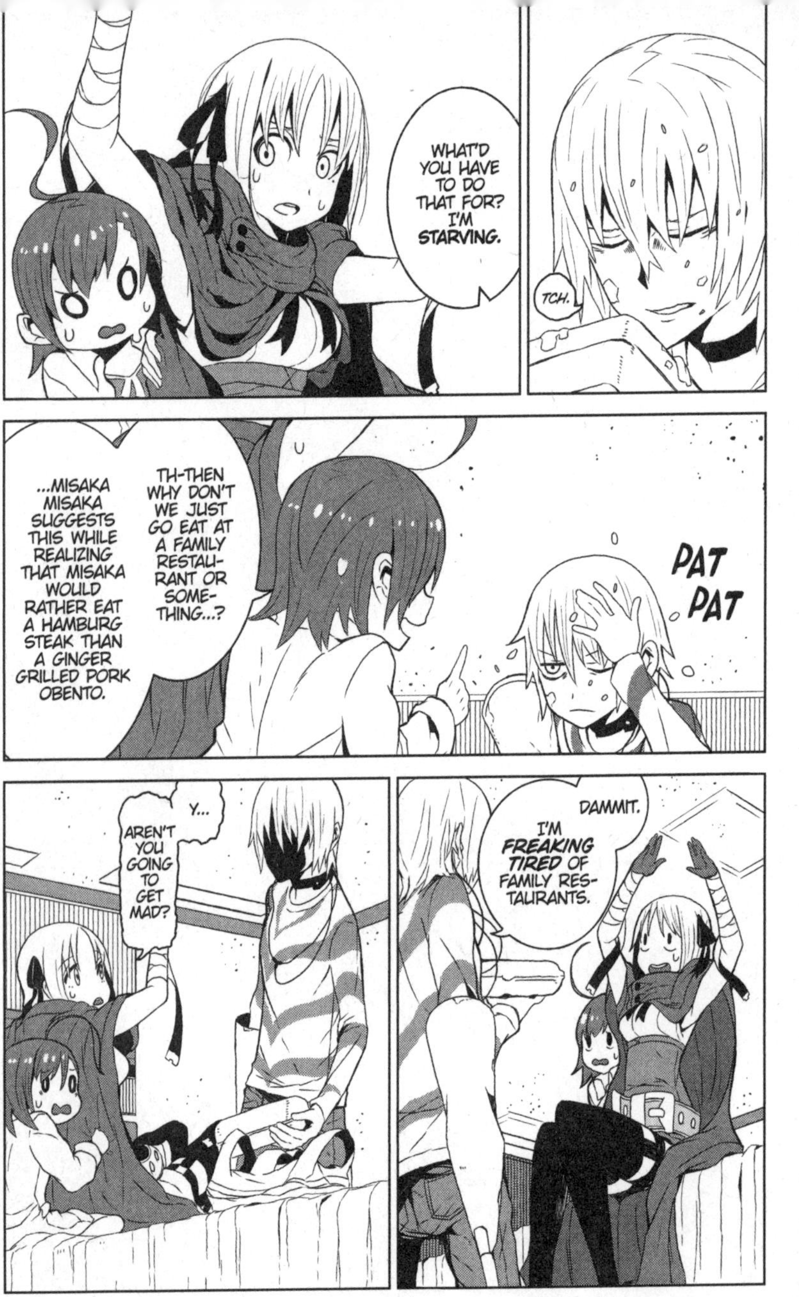
TCH.
WHAT'D YOU HAVE TO DO THAT FOR? I'M STARVING.
PAT PAT
TH-THEN WHY DON'T WE JUST GO EAT AT A FAMILY RESTAU-RANT OR SOME-THING...?
...MISAKA MISAKA SUGGESTS THIS WHILE REALIZING THAT MISAKA WOULD RATHER EAT A HAMBURG STEAK THAN A GINGER GRILLED PORK OBENTO.
DAMMIT. I'M FREAKING TIRED OF FAMILY RES-TAURANTS.
Y... AREN'T YOU GOING TO GET MAD?

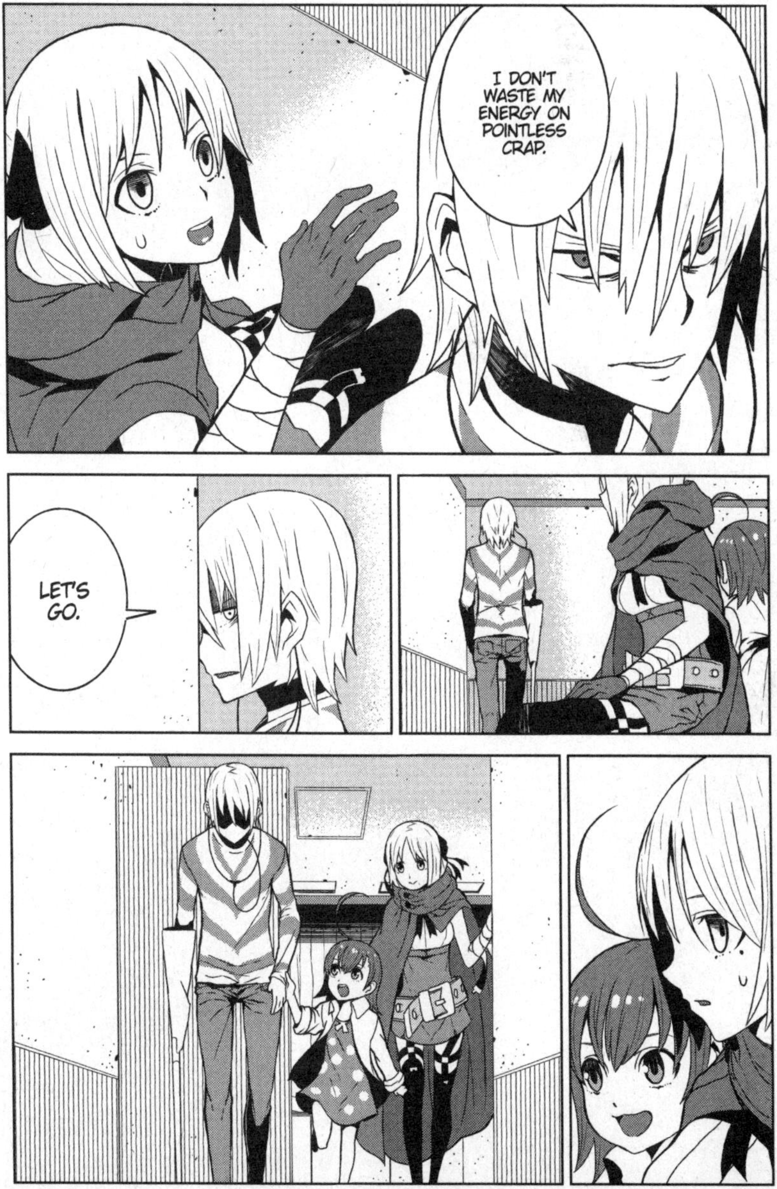
I DON'T WASTE MY ENERGY ON POINTLESS CRAP.
LET'S GO.

a certain
SCIENTIFIC
ACCELERATOR

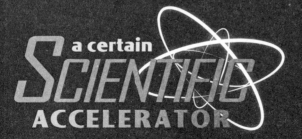

とある科学の一方通行

とある魔術の禁書目録外伝

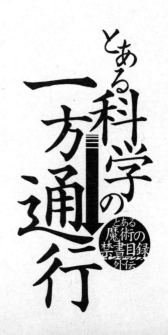

CHAPTER 3

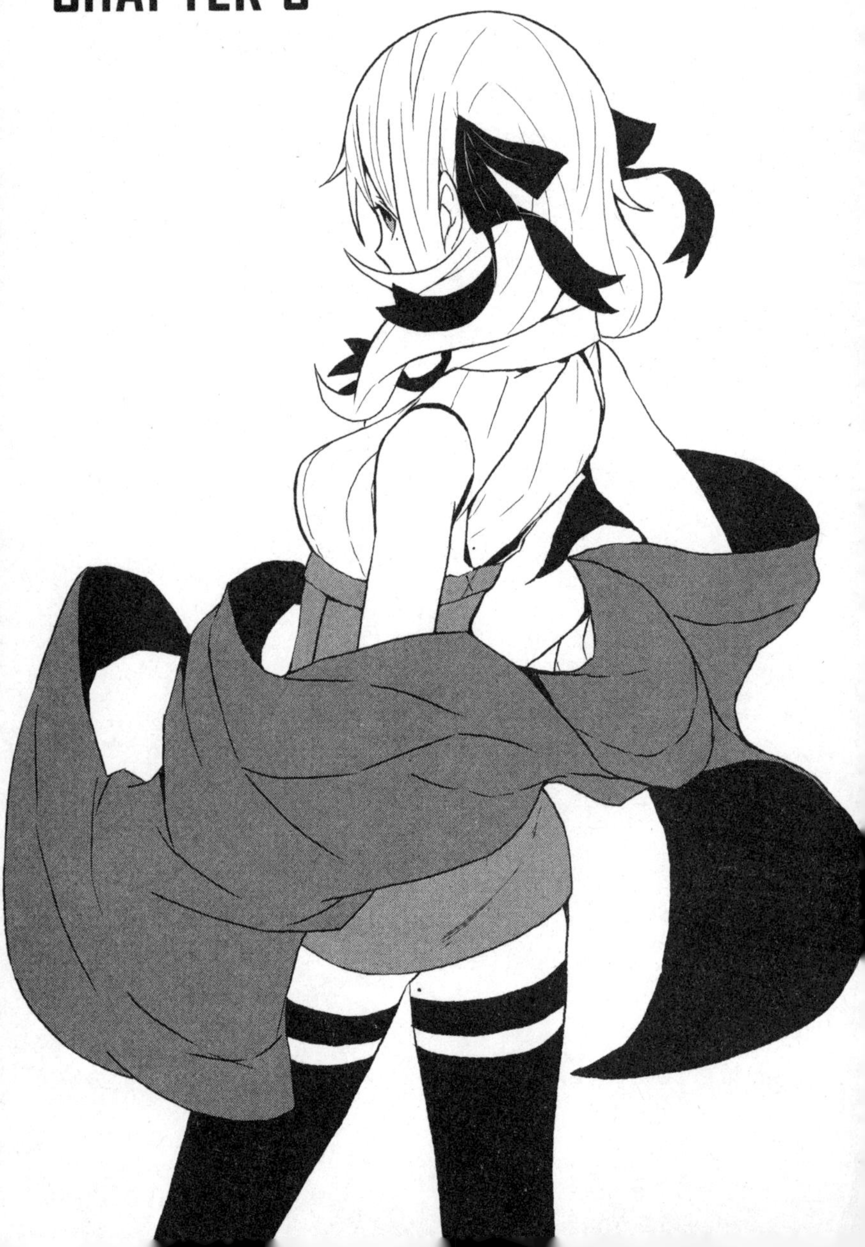

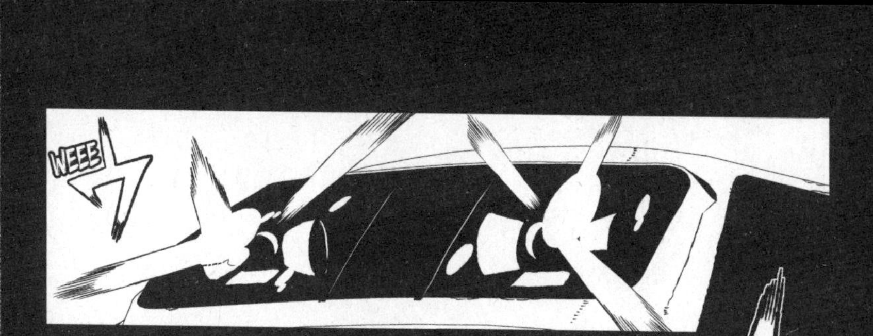
WEEEE
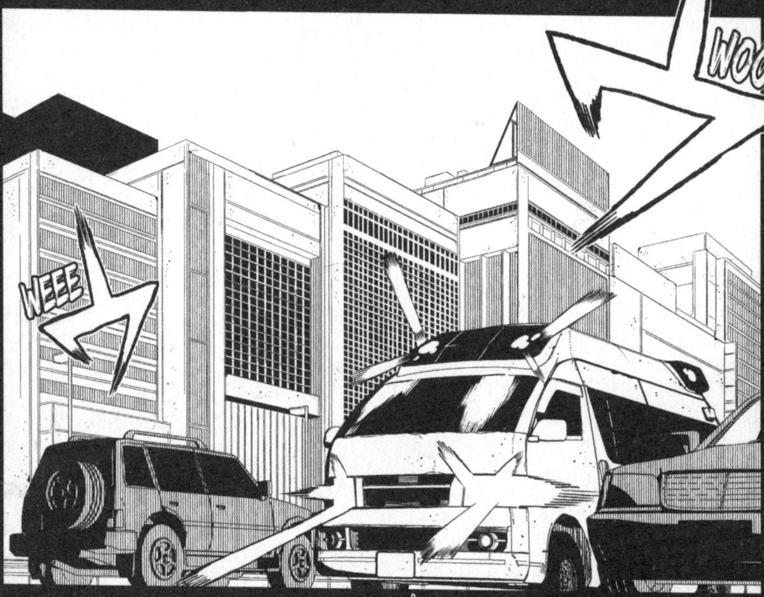
WOOO
WEEE
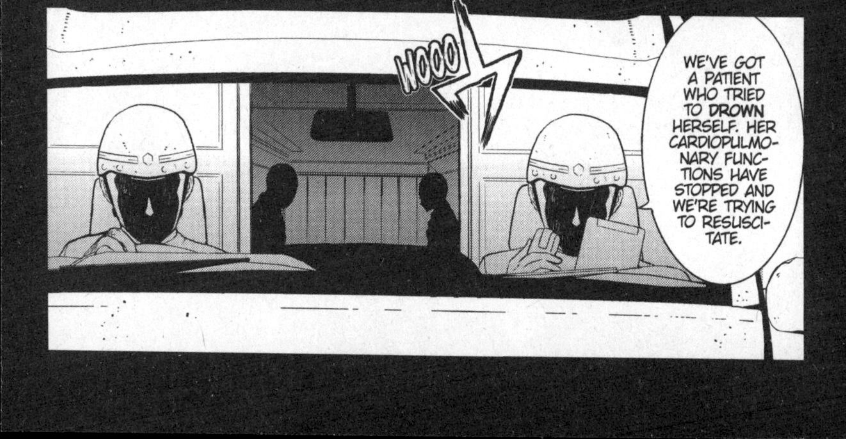
WOOO
WE'VE GOT A PATIENT WHO TRIED TO DROWN HERSELF. HER CARDIOPULMONARY FUNCTIONS HAVE STOPPED AND WE'RE TRYING TO RESUSCITATE.

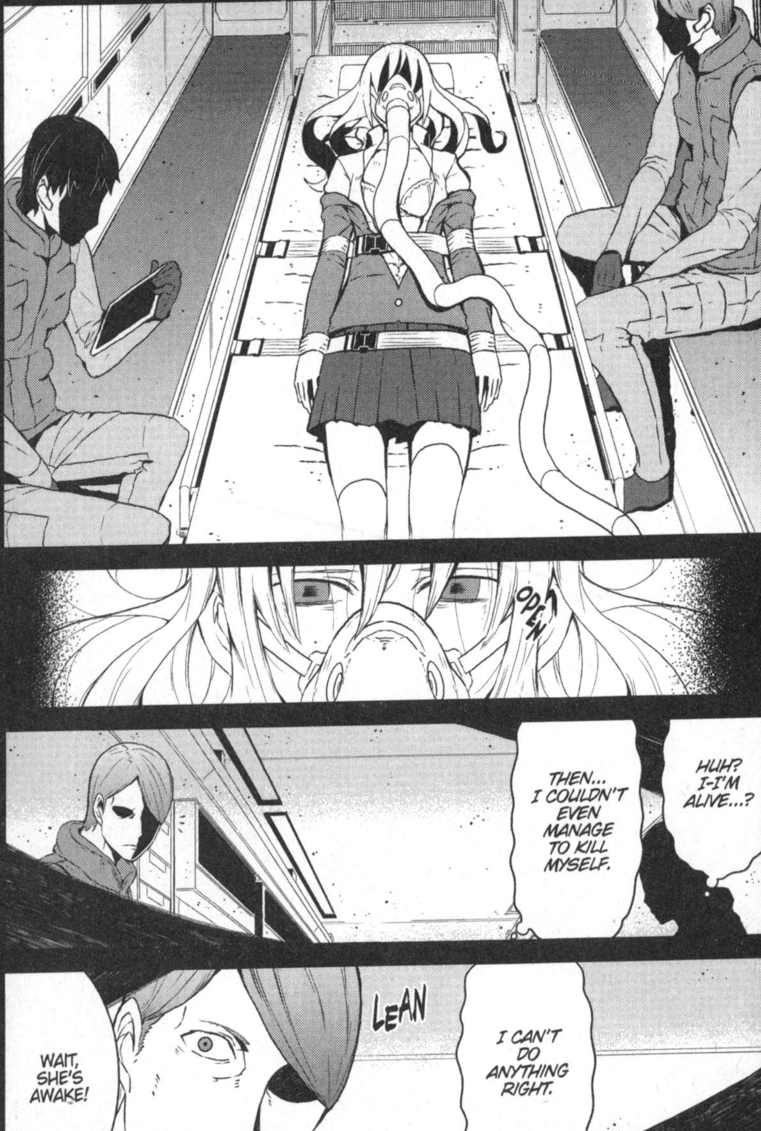
OPEN
HUH? I-I'M ALIVE...?
THEN... I COULDN'T EVEN MANAGE TO KILL MYSELF.
I CAN'T DO ANYTHING RIGHT.
LEAN
WAIT, SHE'S AWAKE!

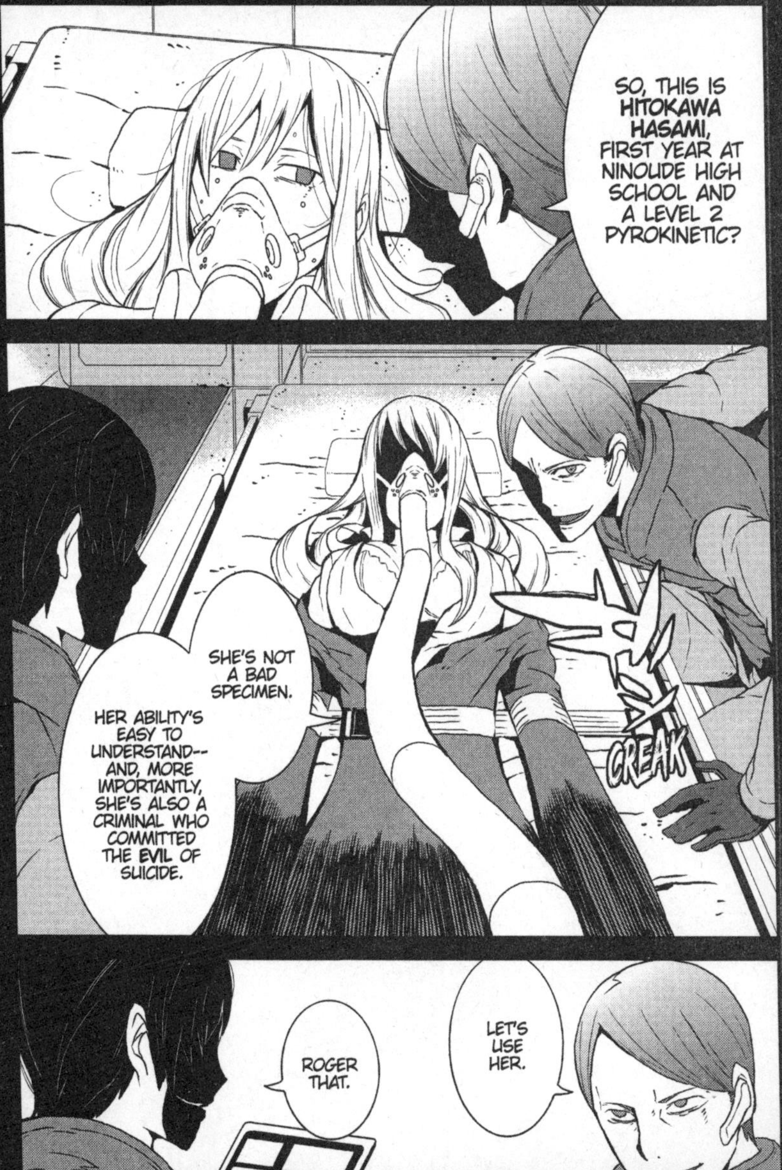
SO, THIS IS HITOKAWA HASAMI, FIRST YEAR AT NINOUDE HIGH SCHOOL AND A LEVEL 2 PYROKINETIC?
CREAK
SHE'S NOT A BAD SPECIMEN.
HER ABILITY'S EASY TO UNDERSTAND-- AND, MORE IMPORTANTLY, SHE'S ALSO A CRIMINAL WHO COMMITTED THE EVIL OF SUICIDE.
LET'S USE HER.
ROGER THAT.

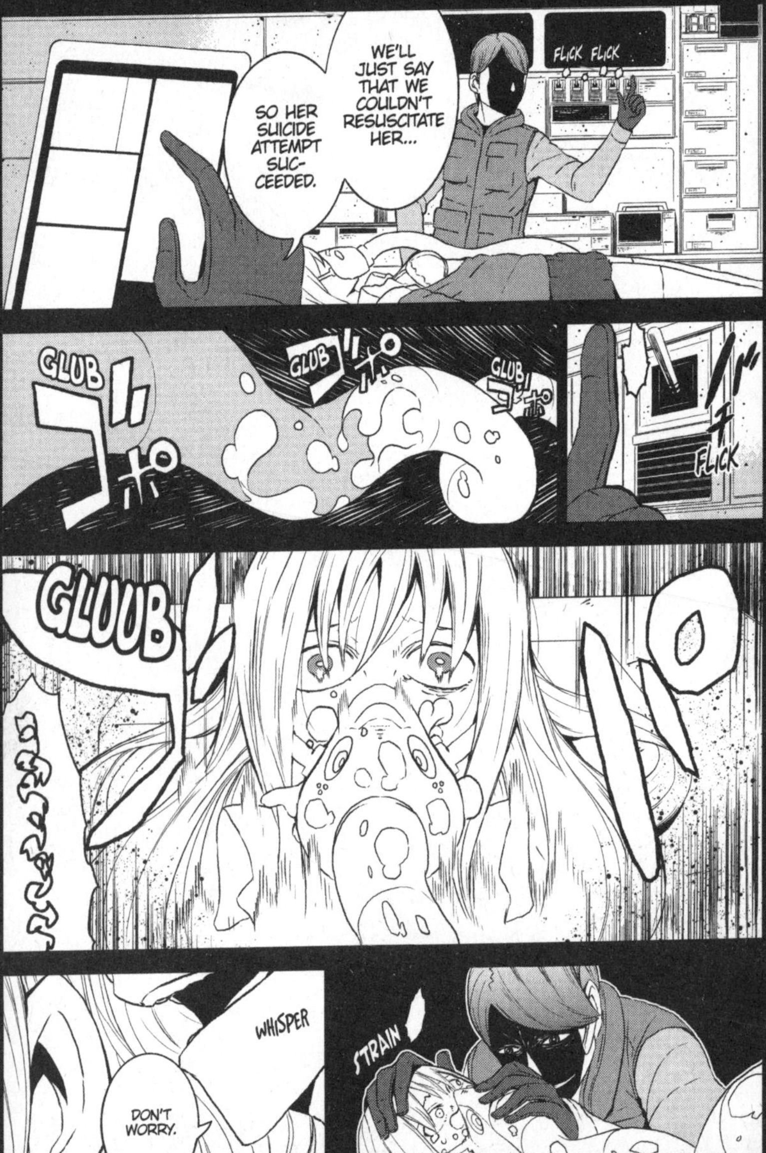
FLICK FLICK
WE'LL JUST SAY THAT WE COULDN'T RESUSCITATE HER...
SO HER SUICIDE ATTEMPT SUC-CEEDED.
FLICK
GLUB
GLUB
GLUB
GLUUB
STRAIN
WHISPER
DON'T WORRY.

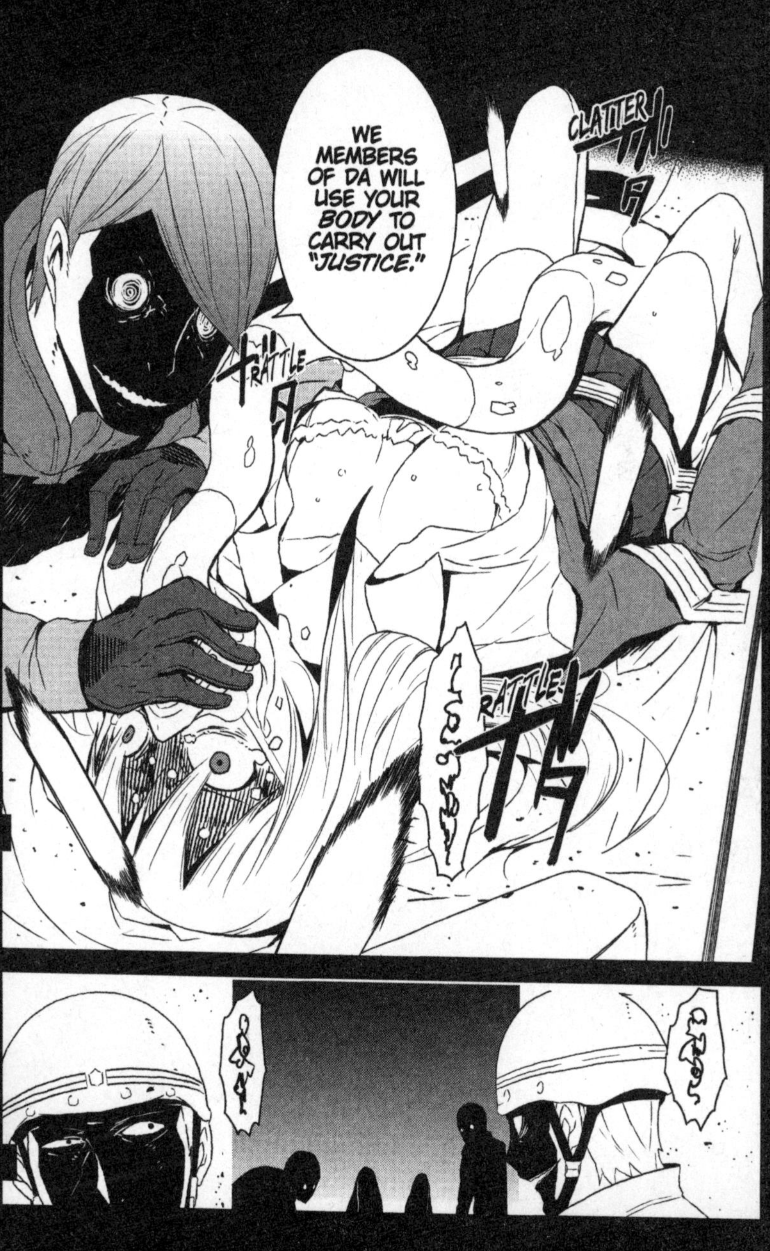
CLATTER
WE MEMBERS OF DA WILL USE YOUR BODY TO CARRY OUT "JUSTICE."
RATTLE
RATTLE

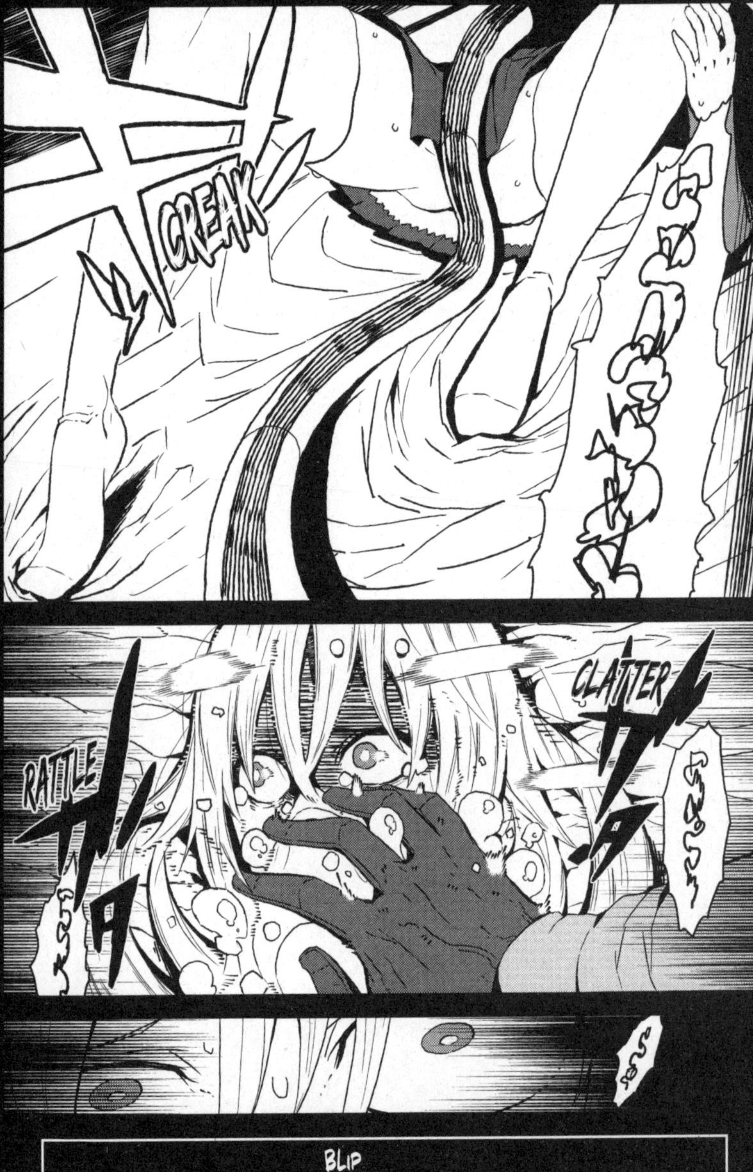
CREAK
CLATTER
RATTLE
BLIP

TURN

TUG

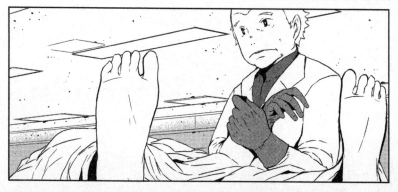

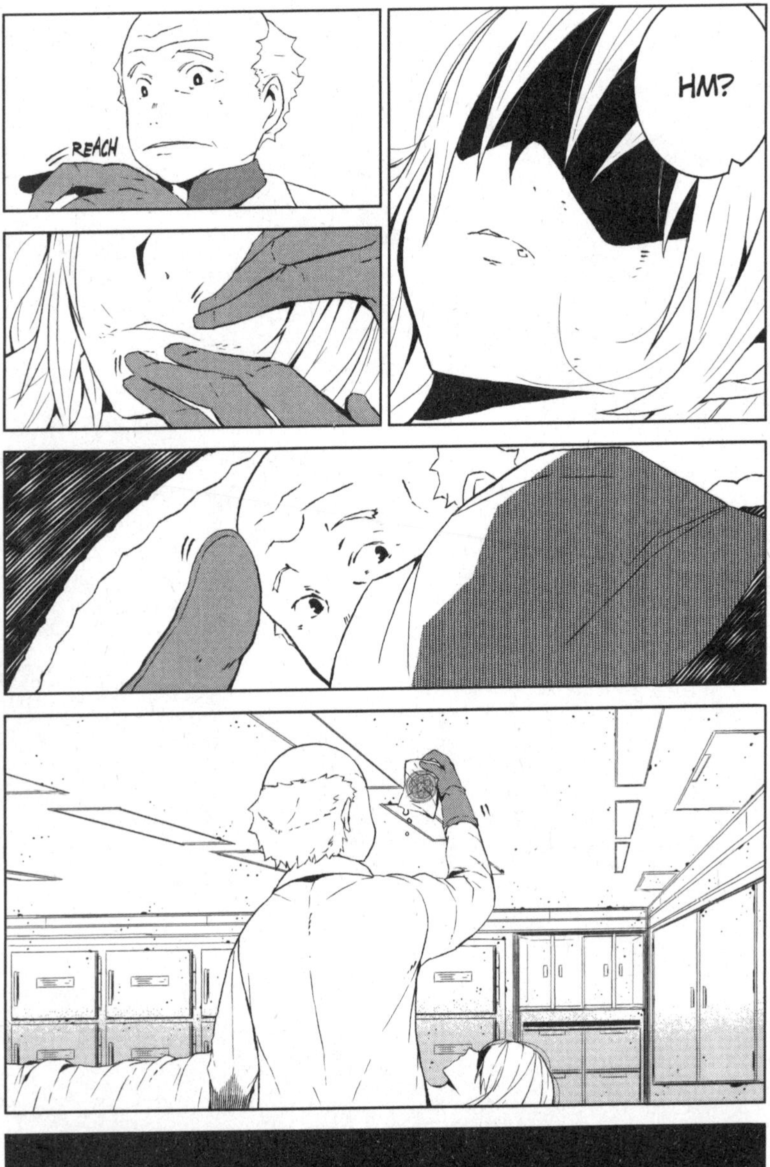
HM?
REACH

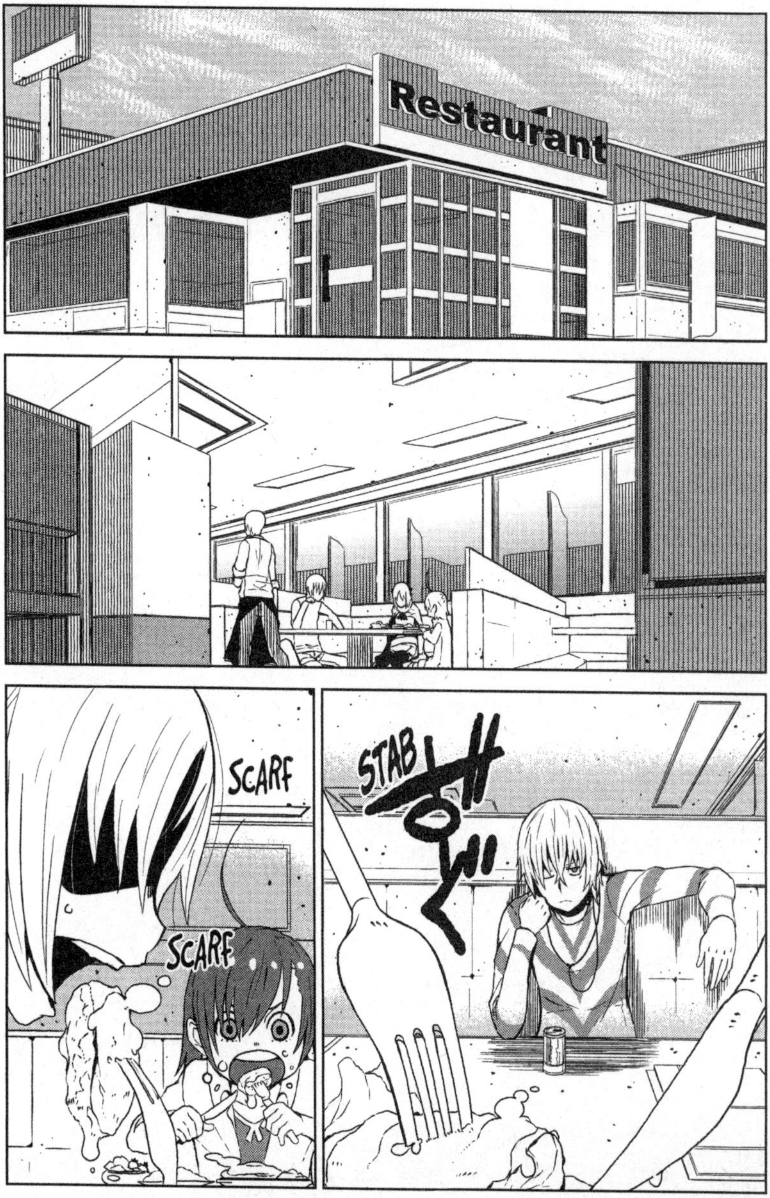
Restaurant
STAB
SCARF
SCARF

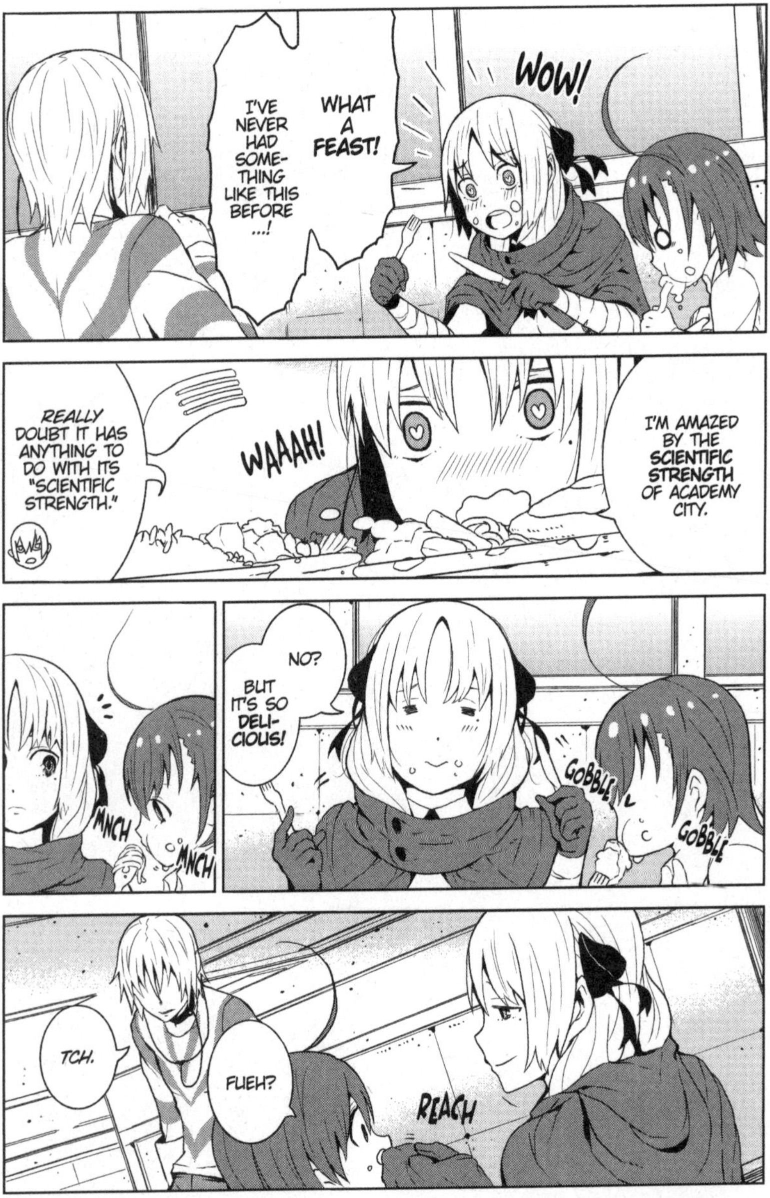
WOW!
WHAT A FEAST! I'VE NEVER HAD SOME-THING LIKE THIS BEFORE ...!
I'M AMAZED BY THE SCIENTIFIC STRENGTH OF ACADEMY CITY.
WAAAH!
REALLY DOUBT IT HAS ANYTHING TO DO WITH ITS "SCIENTIFIC STRENGTH."
GOBBLE
GOBBLE
NO? BUT IT'S SO DELICIOUS!
MNCH
MNCH
REACH
FUEH?
TCH.

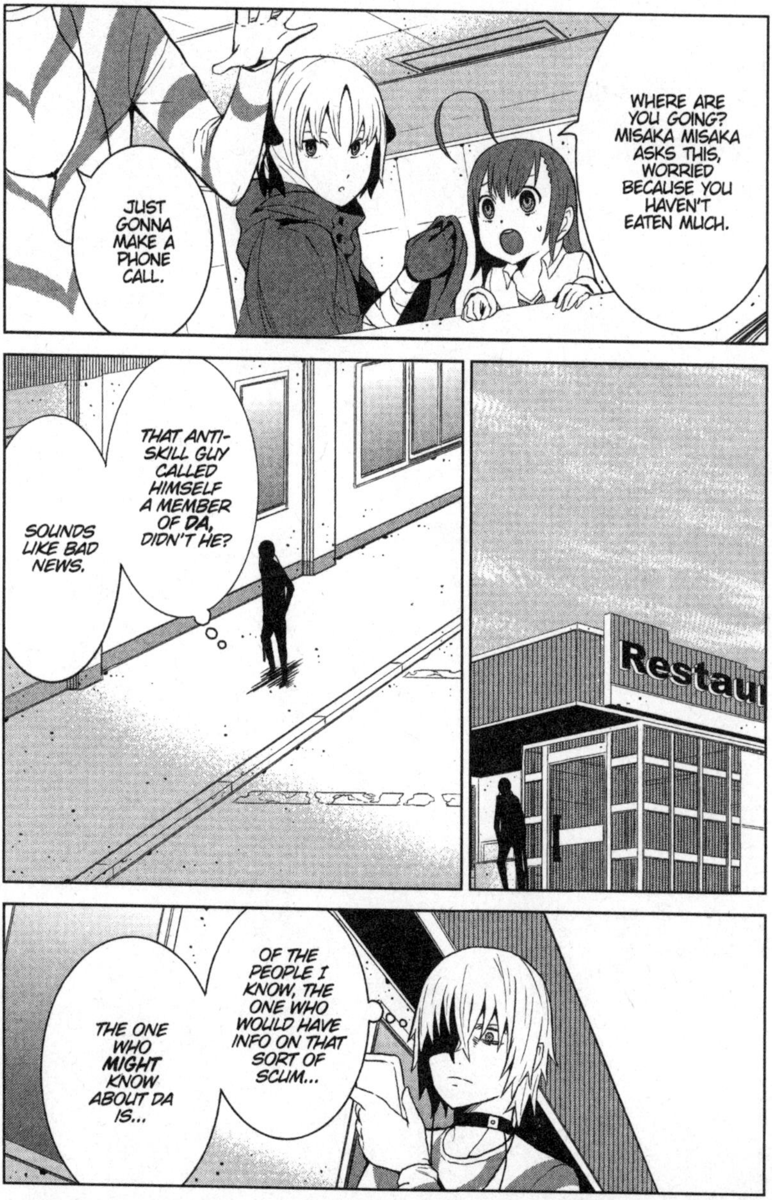
WHERE ARE YOU GOING? MISAKA MISAKA ASKS THIS, WORRIED BECAUSE YOU HAVEN'T EATEN MUCH.
JUST GONNA MAKE A PHONE CALL.
Restau
THAT ANTI-SKILL GUY CALLED HIMSELF A MEMBER OF **DA**, DIDN'T HE?
SOUNDS LIKE BAD NEWS.
OF THE PEOPLE I KNOW, THE ONE WHO WOULD HAVE INFO ON THAT SORT OF SCUM...
THE ONE WHO **MIGHT** KNOW ABOUT DA IS...

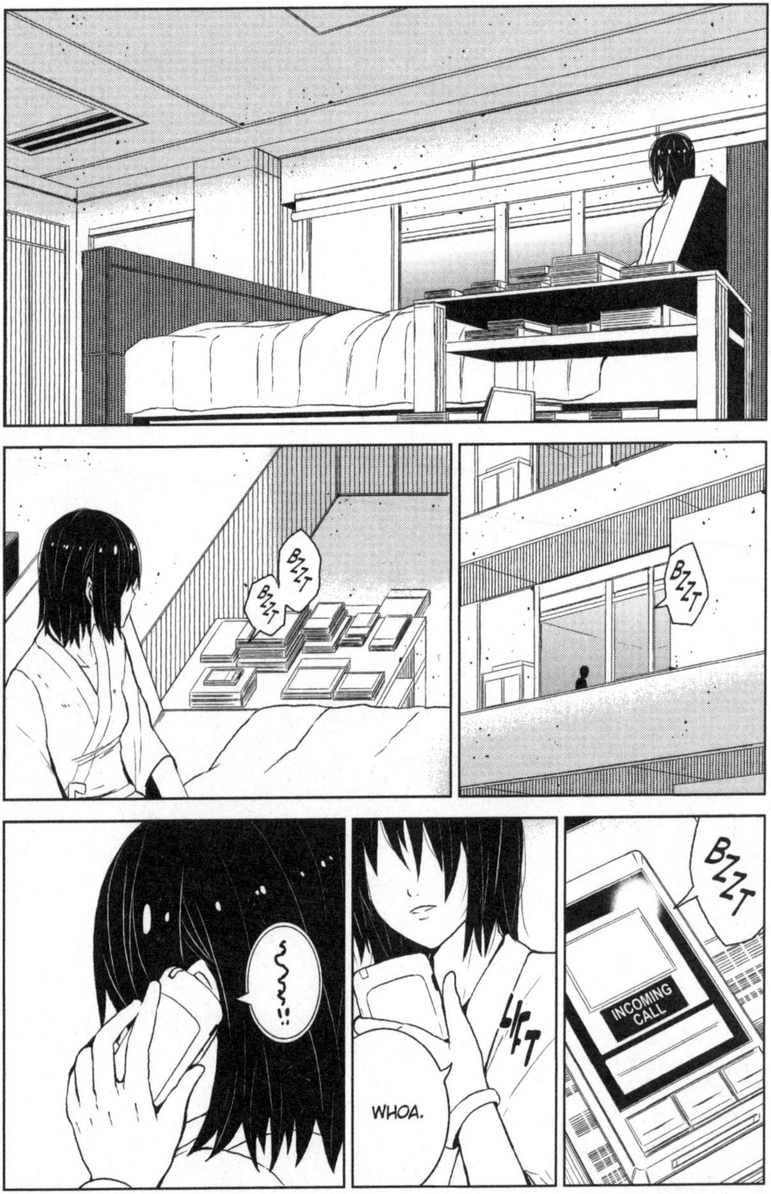
BZZT
BZZT
BZZT
BZZT
INCOMING CALL
LIFT
WHOA.

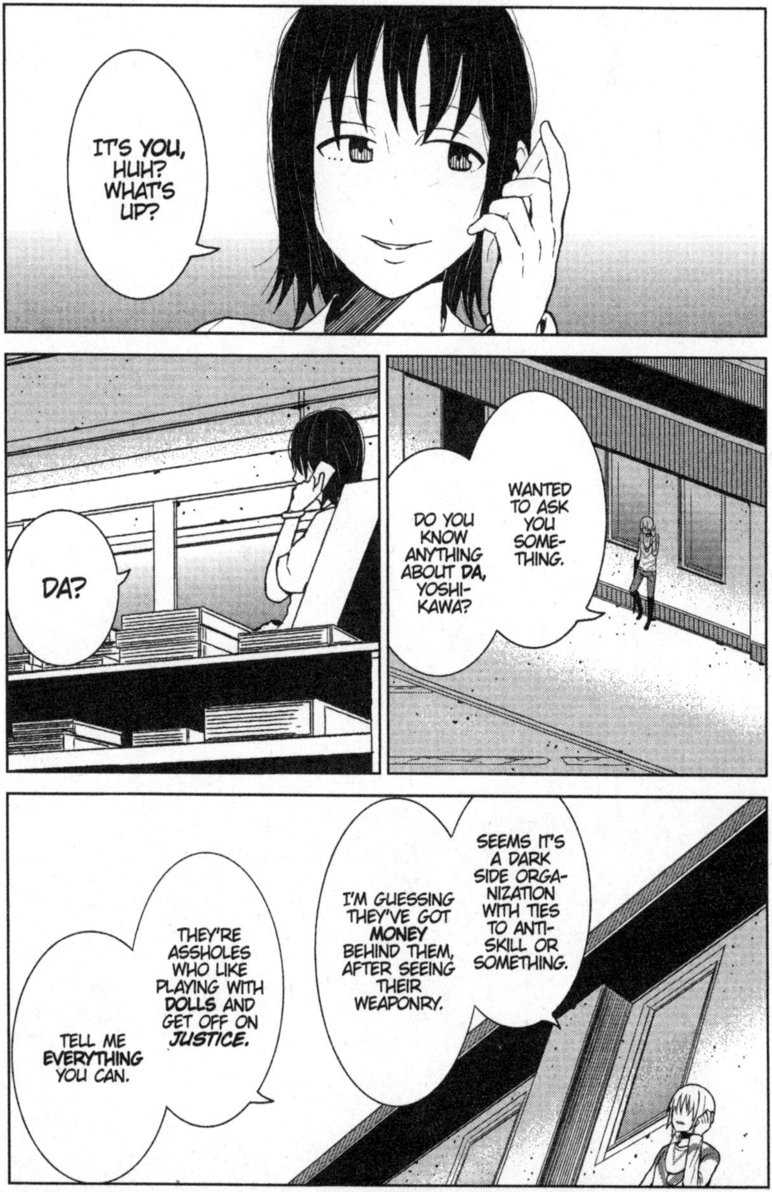
IT'S YOU, HUH? WHAT'S UP?
WANTED TO ASK YOU SOME-THING.
DO YOU KNOW ANYTHING ABOUT DA, YOSHI-KAWA?
DA?
SEEMS IT'S A DARK SIDE ORGA-NIZATION WITH TIES TO ANTI-SKILL OR SOMETHING.
I'M GUESSING THEY'VE GOT MONEY BEHIND THEM, AFTER SEEING THEIR WEAPONRY.
THEY'RE ASSHOLES WHO LIKE PLAYING WITH DOLLS AND GET OFF ON JUSTICE.
TELL ME EVERYTHING YOU CAN.

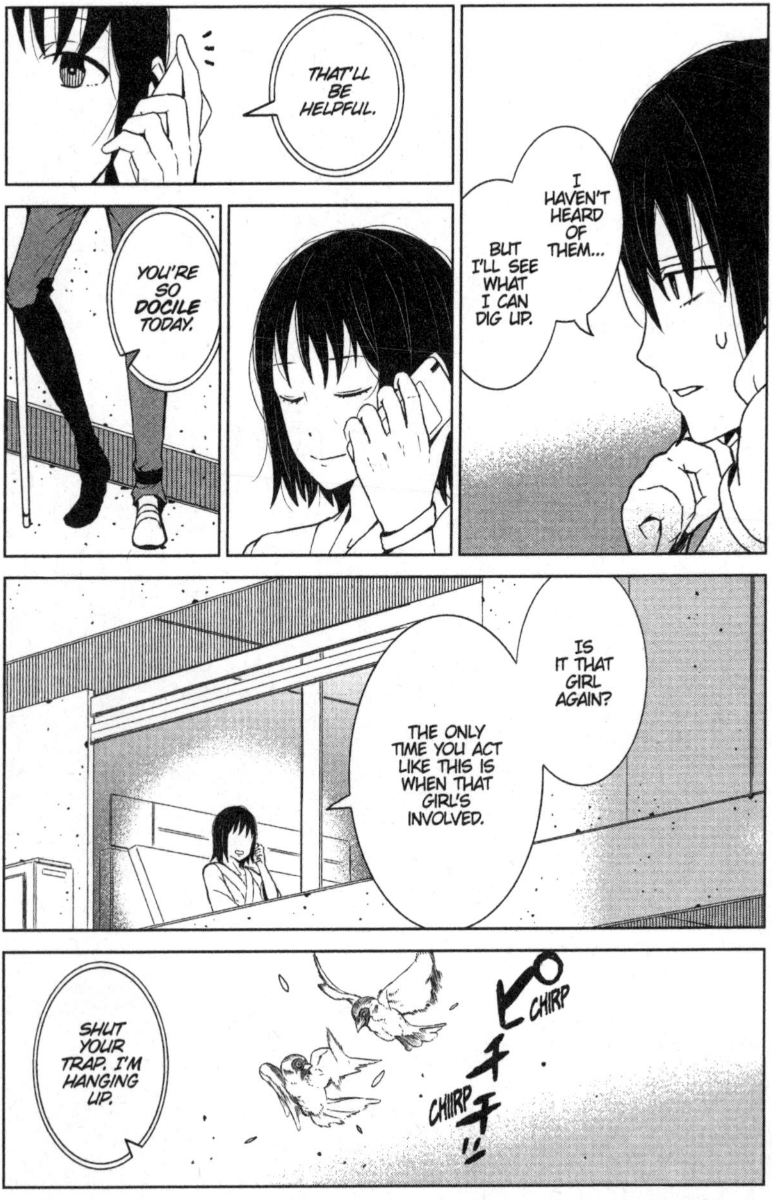
I HAVEN'T HEARD OF THEM...
BUT I'LL SEE WHAT I CAN DIG UP.
THAT'LL BE HELPFUL.
YOU'RE SO DOCILE TODAY.
IS IT THAT GIRL AGAIN?
THE ONLY TIME YOU ACT LIKE THIS IS WHEN THAT GIRL'S INVOLVED.
CHIRP
CHIRP
SHUT YOUR TRAP. I'M HANGING UP.

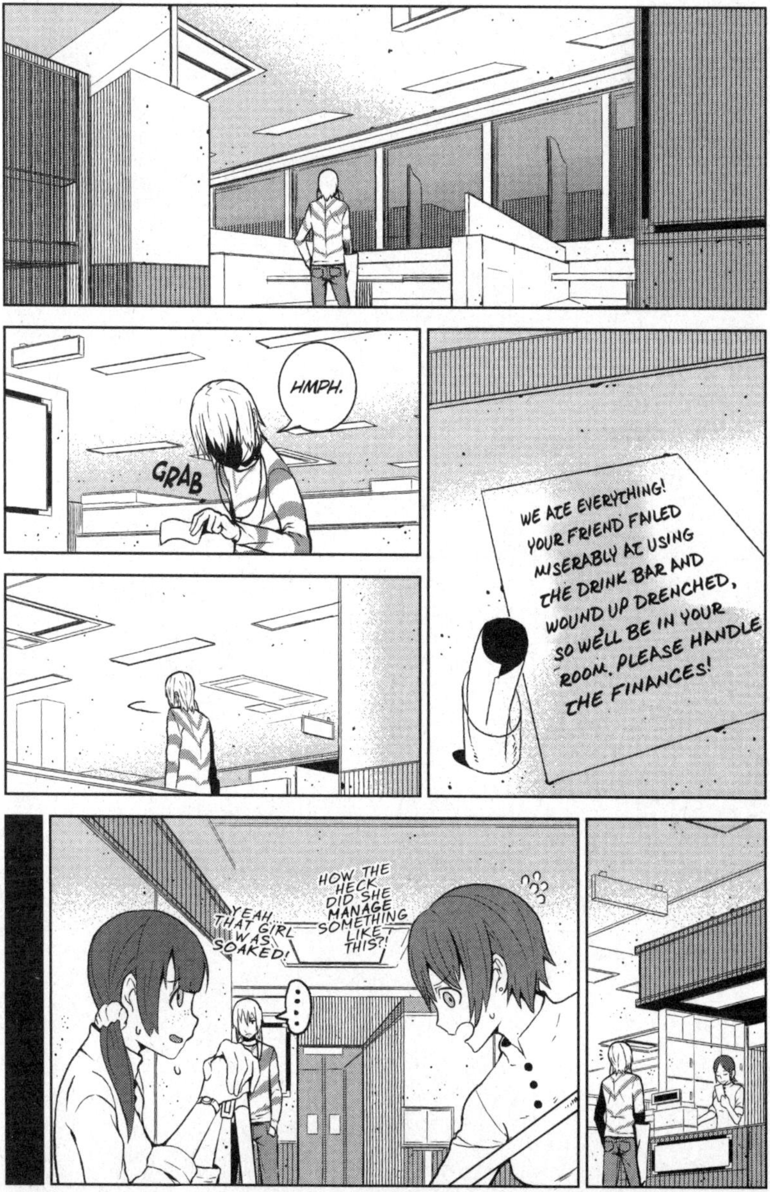
WE ATE EVERYTHING!
YOUR FRIEND FAILED
MISERABLY AT USING
THE DRINK BAR AND
WOUND UP DRENCHED,
SO WELL BE IN YOUR
ROOM. PLEASE HANDLE
THE FINANCES!
HMPH.
GRAB
HOW THE HECK DID SHE MANAGE SOMETHING LIKE THIS?!
YEAH... THAT GIRL WAS SOAKED!
...

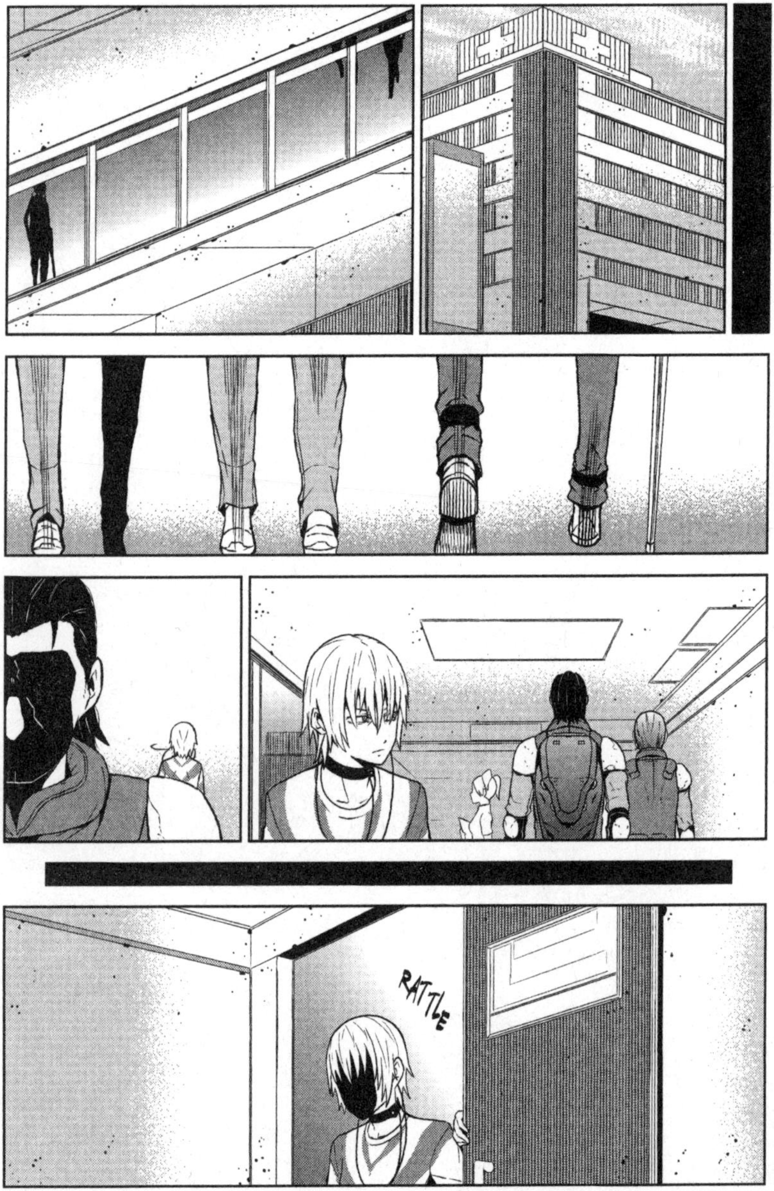
RATTLE

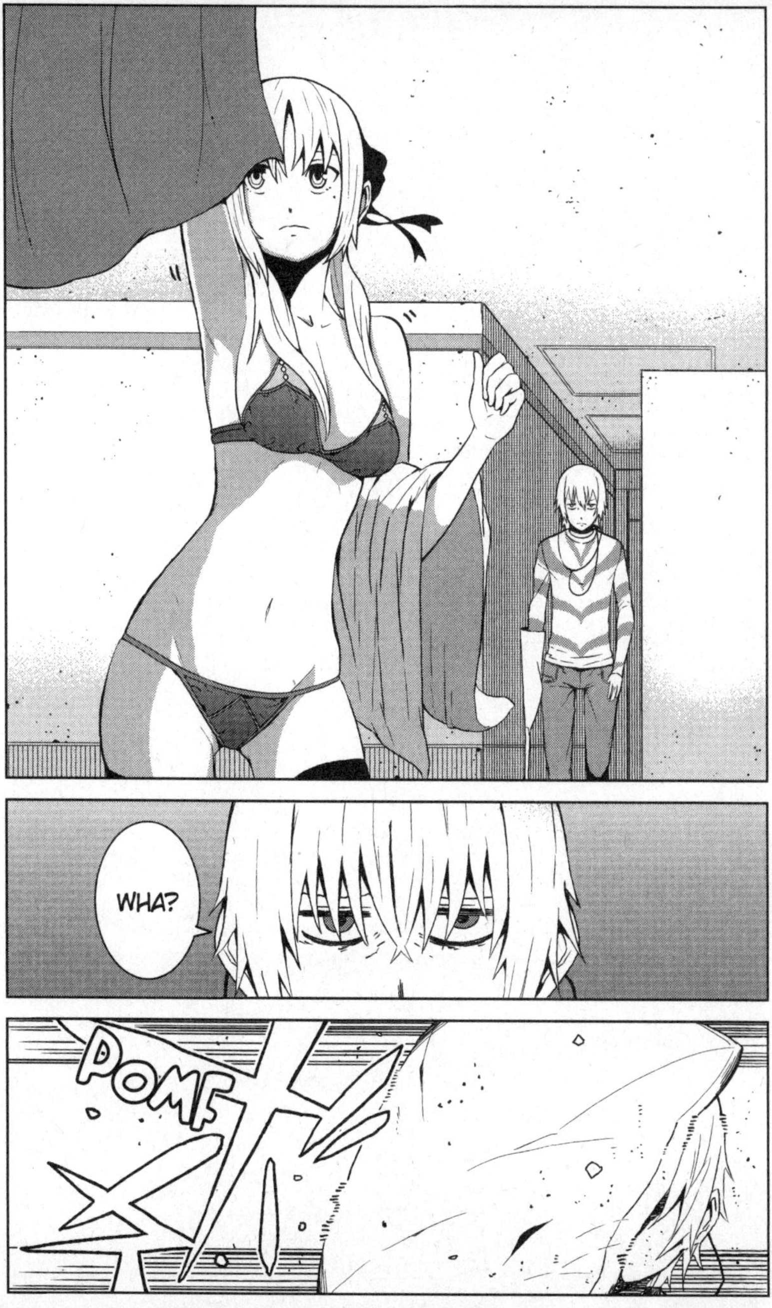
WHA?
POMF

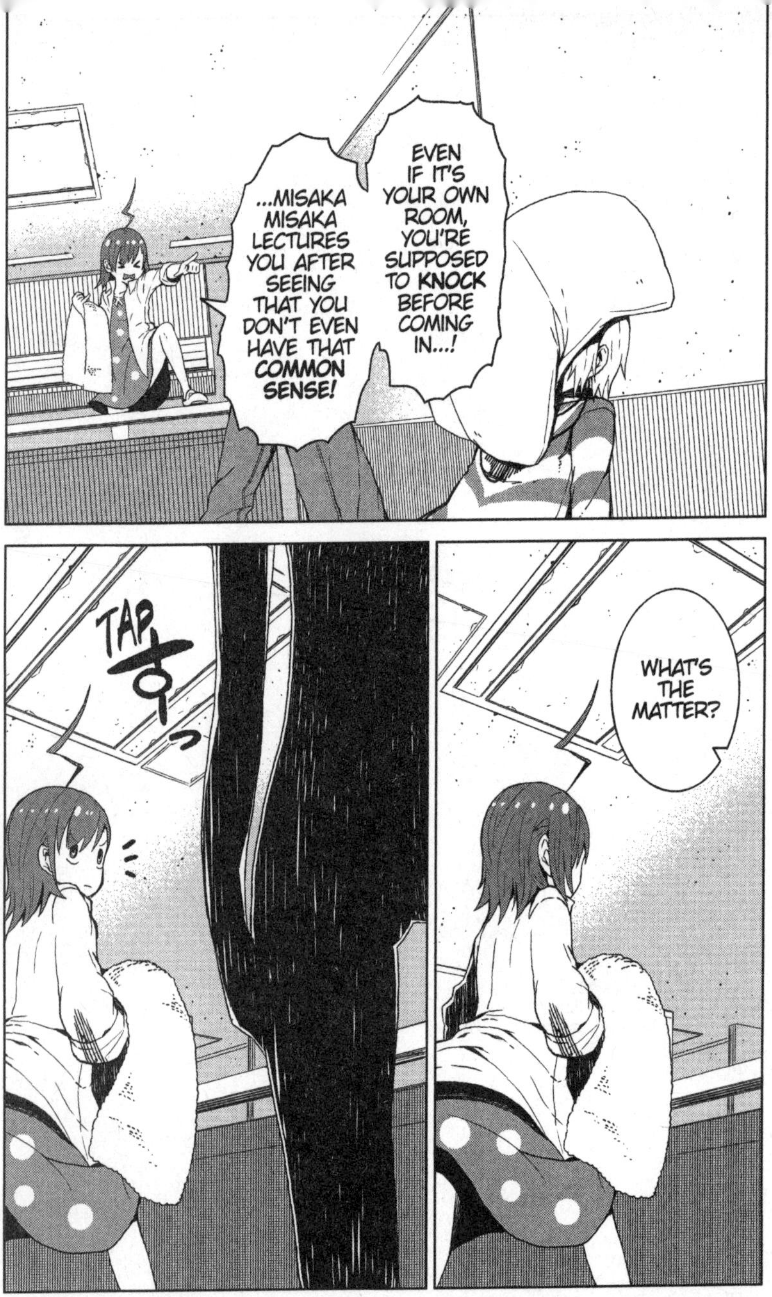
EVEN IF IT'S YOUR OWN ROOM, YOU'RE SUPPOSED TO KNOCK BEFORE COMING IN...!
...MISAKA MISAKA LECTURES YOU AFTER SEEING THAT YOU DON'T EVEN HAVE THAT COMMON SENSE!
WHAT'S THE MATTER?
TAP

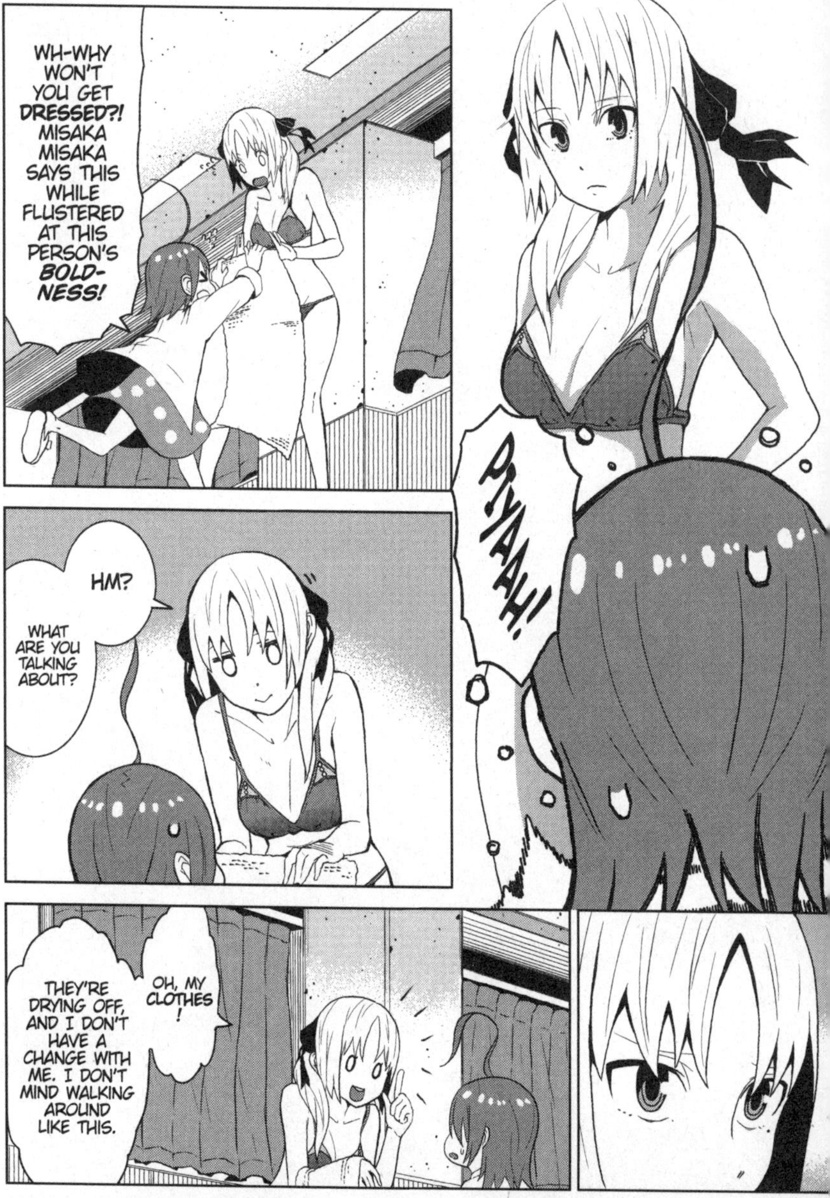
PIYAAH!
WH-WHY WON'T YOU GET DRESSED?! MISAKA MISAKA SAYS THIS WHILE FLUSTERED AT THIS PERSON'S BOLDNESS!
HM?
WHAT ARE YOU TALKING ABOUT?
OH, MY CLOTHES!
THEY'RE DRYING OFF, AND I DON'T HAVE A CHANGE WITH ME. I DON'T MIND WALKING AROUND LIKE THIS.

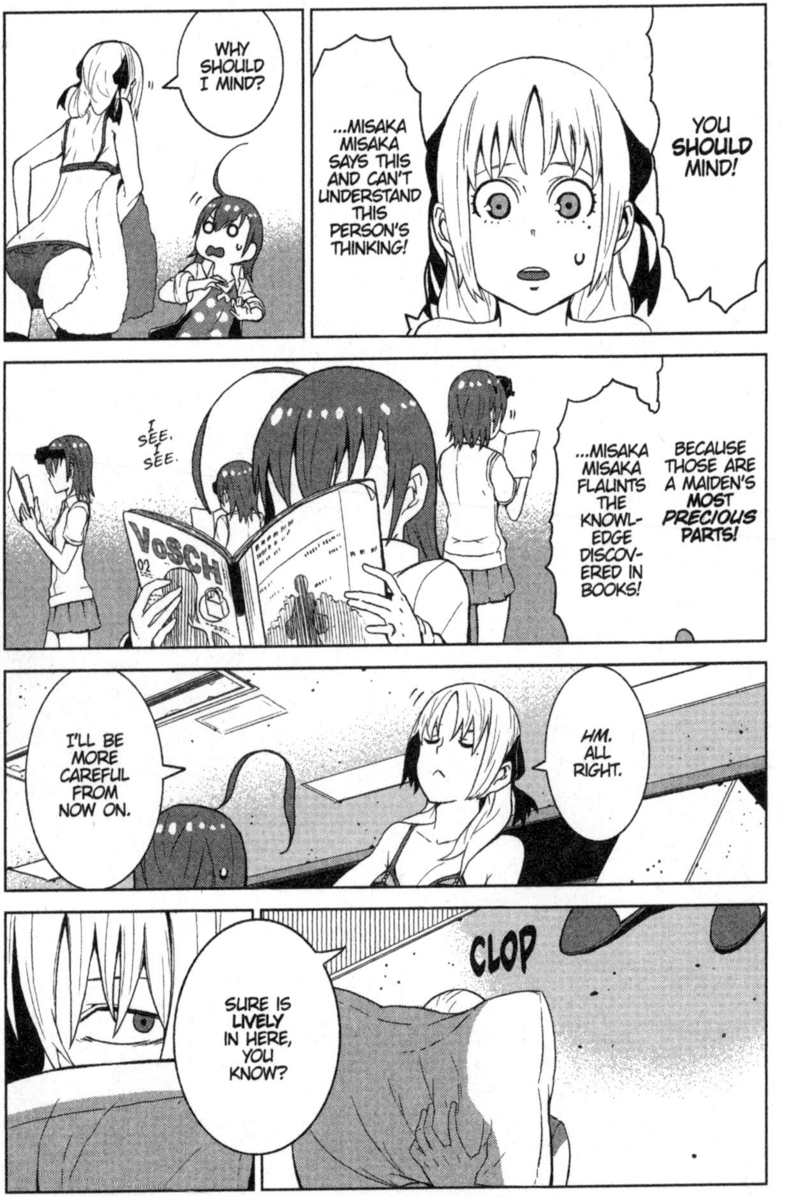
WHY SHOULD I MIND?
YOU SHOULD MIND!
...MISAKA MISAKA SAYS THIS AND CAN'T UNDERSTAND THIS PERSON'S THINKING!
I SEE, I SEE.
VoSCH 02
BECAUSE THOSE ARE A MAIDEN'S MOST PRECIOUS PARTS!
...MISAKA MISAKA FLAUNTS THE KNOWL-EDGE DISCOV-ERED IN BOOKS!
I'LL BE MORE CAREFUL FROM NOW ON.
HM. ALL RIGHT.
SURE IS LIVELY IN HERE, YOU KNOW?
CLOP

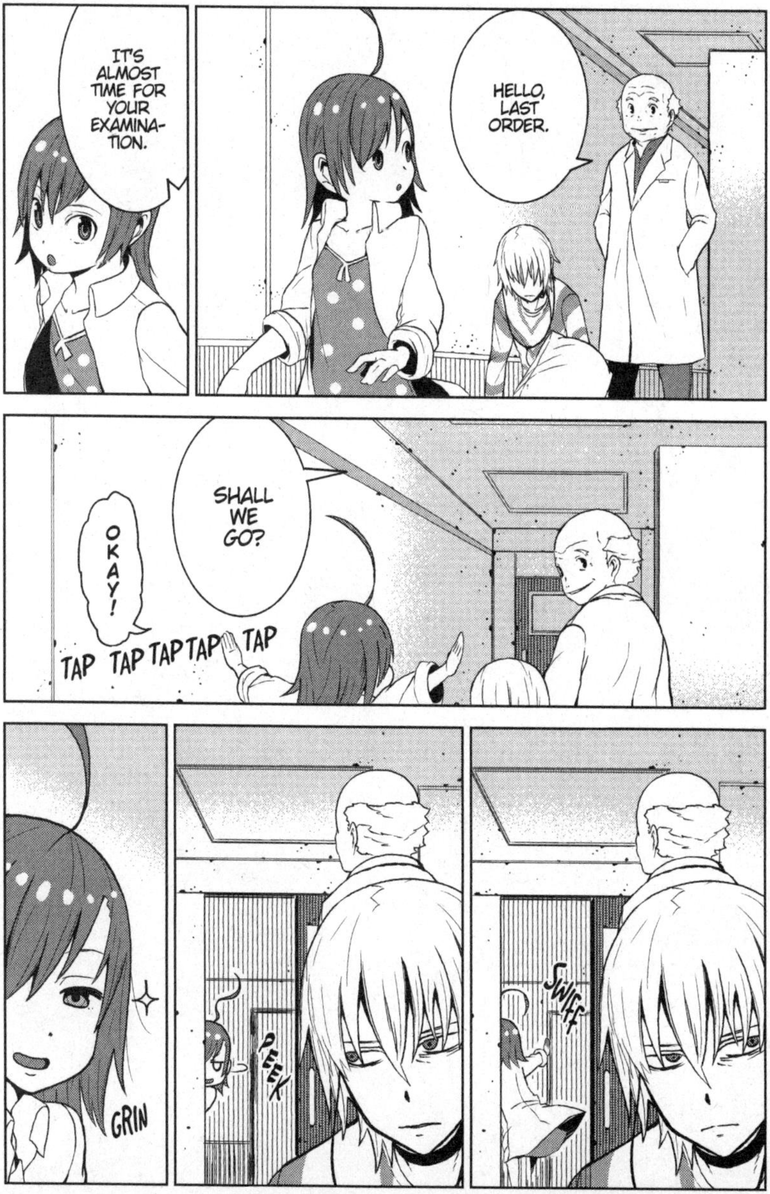
HELLO, LAST ORDER.
IT'S ALMOST TIME FOR YOUR EXAMINATION.
SHALL WE GO?
OKAY!
TAP TAP TAP TAP TAP
SWIFF
PEEK
GRIN

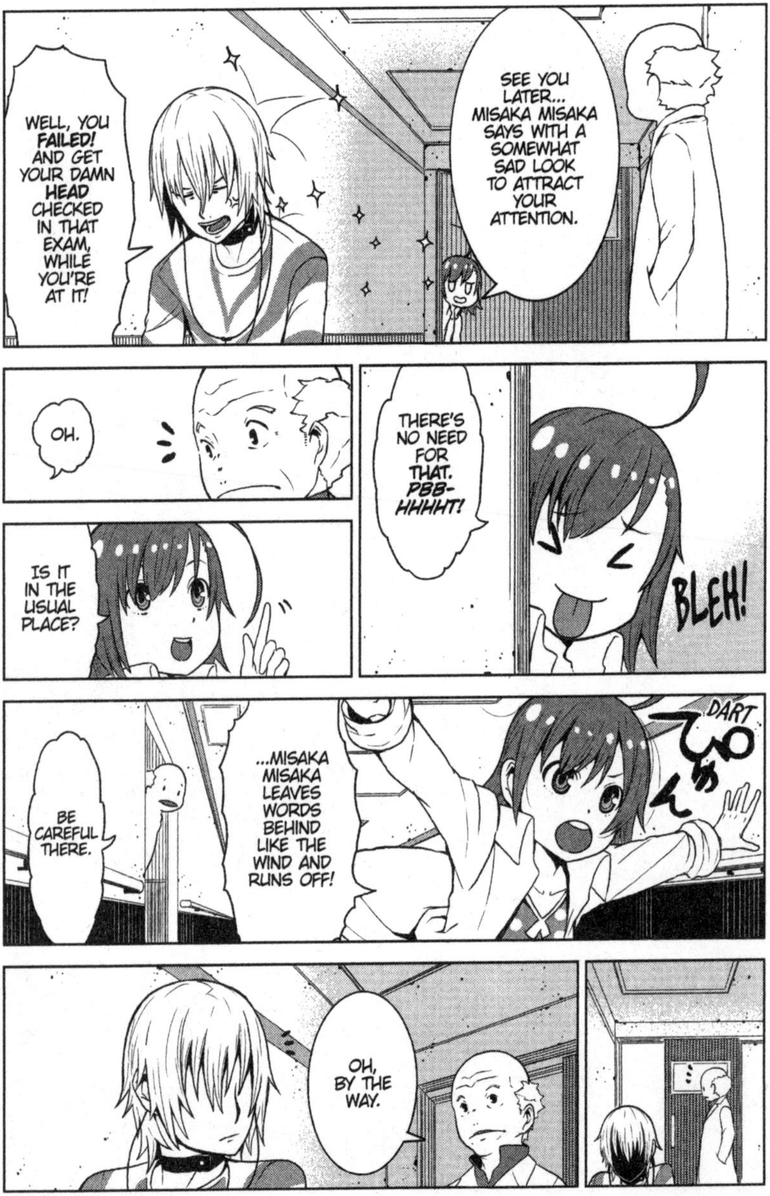
SEE YOU LATER... MISAKA MISAKA SAYS WITH A SOMEWHAT SAD LOOK TO ATTRACT YOUR ATTENTION.
WELL, YOU FAILED! AND GET YOUR DAMN HEAD CHECKED IN THAT EXAM, WHILE YOU'RE AT IT!
THERE'S NO NEED FOR THAT. PBB-HHHHT!
BLEH!
OH.
IS IT IN THE USUAL PLACE?
DART
...MISAKA MISAKA LEAVES WORDS BEHIND LIKE THE WIND AND RUNS OFF!
BE CAREFUL THERE.
OH, BY THE WAY.

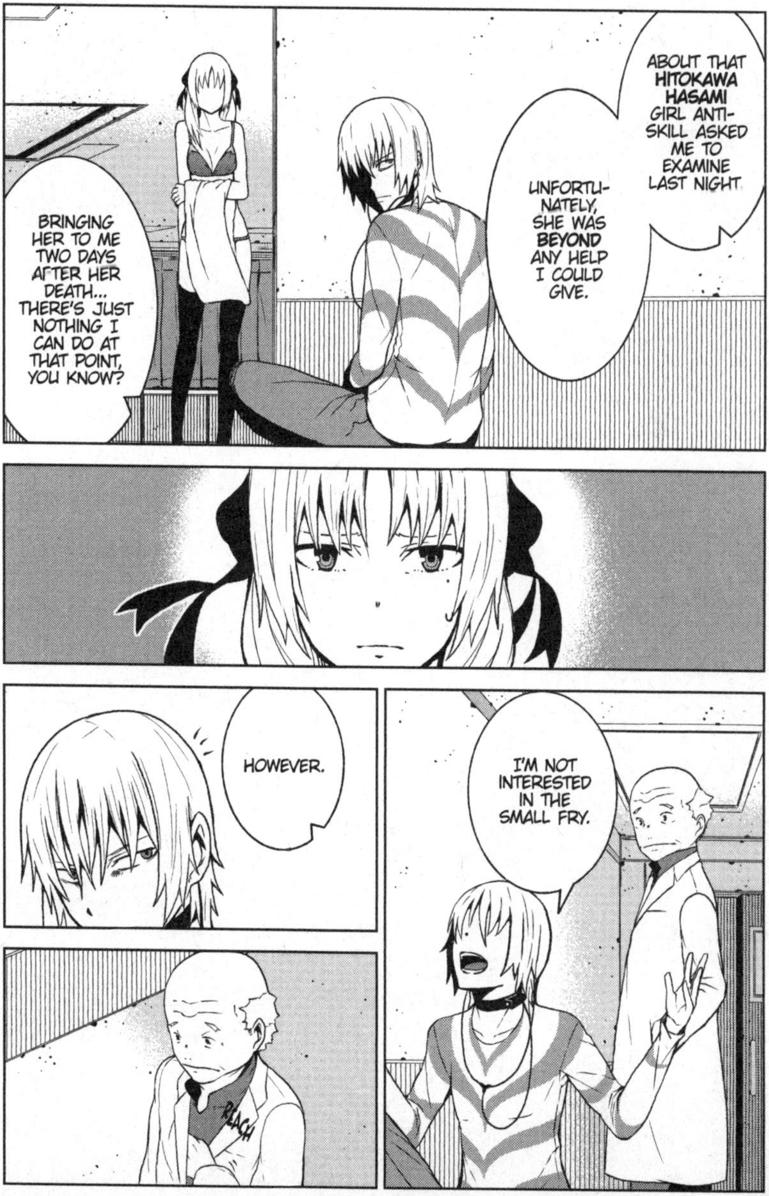
ABOUT THAT HITOKAWA HASAMI GIRL ANTI-SKILL ASKED ME TO EXAMINE LAST NIGHT.
UNFORTUNATELY, SHE WAS BEYOND ANY HELP I COULD GIVE.
BRINGING HER TO ME TWO DAYS AFTER HER DEATH... THERE'S JUST NOTHING I CAN DO AT THAT POINT, YOU KNOW?
I'M NOT INTERESTED IN THE SMALL FRY.
HOWEVER.
REACH

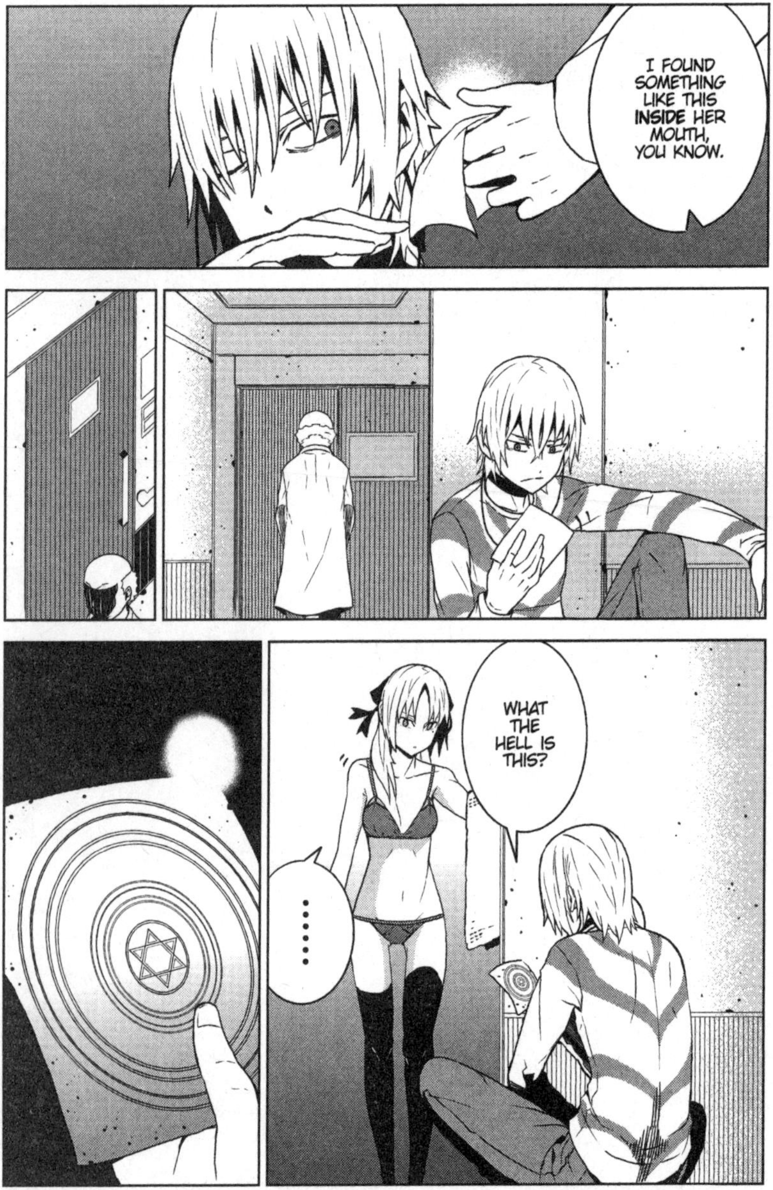
I FOUND SOMETHING LIKE THIS INSIDE HER MOUTH, YOU KNOW.
WHAT THE HELL IS THIS?
......

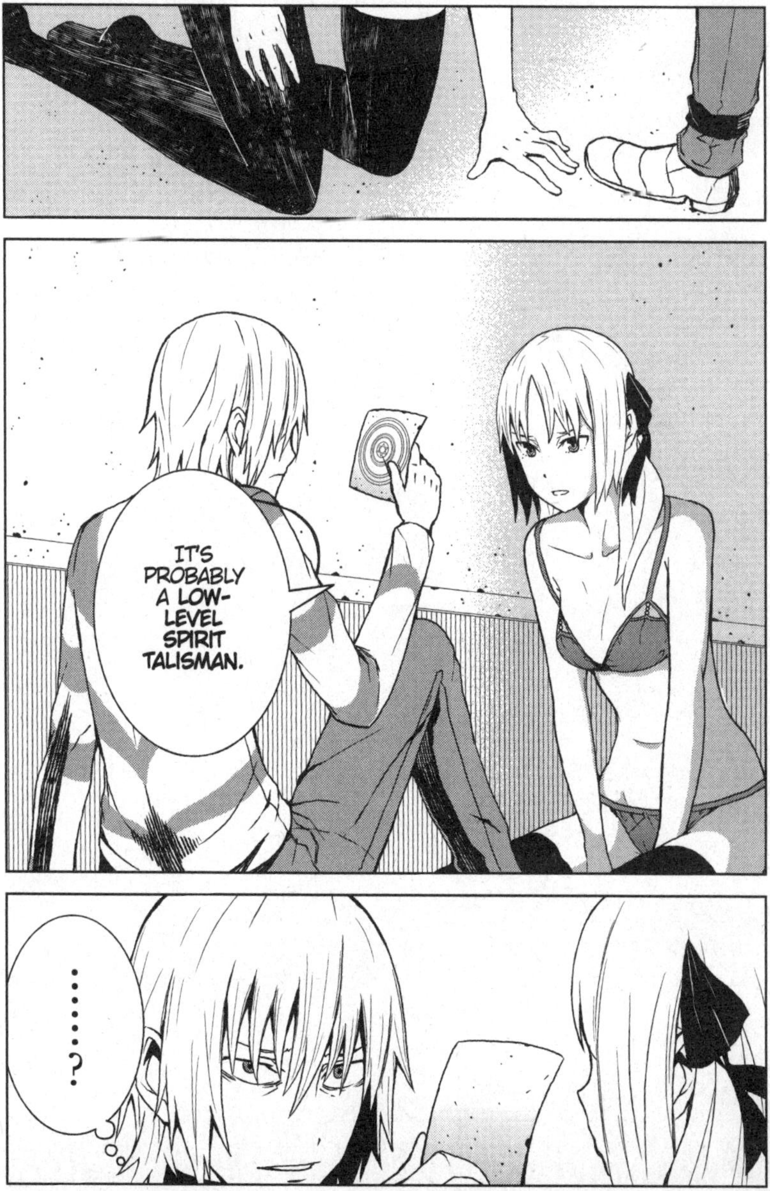
IT'S PROBABLY A LOW-LEVEL SPIRIT TALISMAN.
......?

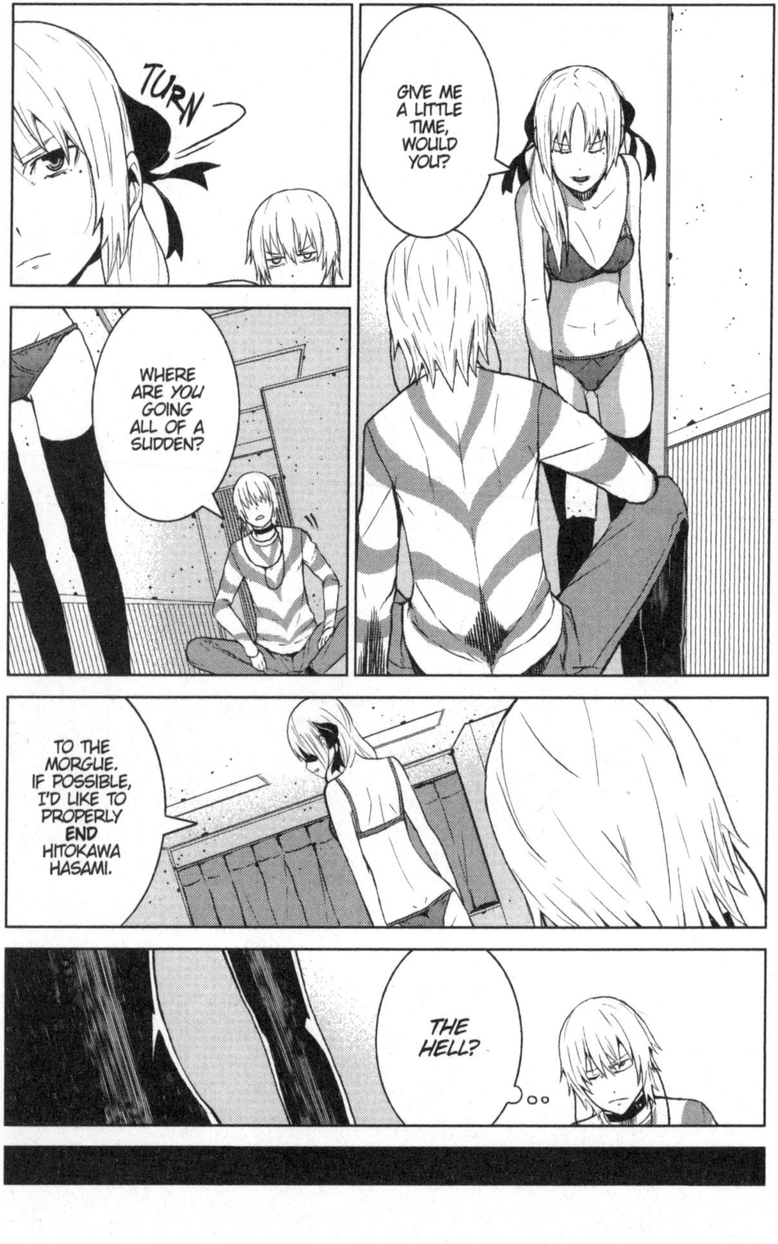
GIVE ME A LITTLE TIME, WOULD YOU?
TURN
WHERE ARE *YOU* GOING ALL OF A SUDDEN?
TO THE MORGUE. IF POSSIBLE, I'D LIKE TO PROPERLY **END** HITOKAWA HASAMI.
THE HELL?

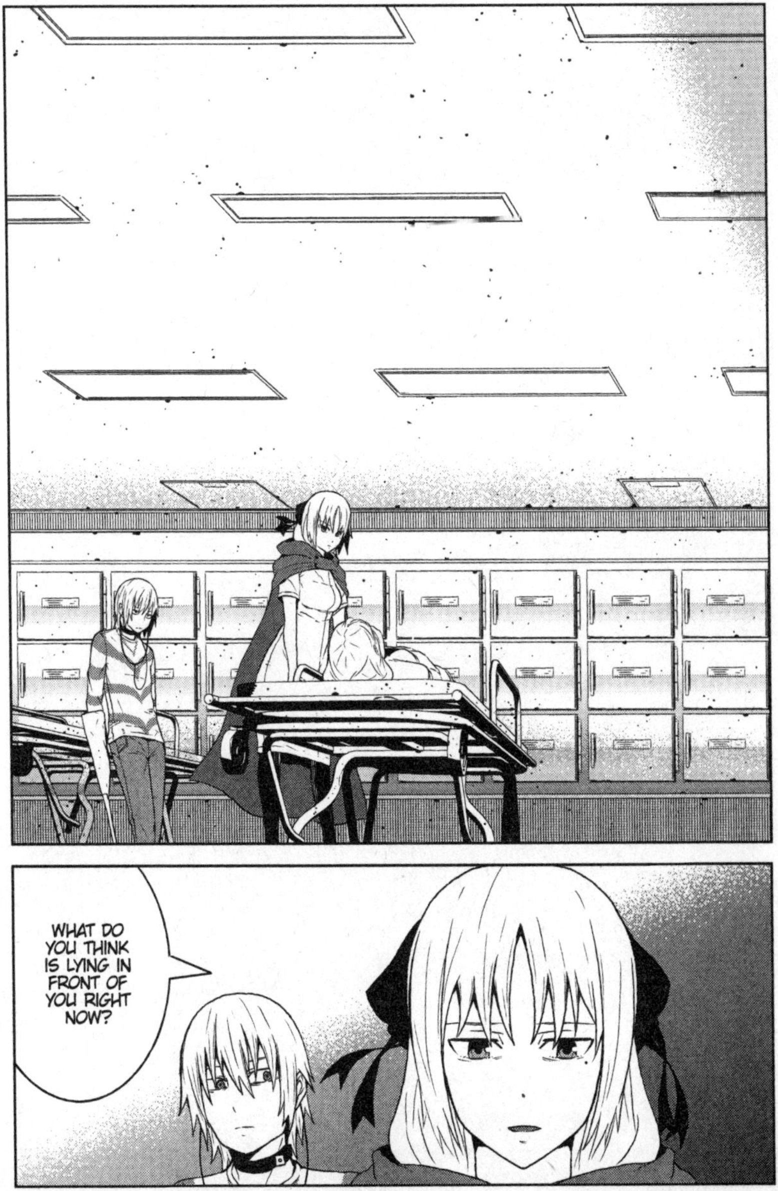
WHAT DO YOU THINK IS LYING IN FRONT OF YOU RIGHT NOW?

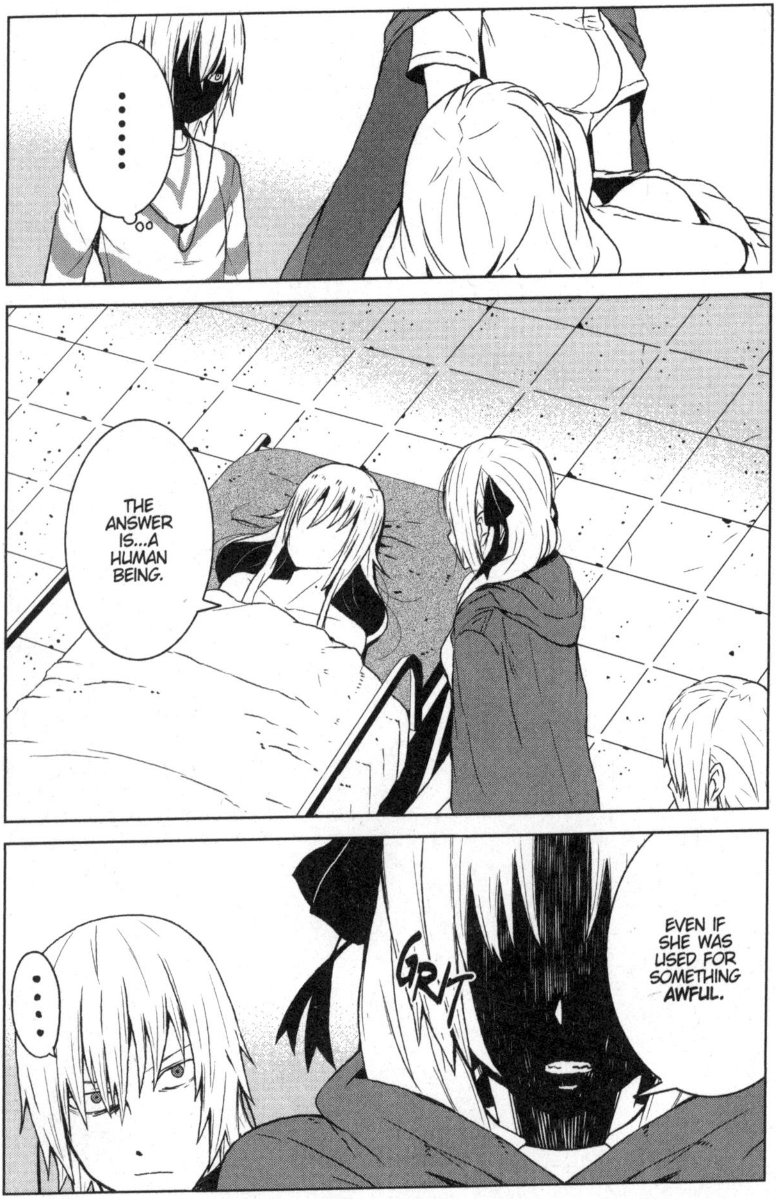
......
THE ANSWER IS...A HUMAN BEING.
EVEN IF SHE WAS USED FOR SOMETHING **AWFUL.**
GRIT
....

YOU'RE GOING TO SHOW ME A LITTLE OF WHAT YOU SAW, OKAY?

INHALE

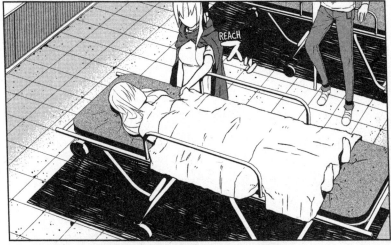

REACH

CRACKLE

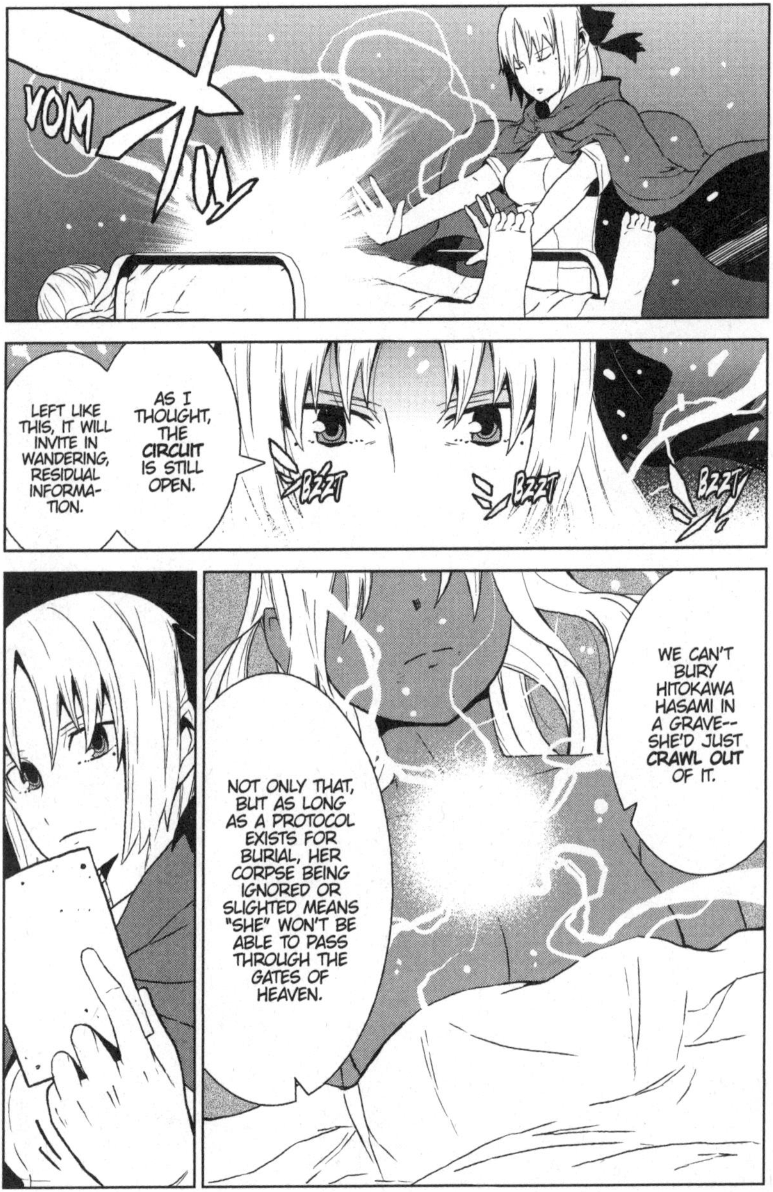
VOM
BZZT
BZZT
BZZT
AS I THOUGHT, THE CIRCUIT IS STILL OPEN.
LEFT LIKE THIS, IT WILL INVITE IN WANDERING, RESIDUAL INFORMATION.
WE CAN'T BURY HITOKAWA HASAMI IN A GRAVE-- SHE'D JUST CRAWL OUT OF IT.
NOT ONLY THAT, BUT AS LONG AS A PROTOCOL EXISTS FOR BURIAL, HER CORPSE BEING IGNORED OR SLIGHTED MEANS "SHE" WON'T BE ABLE TO PASS THROUGH THE GATES OF HEAVEN.

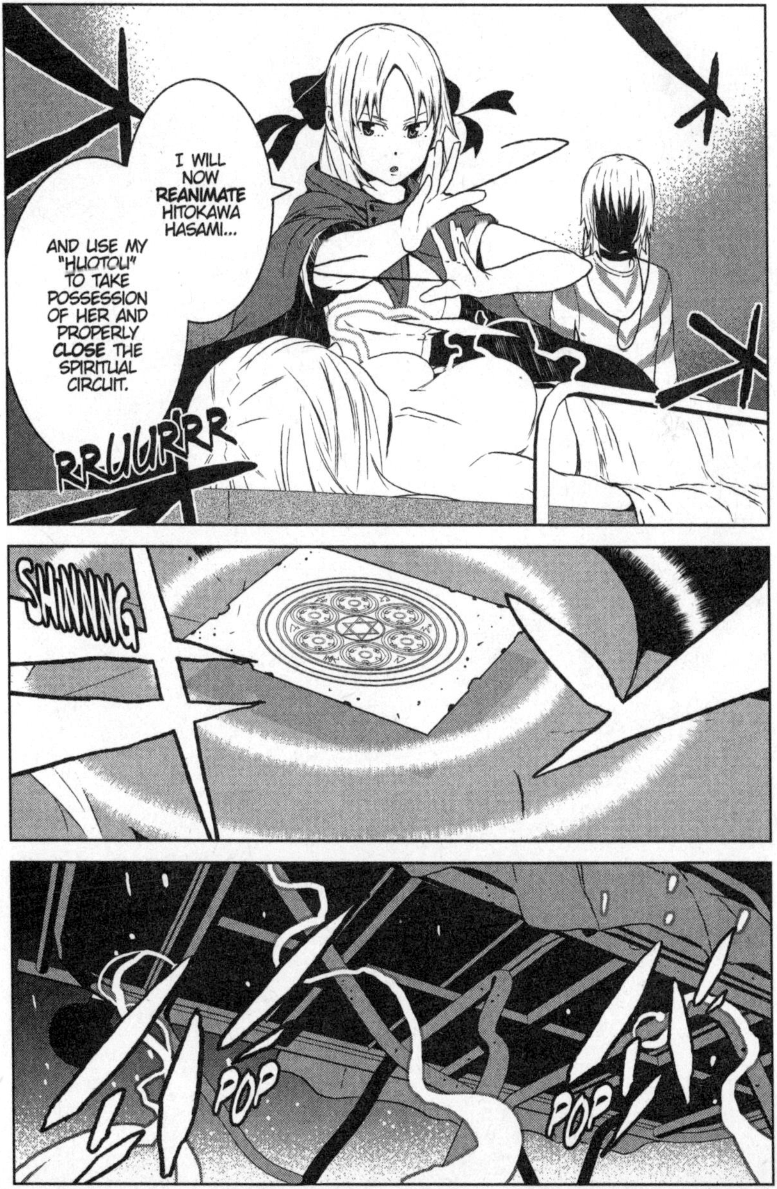
I WILL NOW REANIMATE HITOKAWA HASAMI...
AND USE MY "HUOTOU" TO TAKE POSSESSION OF HER AND PROPERLY CLOSE THE SPIRITUAL CIRCUIT.
RRUUURRR
SHINNNG
POP
POP

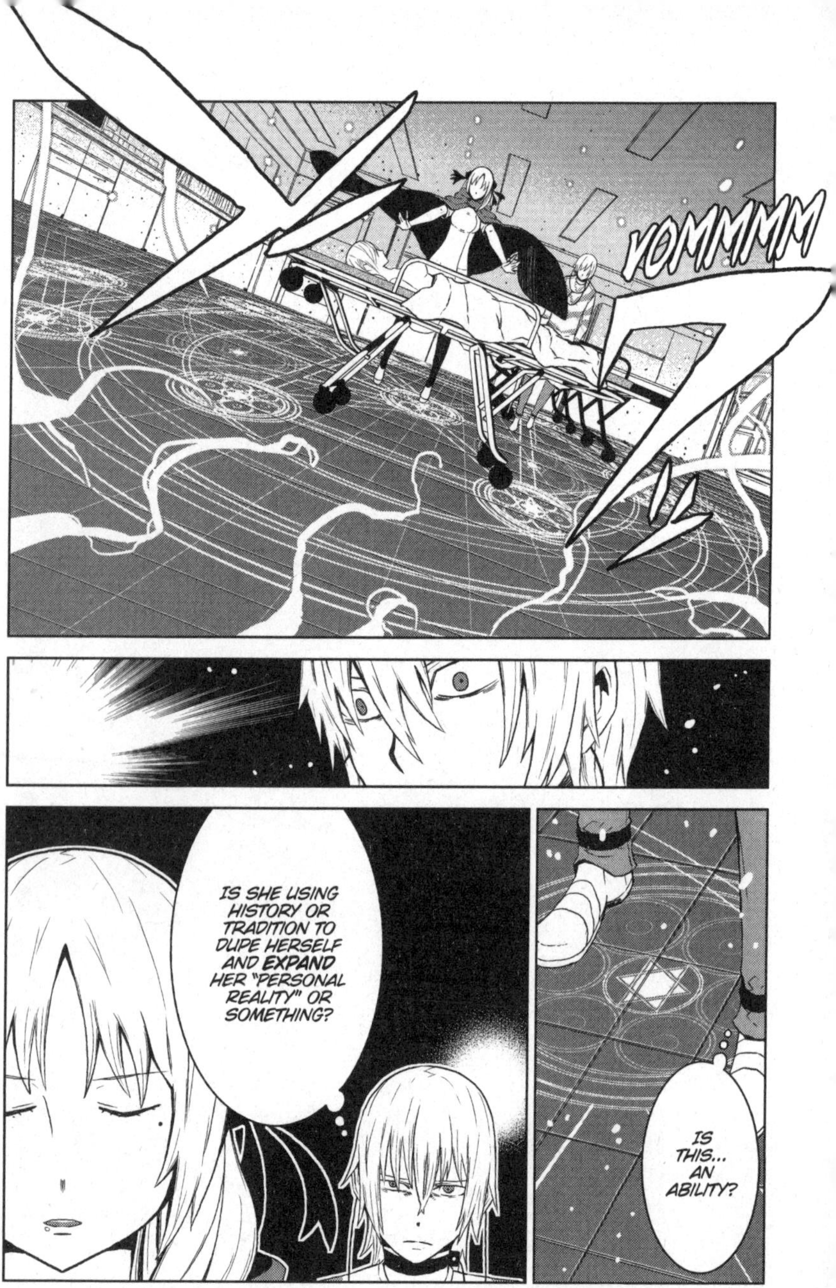
VOMMMMM
IS THIS... AN ABILITY?
IS SHE USING HISTORY OR TRADITION TO DUPE HERSELF AND EXPAND HER "PERSONAL REALITY" OR SOMETHING?

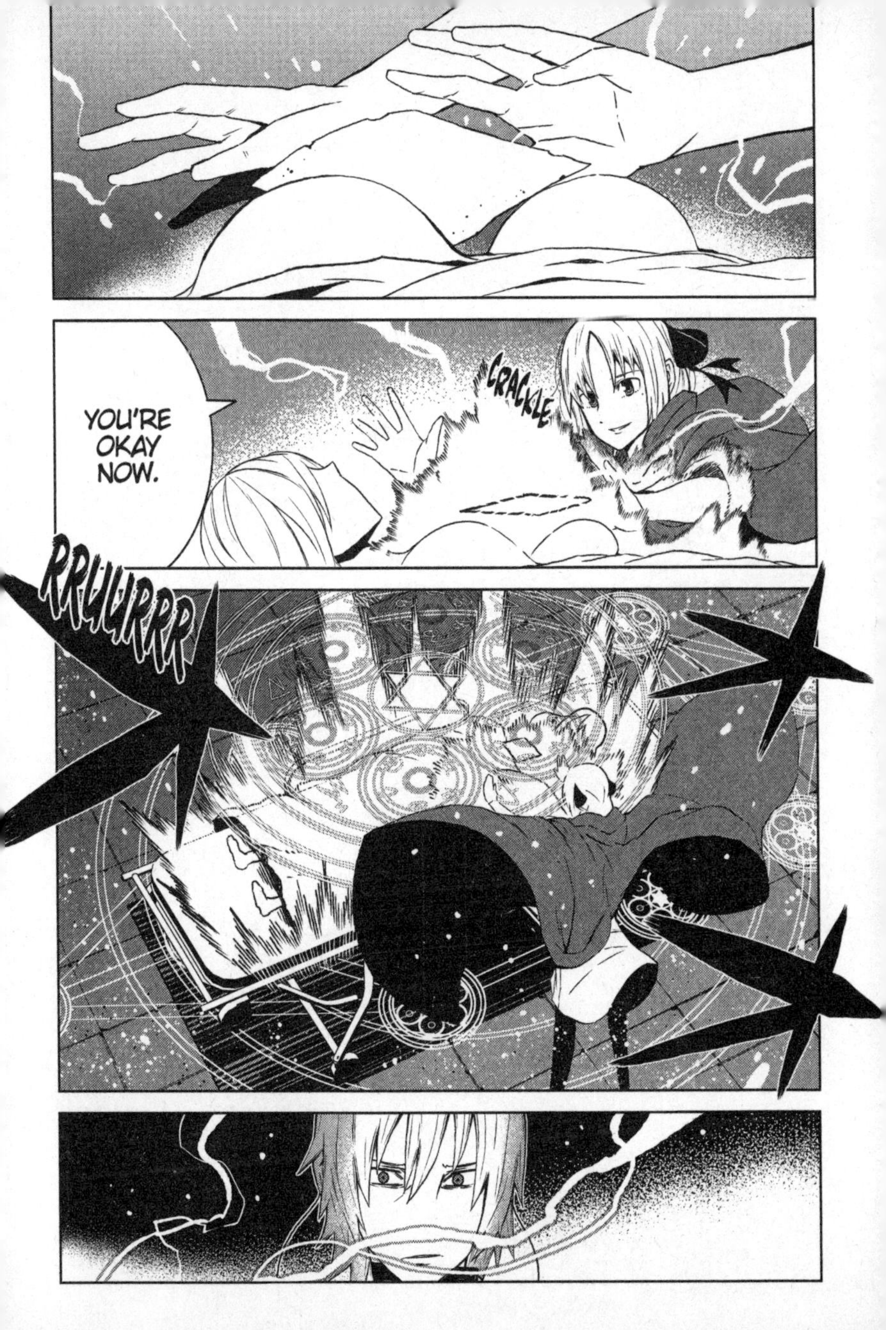
CRACKLE
YOU'RE OKAY NOW.
RRUURRR

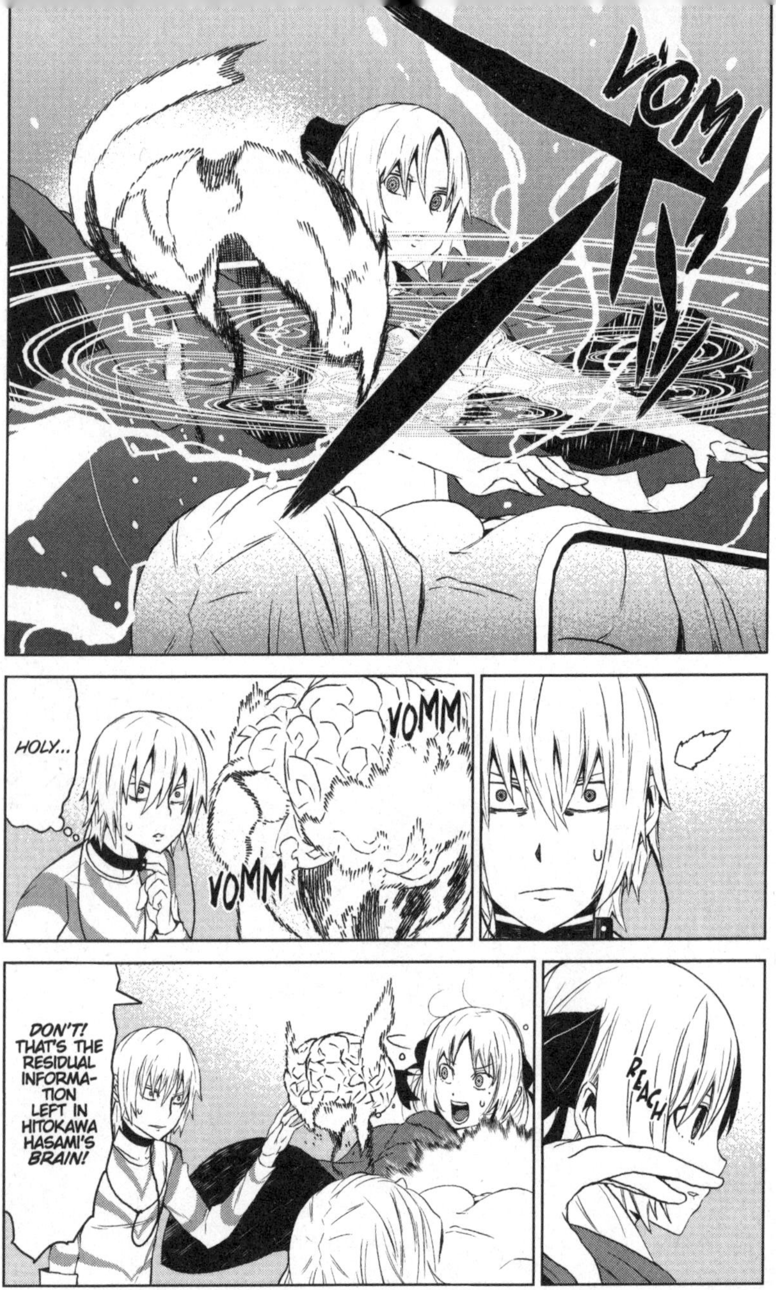
VOM
VOMM
VOMM
HOLY...
REACH
DON'T! THAT'S THE RESIDUAL INFORMATION LEFT IN HITOKAWA HASAMI'S BRAIN!

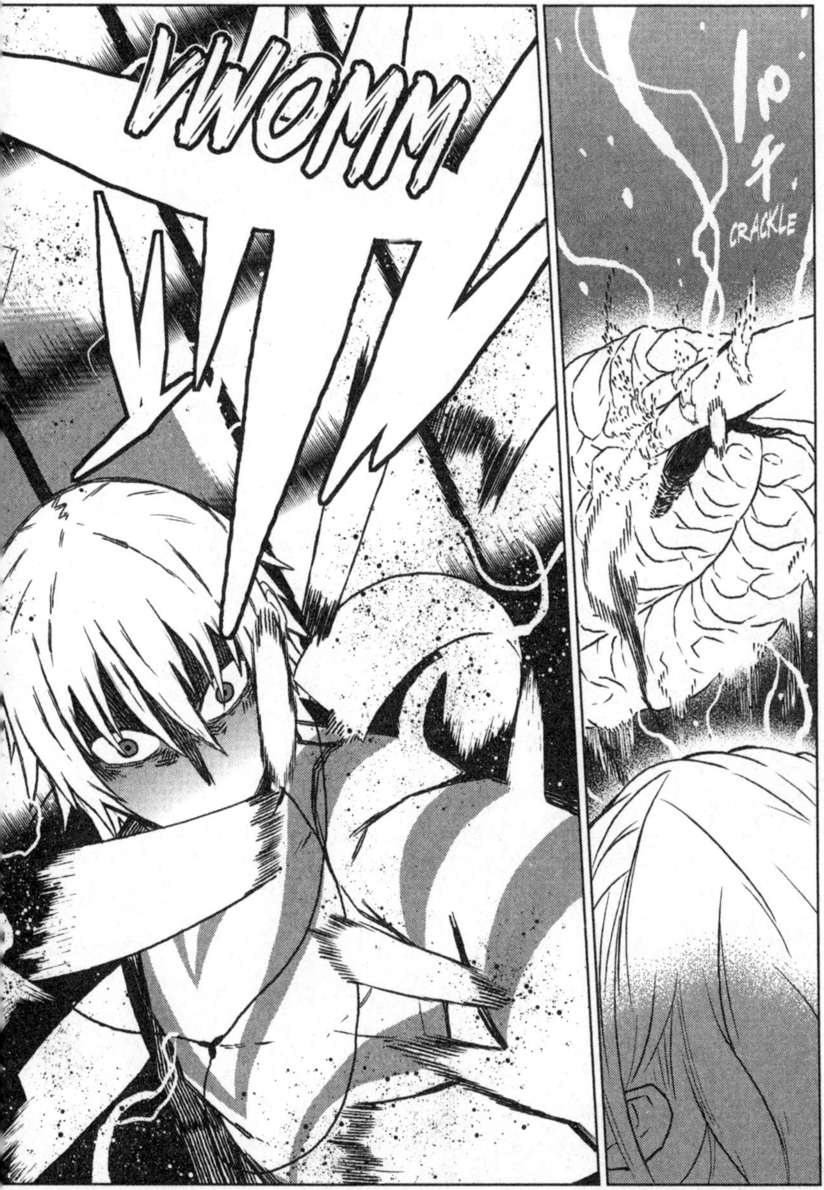
CRACKLE
VWOMM

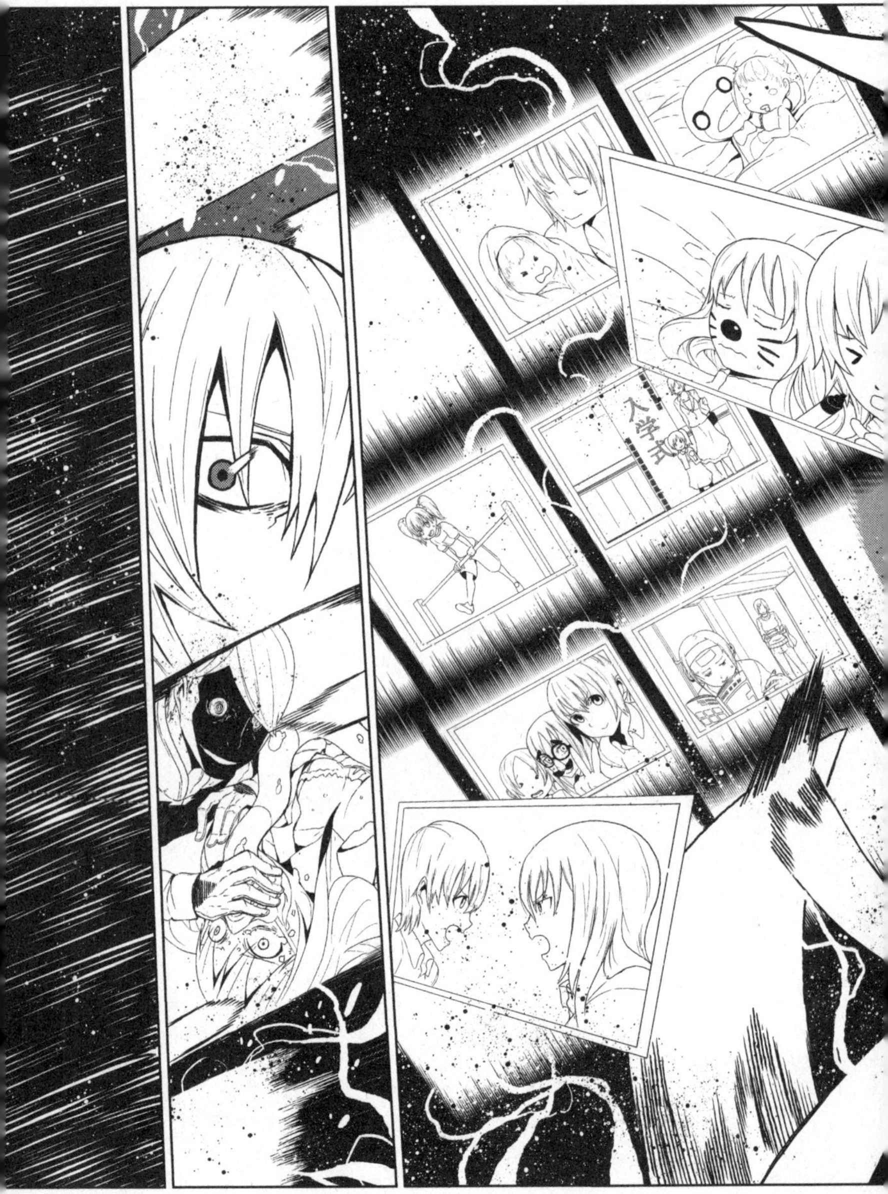
入学式

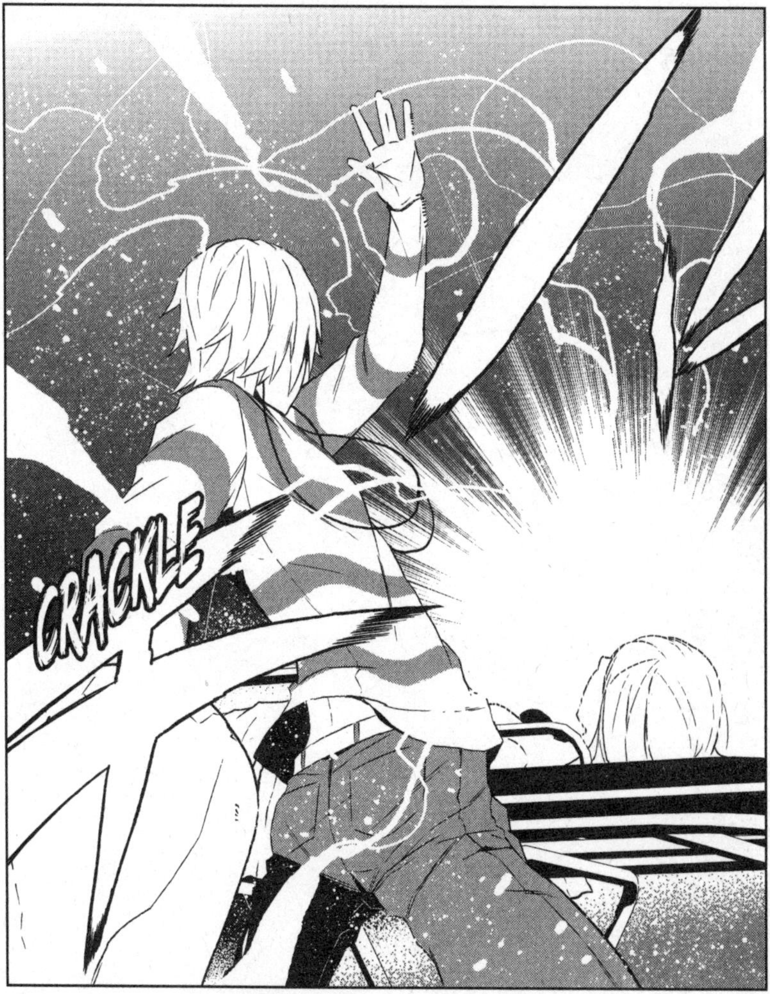
CRACKLE
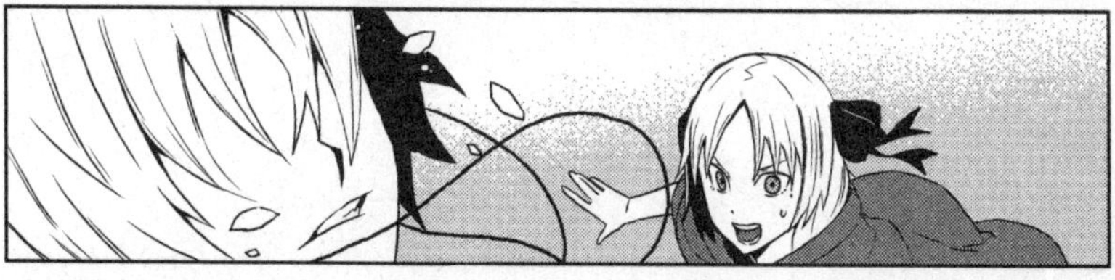

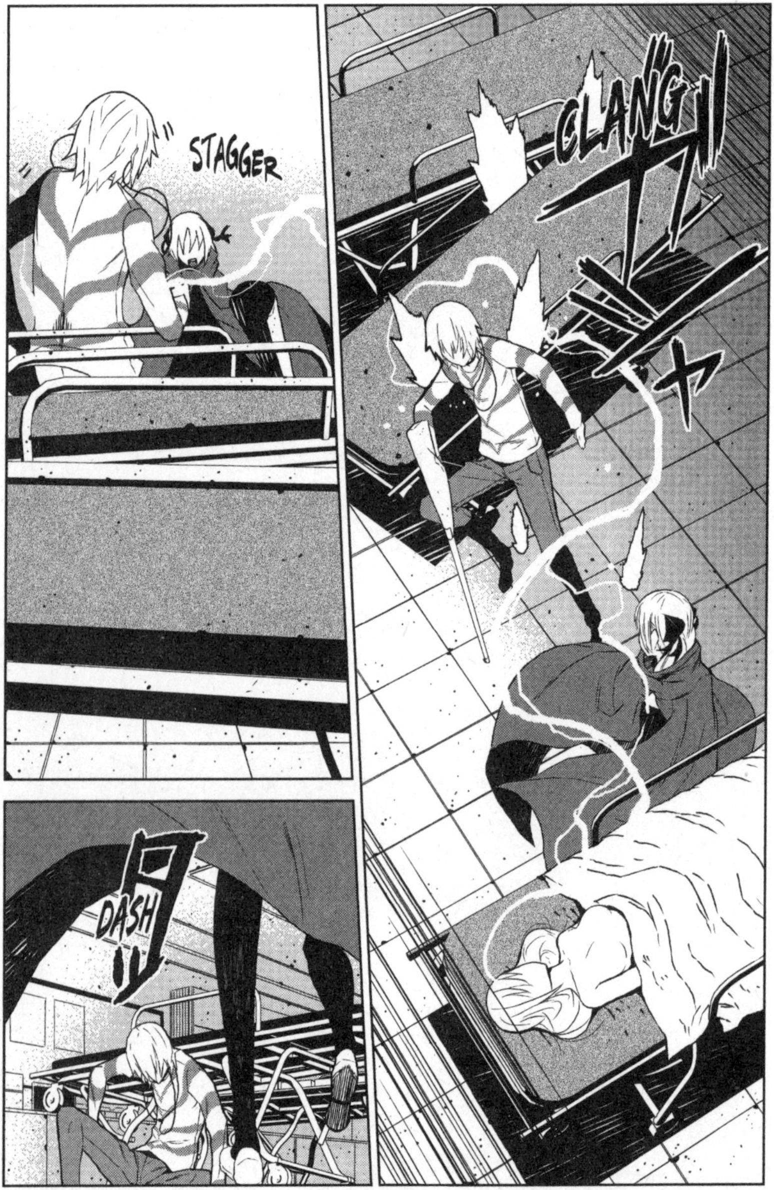
CLANG!!
STAGGER
DASH

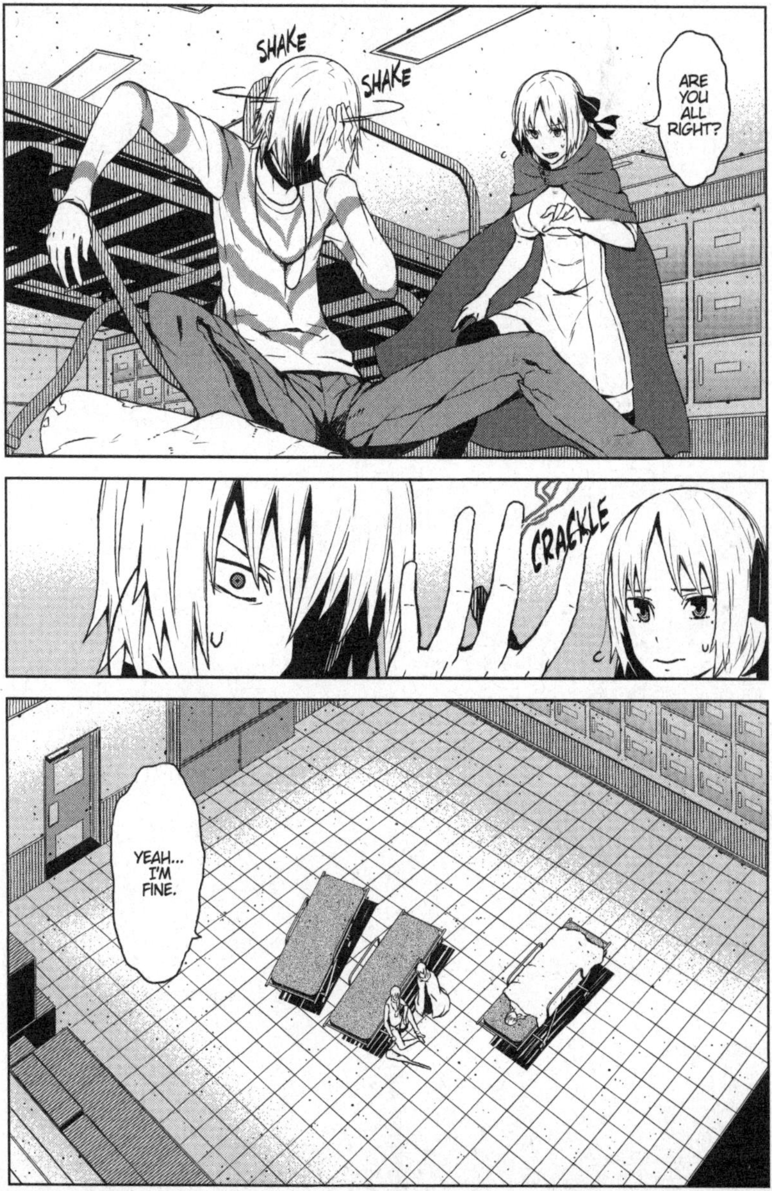
ARE YOU ALL RIGHT?
SHAKE
SHAKE
CRACKLE
YEAH... I'M FINE.

To be continued...

a certain
SCIENTIFIC
ACCELERATOR

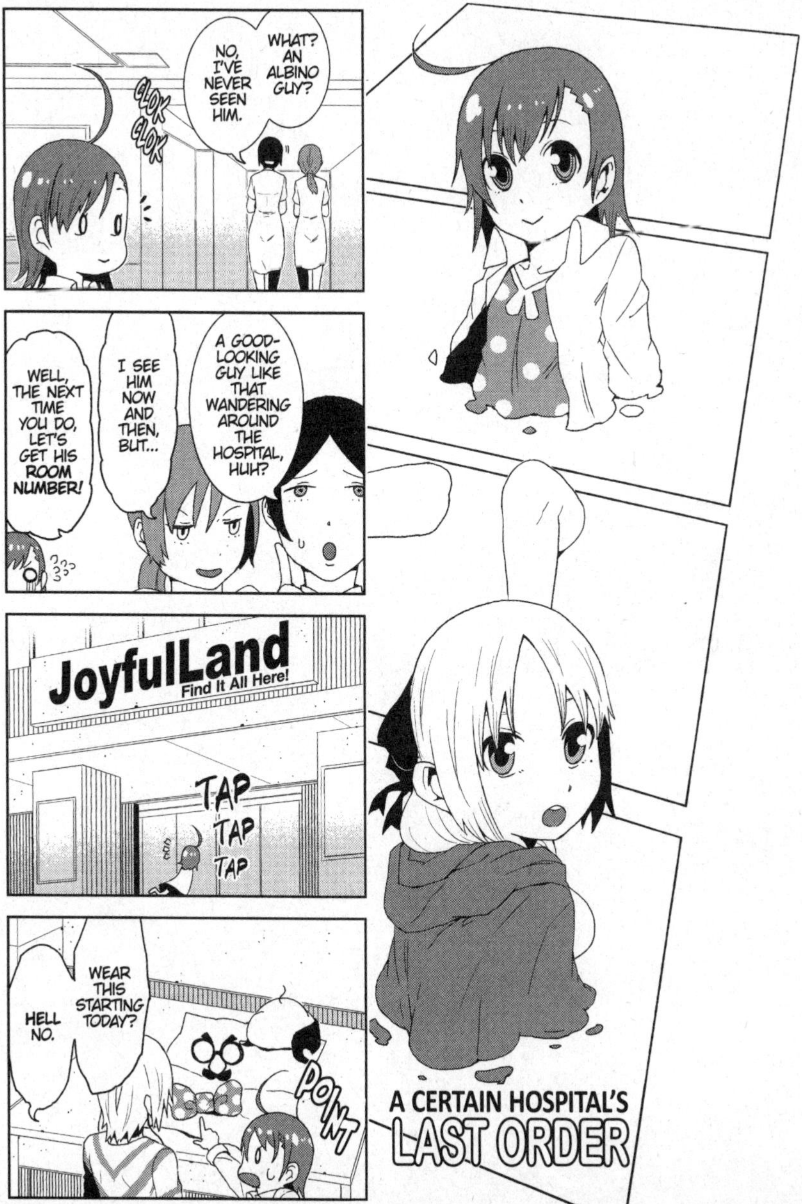
A CERTAIN HOSPITAL'S
LAST ORDER
WHAT? AN ALBINO GUY?
NO, I'VE NEVER SEEN HIM.
CLOK CLOK
A GOOD-LOOKING GUY LIKE THAT WANDERING AROUND THE HOSPITAL, HUH?
I SEE HIM NOW AND THEN, BUT...
WELL, THE NEXT TIME YOU DO, LET'S GET HIS ROOM NUMBER!
JoyfulLand
Find It All Here!
TAP TAP TAP
POINT
WEAR THIS STARTING TODAY?
HELL NO.

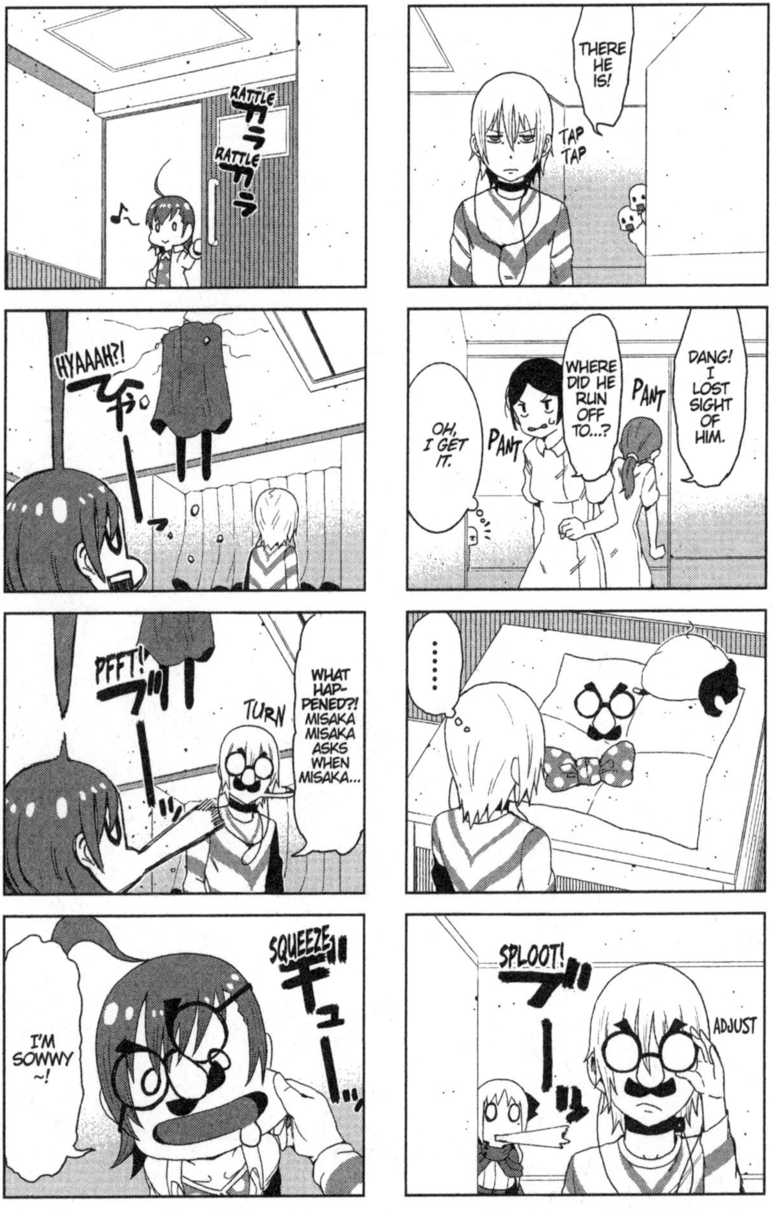
THERE HE IS!
TAP TAP
DANG! I LOST SIGHT OF HIM.
PANT
WHERE DID HE RUN OFF TO...?
PANT
OH, I GET IT.
......
SPLOOT!
ADJUST
RATTLE
RATTLE
HYAAAH?!
WHAT HAP-PENED?! MISAKA MISAKA ASKS WHEN MISAKA...
TURN
PFFT!
SQUEEZE
I'M SOWWY ~!

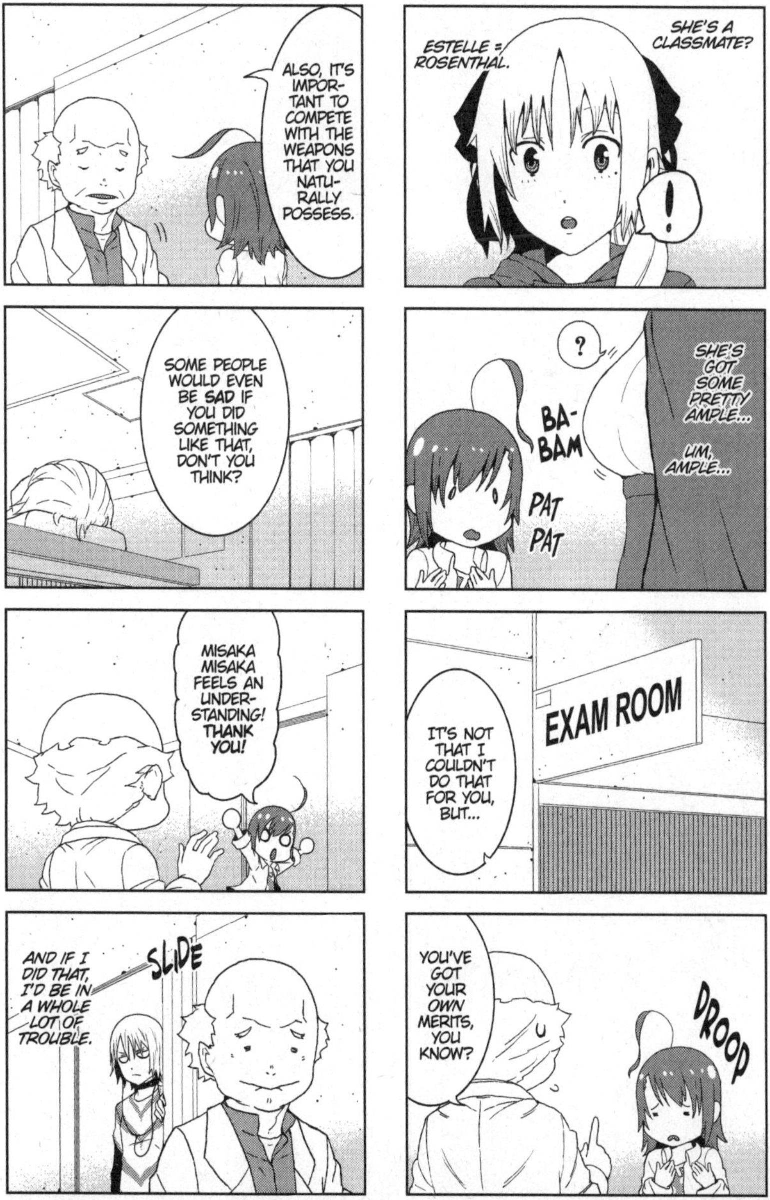
SHE'S A CLASSMATE?
ESTELLE = ROSENTHAL.
!
SHE'S GOT SOME PRETTY AMPLE...
UM, AMPLE...
?
BA-BAM
PAT PAT
EXAM ROOM
IT'S NOT THAT I COULDN'T DO THAT FOR YOU, BUT...
DROOP
YOU'VE GOT YOUR OWN MERITS, YOU KNOW?
ALSO, IT'S IMPOR-TANT TO COMPETE WITH THE WEAPONS THAT YOU NATU-RALLY POSSESS.
SOME PEOPLE WOULD EVEN BE SAD IF YOU DID SOMETHING LIKE THAT, DON'T YOU THINK?
MISAKA MISAKA FEELS AN UNDER-STANDING! THANK YOU!
SLIDE
AND IF I DID THAT, I'D BE IN A WHOLE LOT OF TROUBLE.

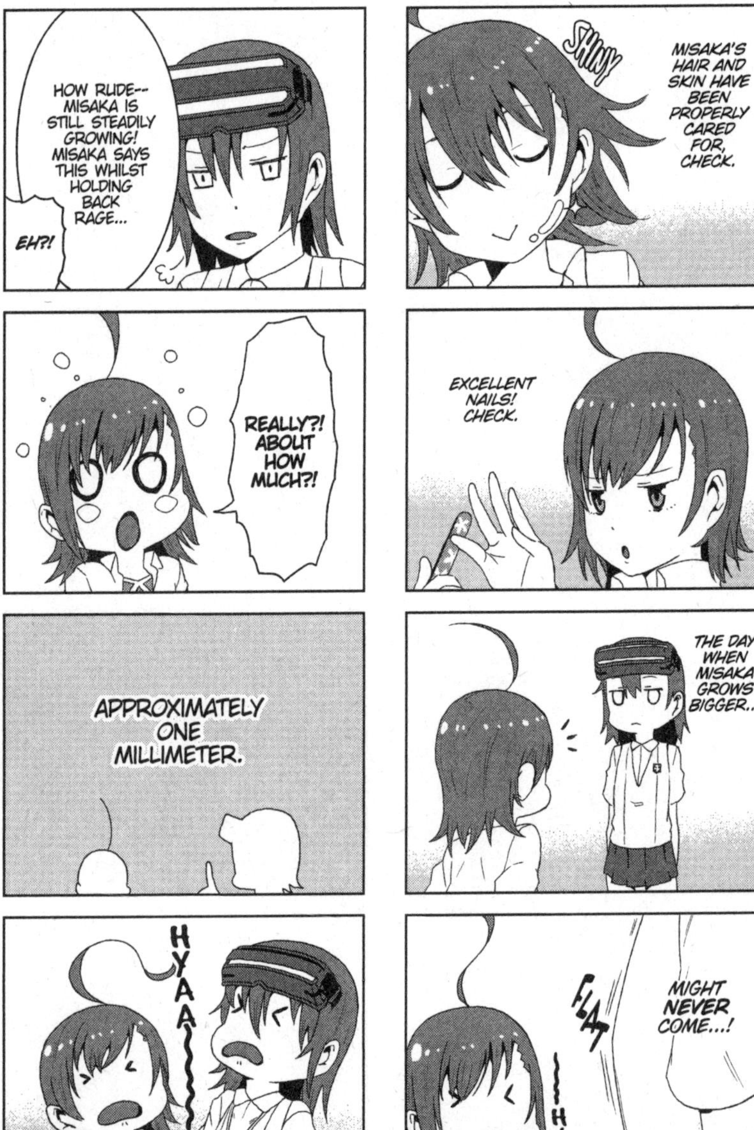
SHINY
MISAKA'S HAIR AND SKIN HAVE BEEN PROPERLY CARED FOR, CHECK.
EXCELLENT NAILS! CHECK.
THE DAY WHEN MISAKA GROWS BIGGER...
MIGHT NEVER COME...!
FLAT
~~H!
HOW RUDE-- MISAKA IS STILL STEADILY GROWING! MISAKA SAYS THIS WHILST HOLDING BACK RAGE...
EH?!
REALLY?! ABOUT HOW MUCH?!
APPROXIMATELY ONE MILLIMETER.
HYAAA~~~H!

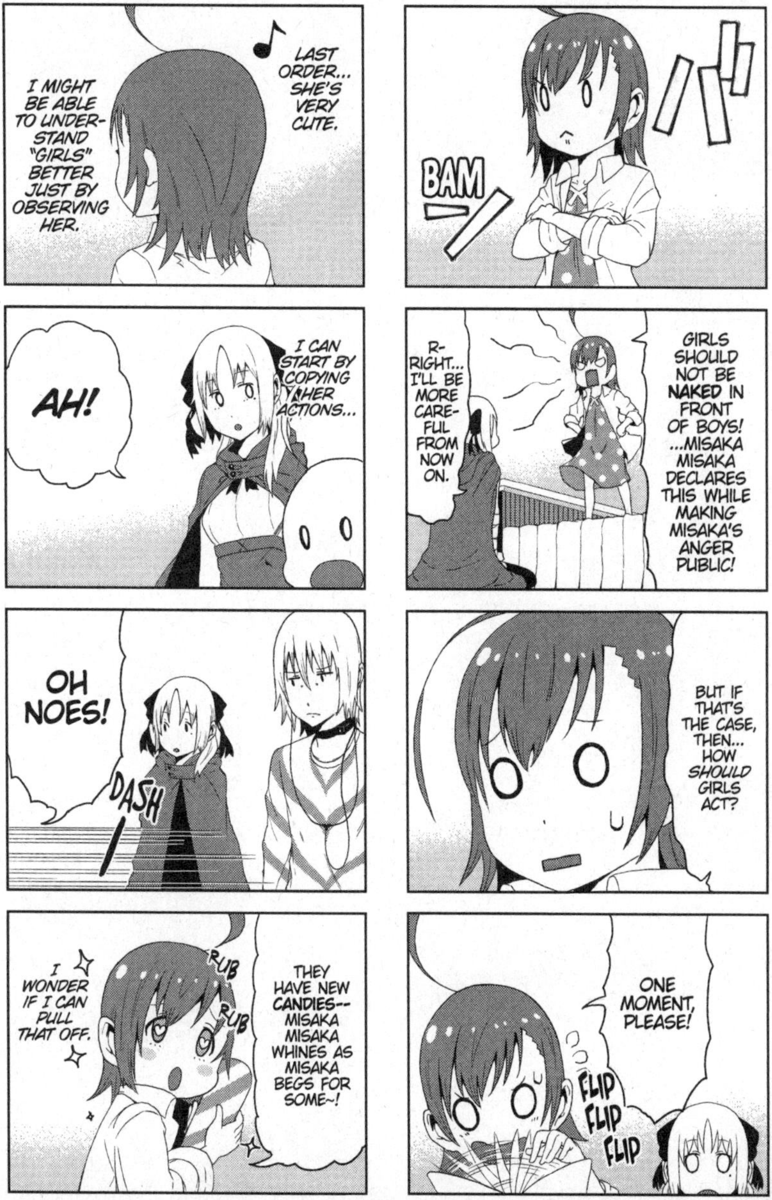
BAM
GIRLS SHOULD NOT BE NAKED IN FRONT OF BOYS! ...MISAKA MISAKA DECLARES THIS WHILE MAKING MISAKA'S ANGER PUBLIC!
R-RIGHT... I'LL BE MORE CARE-FUL FROM NOW ON.
BUT IF THAT'S THE CASE, THEN... HOW SHOULD GIRLS ACT?
ONE MOMENT, PLEASE!
FLIP FLIP FLIP
LAST ORDER... SHE'S VERY CUTE.
I MIGHT BE ABLE TO UNDER-STAND "GIRLS" BETTER JUST BY OBSERVING HER.
I CAN START BY COPYING HER ACTIONS...
AH!
OH NOES!
DASH
THEY HAVE NEW CANDIES-- MISAKA MISAKA WHINES AS MISAKA BEGS FOR SOME~!
RUB RUB
I WONDER IF I CAN PULL THAT OFF.

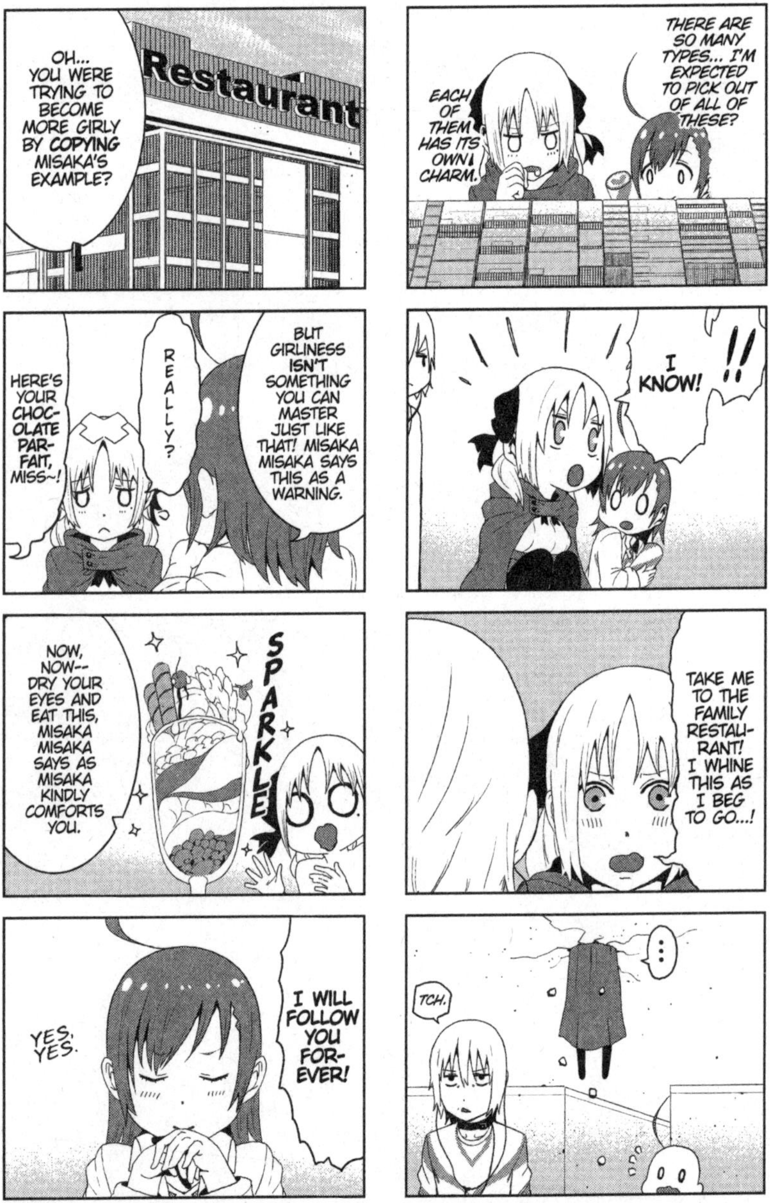
THERE ARE SO MANY TYPES... I'M EXPECTED TO PICK OUT OF ALL OF THESE?
EACH OF THEM HAS ITS OWN CHARM.
!!
I KNOW!
TAKE ME TO THE FAMILY RESTAURANT! I WHINE THIS AS I BEG TO GO...!
...
TCH.
Restaurant
OH... YOU WERE TRYING TO BECOME MORE GIRLY BY COPYING MISAKA'S EXAMPLE?
BUT GIRLINESS ISN'T SOMETHING YOU CAN MASTER JUST LIKE THAT! MISAKA MISAKA SAYS THIS AS A WARNING.
REALLY?
HERE'S YOUR CHOCOLATE PARFAIT, MISS~!
SPARKLE
NOW, NOW-- DRY YOUR EYES AND EAT THIS, MISAKA MISAKA SAYS AS MISAKA KINDLY COMFORTS YOU.
I WILL FOLLOW YOU FOREVER!
YES, YES.

To be continued...?

DA intensifies their efforts to make their brand of "Justice" a reality.

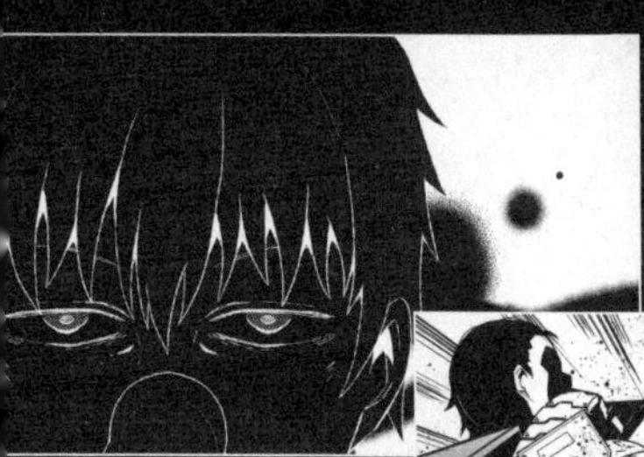

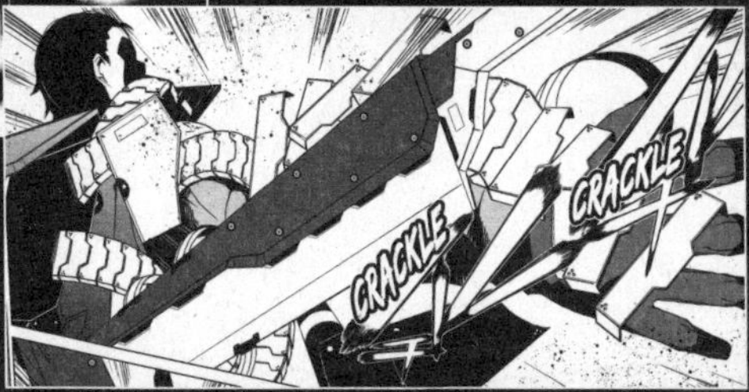
CRACKLE
CRACKLE

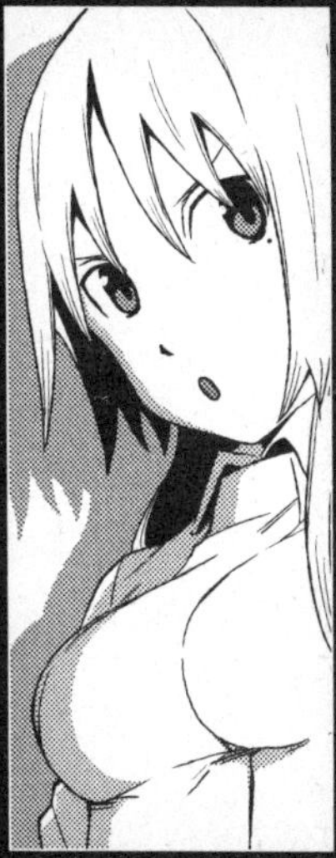

Working to stop them is Estelle, who uses Necromancy and the reanimated corpse of a girl!

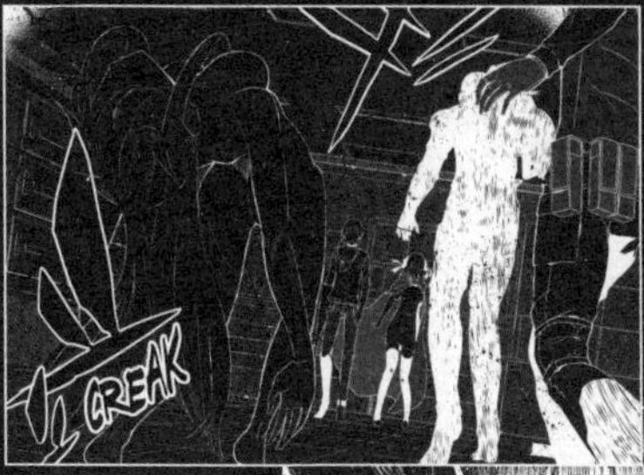
CREAK

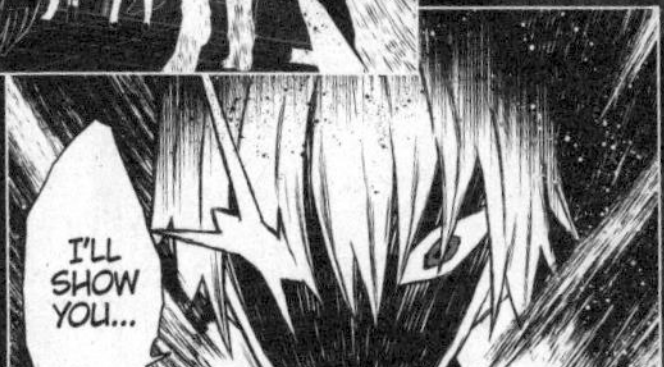
I'LL SHOW YOU...

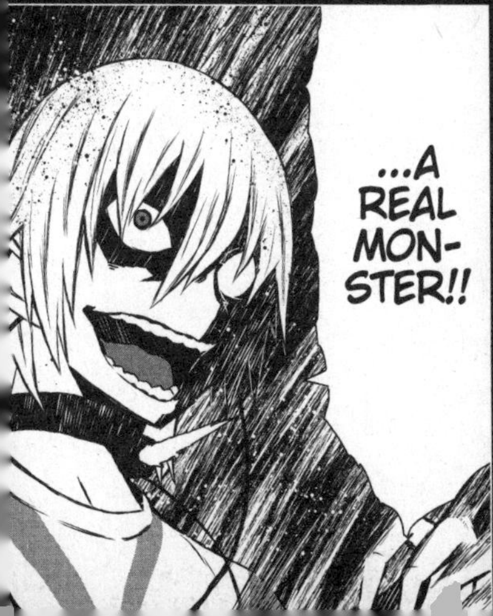
...A REAL MONSTER!!

In the midst of it all, who becomes Accelerator's target?!

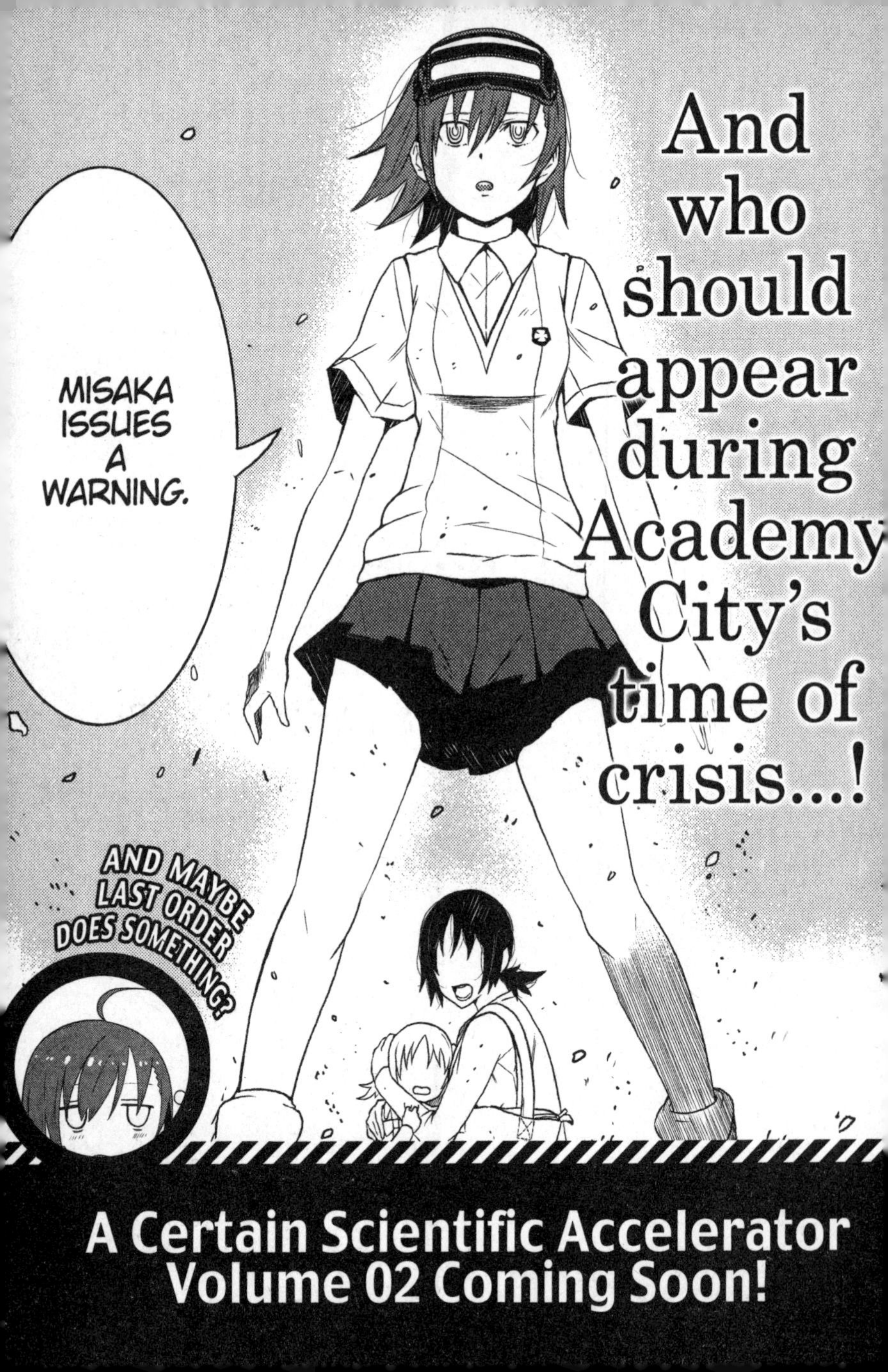

And who should appear during Academy City's time of crisis...!
MISAKA ISSUES A WARNING.
AND MAYBE LAST ORDER DOES SOMETHING?
A Certain Scientific Accelerator Volume 02 Coming Soon!

SEVEN SEAS ENTERTAINMENT PRESENTS

a certain SCIENTIFIC ACCELERATOR
volume 1

story by KAZUMA KAMACHI / art by ARATA YAMAJI

TRANSLATION
Nan Rymer

ADAPTATION
Maggie Danger

LETTERING
Roland Amago

LAYOUT
Bambi Eloriaga-Amago

COVER DESIGN
Nicky Lim

PROOFREADER
Shanti Whitesides
Janet Houck

ASSISTANT EDITOR
Lissa Pattillo

MANAGING EDITOR
Adam Arnold

PUBLISHER
Jason DeAngelis

FOLLOW US ONLINE: *www.gomanga.com*

READING DIRECTIONS

The manga prelude and epilogue sections that bookend this light novel read from right to left, Japanese style. If this is your first time reading manga, you start reading from the top right panel on each page and take it from there. If you get lost, just follow the numbered diagram here. Enjoy!!

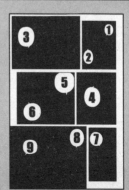

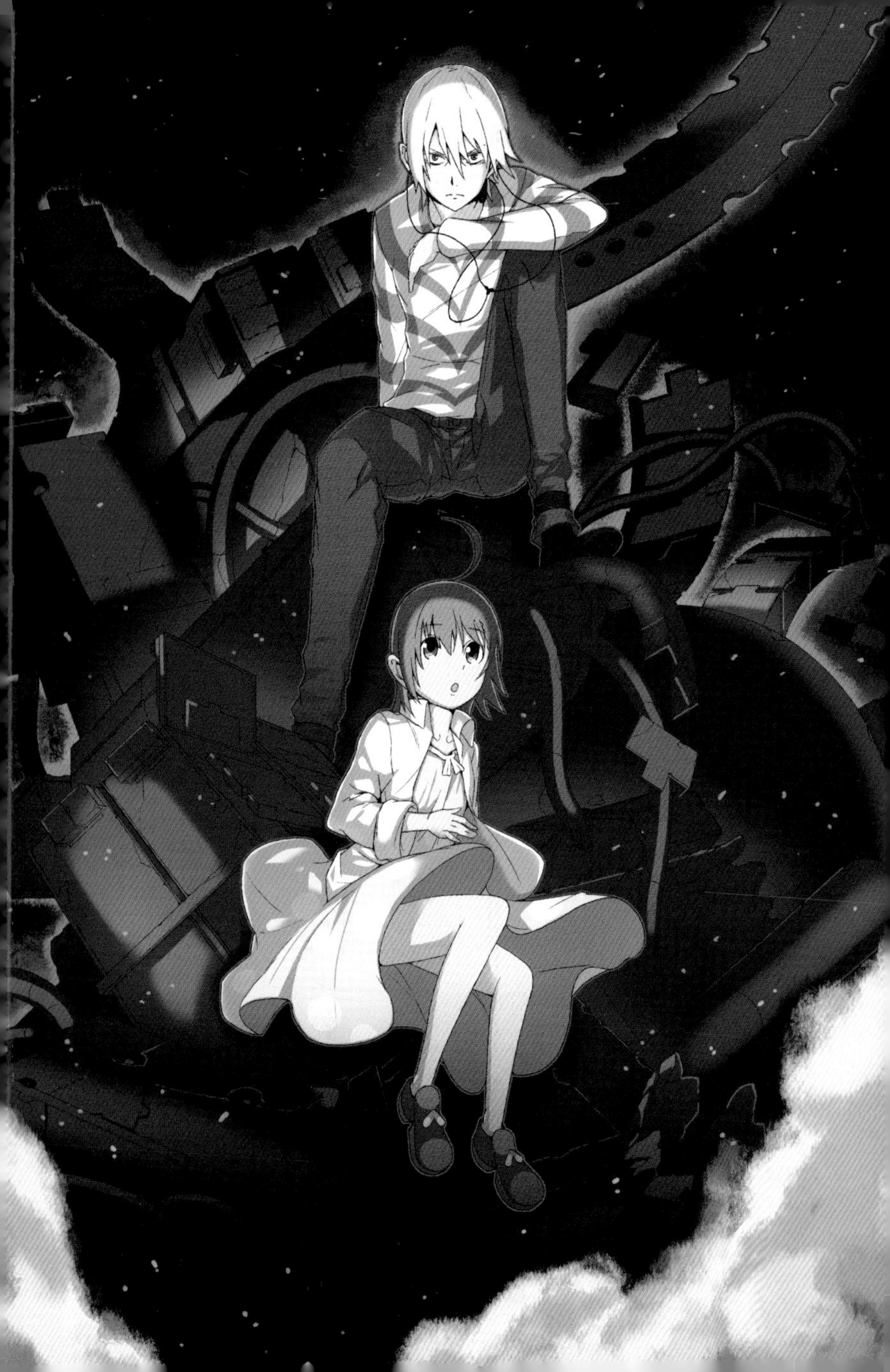

a certain SCIENTIFIC ACCELERATOR 01

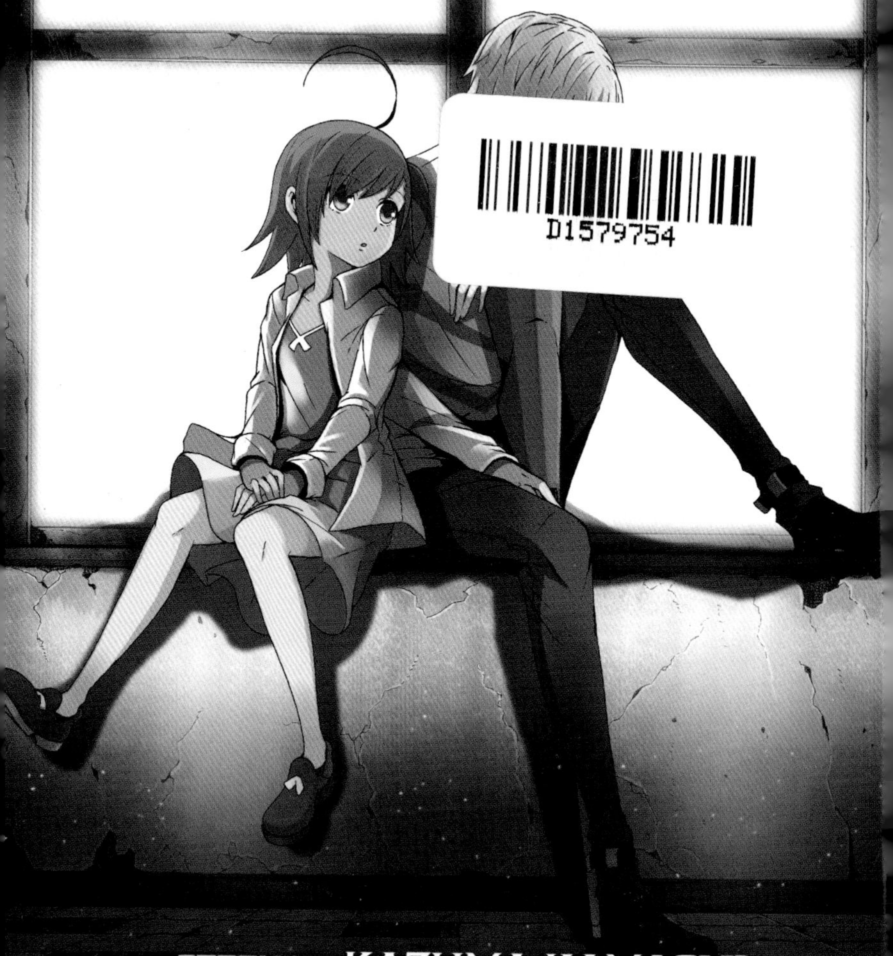

STORY BY KAZUMA KAMACHI

ART BY ARATA YAMAJI

CHARACTER DESIGN BY KIYOTAKA HAIMURA & ARATA YAMAJI